Porridge and Passion

Jonathan Aitken

continuum

Continuum

The Tower Building	15 East 26th Street
11 York Road	New York
London SE1 7NX	NY 10010

www.continuumbooks.com

First published 2005

British Library Cataloguing-in-Publication Data
A catalogue record for this book is available from the British Library.

ISBN 0–8264–7630–9

Designed and typeset by Benn Linfield
Printed and bound by CPI Bath Press, United Kingdom

To

Elizabeth, my 'best mate' in life

and

Mickey, my 'best mate' in prison

Contents

Preface

Porridge[*] *and Passion* is a second volume of autobiography following on from my previous book *Pride and Perjury*.

In these pages I have tried to tell the story, laced with humour and human interest, of my prison sentence followed by my release into a world that was full of paradoxical reactions. Taken as a whole the journey was a roller-coaster ride. It led me through three prisons, two courtroom dramas, a bitter bankruptcy, an Oxford college and a joyful marriage. Along the way I engaged with a cast of characters who introduced me to scenes, sagas and emotions that I could never have imagined, let alone encountered, in my previously sheltered life as a politician.

Although I was humbled by some of these experiences I was also enriched by them. The enrichment was only possible because of three pillars in my life which I came to call my three F's – faith, family and friends. The inter-reaction of these three F's with the pressures and problems of my journey eventually grew into a mysterious mixture of passions, from suffering to rejoicing, which have blended into a new life which is far more fulfilled, happier and deeper than the life I was leading before my troubles began.

Some readers may pick up this book with little or no knowledge of the events prior to my prison sentence as recounted in *Pride and Perjury* and in many thousands of media reports. So for the benefit of these new readers I hope the following paragraphs will act as a scene setter for this book.

In 1994, after twenty years in the House of Commons and two years as Minister of State for Defence I was promoted into the Cabinet

[*] Porridge is the vernacular term among criminals for a prison sentence, popularized to a wider audience by the TV series of that name.

as Chief Secretary to the Treasury. My arrival at the top table of British politics was greeted with considerable media interest. This ranged from positive suggestions that I was a future Prime Minister to negative allegations, exclusively published by the *Guardian*, that I was a pimp, an illegal arms dealer and a corrupt minister who had amassed a huge fortune from my secret connections with prominent Saudi Arabians. Confident that I could disprove these charges I launched a libel action against the *Guardian* and against two sub-sequent Granada Television *World in Action* programmes based on the *Guardian*'s reports.

In the course of a dramatic libel action in the High Court I had considerable success during the first ten days of the trial in dis-proving many of the serious charges that had been made against me. After the defendants withdrew all their defences of justification to their arms-dealing allegations it looked as though I was on course for victory, a view which we now know was shared by many of the leading protagonists at the *Guardian* and Granada Television.

However one fiercely contested matter in the libel case was the issue of who had paid a £900 bill for my stay in the Ritz Hotel in Paris in 1992. The *Guardian*, with the help of the hotel's owner Mr Mohammed Al Fayed and some forged correspondence on House of Commons notepaper, thought they could prove that my bill had been paid by a Saudi friend, thus establishing that as a Minister I had improperly received hospitality. I denied this allegation saying on oath that my wife had paid the bill.

For the first two and a half weeks of the libel trial the Ritz bill issue remained unprovable either way in the absence of decisive evidence. However on the 11th day of the trial the *Guardian* unex-pectedly produced new evidence in the form of British Airways air tickets which proved that my wife could not have paid the bill. This was also clear proof that I had told a lie on oath. I had to with-draw my libel action, and the case collapsed amidst justified media vilification of me. The *Guardian* launched an editorial campaign to have me prosecuted for the crime of perjury.

There was a delay of almost eighteen months before the *Guardian*'s campaign succeeded. During that time I went through an agony of remorse accompanied by a spiritual journey of prayer, repentance, and commitment to a new life in Christ. One consequence of this journey, and of the prayer life I was sharing with a group of new Christian friends, was that I issued a confession statement to the prosecuting authorities at the earliest opportunity. I also took the earliest opportunity to enter a plea of guilty. My world fell apart still further when my wife divorced me. This event plus the arrival of legal bills from the *Guardian* and Granada of some £2.4 million drove me into bankruptcy. Against a background of defeat, disgrace, divorce, bankruptcy and the certainty of jail I was summoned to the Central Criminal Court on Tuesday 8th June 1999 to be sentenced. Now read on ...

CHAPTER 1

Sentencing Day

The morning began with the butler shimmering into my darkened bedroom at 7.15 a.m., pulling back the curtains, pouring out a cup of my favourite Jamaica Blue Mountain coffee, hanging up the suit he had just pressed and reporting in his most theatrical stage whisper that there were 'at *least* a hundred photographers *already* sir' camped outside my front door in Lord North Street.

Eighteen hours later my evening ended less comfortably. I was perched on an iron bedstead inside a cell at HMP Belmarsh, drinking tap water, nibbling at a stale bread roll and listening fearfully to my fellow prisoners chanting obscene threats about what they were going to do to various parts of my anatomy. It was to be a day of high drama, low moments and sharp contrasts.

Although the butler was performing his duties rather excitably as he laid out my shirt and tie with much ruffling and flourishing, I was touched to have him in the house on that midsummer morning of 8 June 1999. For 72-year-old Clifford Berwick, who had worked for me on and off for the past 17 years, had volunteered to come out of retirement for my last hours of freedom. 'Oh sir, I couldn't possibly leave you on your own today of all days could I now?' said Cliff as I thanked him for coming in so early. 'And with 22 for breakfast, Inez can do with an extra pair of hands in the kitchen can't she?'

The 22 breakfasters included my four children. Were they awake yet? I asked. 'Oh yes sir, Miss Petrina was up and doing when I came in at half six. And young Trouble is watching the telly with Ally and Vicky. Part of the news was live from Lord North Street.

1

They even had me letting myself in through the front door. Apparently the reporter said I was one of your lawyers!'

I laughed, partly at Cliff's enjoyment of his own televised entrance and partly at his distinction between 'Miss Petrina' and 'Young Trouble' which was a nickname he had used for my 16-year-old son William ever since he was a toddler. Cliff's formality towards 'Miss Petrina' was because he hardly knew her. She had only been discovered to be my daughter six months earlier as a result of a DNA test. We had immediately and lovingly welcomed her into the family, but last night had been the first night she had slept over in our house. She had asked to stay to show solidarity with her new-found father, sisters and brothers in the tough hours that lay ahead.

The next person entering the house to be inaccurately described on television as one of my lawyers was Charles W. Colson. This former White House aide and so-called 'hatchet man' to President Richard Nixon had once been an even more vilified figure in the eyes of the US media than I now was to the British media. After serving seven months in prison for Watergate-related offences, Colson had founded Prison Fellowship, a ministry to prisoners which over the past 25 years had made him America's best-known Christian leader after Billy Graham. I had first met Colson in 1987 when he was a most helpful source for my biography of Nixon. More importantly, in the last two years Colson had become an inspirational influence on my journey of repentance and spiritual searching ever since I had been caught telling a lie on oath in my ill-judged libel action against the *Guardian*.

Colson and his wife Patty were the first of several friends for what my son William called 'the last breakfast'. William did justice to it by consuming three helpings of eggs, bacon, tomatoes and sausages followed by two large slices of cheese on toast. I confined myself to coffee. My fasting and my son's gorging were probably our different ways of coping with the high state of nervous tension we were both feeling.

Real lawyers now started coming through the front door. Bruce Streather, who was my solicitor for the criminal charges of perjury to which I had already pleaded guilty, had some last-minute queries on points of detail for the plea of mitigation. The solicitor handling my bankruptcy, Michael Coleman, opened a letter from the bailiffs acting for my creditors. It said that all the contents of 8 Lord North Street would be forcibly removed next week. 'They can't do that,' said Coleman. 'You have a child under 18 living at home, which protects it for a year under the Insolvency Act, and in any case your ex-wife has a valid case on the chattels.' His assurance proved correct. Our house did not come under the hammer for another 15 months.

A nicer letter arrived in the middle of breakfast, by special delivery from Lambeth Palace. The Archbishop of Canterbury, George Carey, whom I did not know well, had taken the trouble to send me a handwritten note of great kindness. 'You continue to be in the thoughts and prayers of many Christians. We know that God can redeem any situation and he can bring hope from apparently the most hopeless mess,' wrote Carey. 'We pray that having learnt the lessons and having fully repented of the offences you are guilty of, you too will be able to look forward to a new life'.

As the most immediate life ahead of me was likely to be behind bars, I had to think practically as well as spiritually when we came to the end of breakfast. Much attention was given to preparing the contents of a small bag of personal possessions which I would be allowed to take into prison with me in accordance with the Home Office list of permitted items. My children had been out shopping the previous afternoon for several of them, so my bag (of which more later) included handkerchiefs, socks, underwear, a radio, writing paper, a notebook, biros, stamps and a wash kit containing toothpaste, soap, shampoo and razor.

Having prepared for cleanliness, next up was godliness. In the last few months I had become well versed in the evangelical practice of praying aloud in communal groups, so it seemed natural for us to move from the dining room into the drawing room in order to say some final prayers before going off to court.

Our 44-foot-long drawing room had been the venue for many an interesting gathering. In the 1930s, under the previous owner Brendan Bracken, Winston Churchill used the house as his London political base during his wilderness years. In my two decades as an

MP and minister I had hosted numerous lunches and dinners here. Sometimes they were for dining clubs such as the Conservative Philosophy Group, sometimes in honour of political leaders such as Harold Macmillan, Harold Wilson, Margaret Thatcher, Henry Kissinger, John Major and Richard Nixon. In striking contrast with its past history, the room was now put to use for a prayer meeting on behalf of a prisoner heading for jail.

We kept the prayers short, but they were powerful. Jim Pringle read some verses from Psalm 118; Charles Colson delivered a vigorous plea for justice to be tempered with mercy; Father Philip Chester, the Vicar of St Matthew's, Westminster (our local parish church), gave a blessing; and I said my favourite prayer by Ignatius of Loyola which goes:

Take Lord and receive all my memory, all my will, all my understanding, everything I have and possess. For you gave these things to me and to you I gladly return them. Only dear Lord in your mercy grant me your peace and your grace for these are enough for me. Amen.

After that, we all needed plenty of peace and grace, for it was saying goodbye time followed by paparazzi time.

The farewells inside the house were difficult, for I had no idea when I would next see my family. I imagined I would be sentenced within a couple of hours and might then be incarcerated for a couple of years, as the rules for prison visiting were then unknown to me. So, expecting a long separation, I tried to say something comforting about the enduring continuity of love to each of my four children. It was easier saying goodbye to other friends and relations; the exception was my 88-year-old mother who became understandably tearful when taking her leave of a son bound for jail. She was overtaken in the sobbing stakes, however, by Clifford Berwick the butler. He was so overcome that he had to lie down. His last words, through his abject tears, were based on his youthful experience of spending one night in a prison cell. 'It was terrible sir, terrible. I don't think you'll be able to bear it.'

On that far from reassuring note I set off to court.

The scene outside the Old Bailey on the morning of 8 June was one of confusion. My arrival turned it into chaos. Twenty or so police officers were already having difficulty controlling a crowd of over two hundred pushing and shoving paparazzi, not to mention the crush from many other bystanders. As the Aitken party alighted from our cars, the crowd barriers collapsed and the cameramen charged forward like barbarians on the attack.

My three daughters, Alexandra, Victoria and Petrina, became frightened. Holding on to each other's hands they made a dash towards the doors of the court. The picture of them running together as a terrified trio dominated the front page of that afternoon's *Evening Standard*. It was charmingly captioned, 'THERE TO SEE DADDY JAILED'.

In another part of the media scrimmage, I was pinioned into immobility until rescued by the police. Behind me Charles Colson, in his unmistakable New England twang, declared, 'This is worse than Watergate.' Ahead of me I saw a group of ladies from my former constituency, waving banners. One of them proclaimed, 'Don't persecute Jonathan'. Suddenly a TV camera was thrust towards my face and a BBC reporter wanted to know, 'How are you feeling today, Mr Aitken?' 'At peace,' I replied, an answer which so nonplussed him that he gave me peace from further questioning.

Eventually I did get into the Old Bailey through a side entrance. There was a ten-minute wait before the doors of the court opened. I filled it by talking with two infirm old gentlemen whose unexpected presence in the waiting hall of the Central Criminal Court moved me. One was Father Norman Brown, the other was Lord Longford.

Norman Brown was a Catholic priest from Westminster Cathedral. He had heard my confession (making a special exception for a non-Catholic penitent) back in 1997, a few months after my libel case against the *Guardian* collapsed in disaster. At that time I was almost collapsing under the weight of my remorse and guilt until Norman guided me along the sacramental road to God's forgiveness with a love and pastoral care for which I will always be grateful.

Lord Longford was one of my lifelong heroes. Our family links went back 40 years. Among his many campaigns and causes, one which had never much interested me before was his compassion for prisoners, whom he visited frequently. This was an activity much laughed at by cynics but never by the recipients of his visits. At 94, Frank looked frail and immobile. I realized what a struggle it must have been for him to reach the Old Bailey. But for all his infirmities he talked to me with great vigour, displaying an amusing ambivalence between longing for me not to be sent to jail and longing to visit me in jail as he said, 'Well I do hope the judge will be merciful ... Don't you think a suspended sentence is still on the cards? ... Oh dear, well you're a pessimist but I'm an optimist ... But then if the judge isn't as merciful as we optimists would like, I do hope you will welcome a visit from me ... In the Scrubs I suppose? ... Oh well, Belmarsh – I can get there too I suppose ... No it won't be difficult at all ... I'm very determined you know.'

Lord Longford's determination to visit me in prison was a mark of his character with which I was to become gratefully, if hilariously, familiar with in the coming months. However, this was one of our shorter conversations because it was interrupted by the opening of the courtroom doors. As a thundering herd of journalists rushed to find seats, I, who was destined for the most secluded seat of all, hung around rather awkwardly at the back until a robed court usher beckoned me over. He told me to stand beside him at the door of the dock until he gave me the signal to enter it, then he exhibited a droll sense of humour by saying to me *sotto voce*, 'Do you realize you are in Court No. 1, Mr Aitken? Soon you'll be standing in the most famous dock in Britain ... Among the celebrated defendants tried here were Lord Haw-Haw, Dr Crippen, the Kray Brothers – and now you.'

A second or two later, another court warden's stentorian tones boomed out, 'Be upstanding in court! All persons who have anything to do before my Lords the Queen's Justices of Oyer and Terminer and general gaol delivery draw near and give your attendance. God save the Queen!' To those ancient words, the trial judge Mr Justice Scott-Baker entered the courtroom. The final act of *Regina v Aitken* was about to begin.

*   *   *

As final acts go, it was Wagnerian in length, lasting for over six hours. Despite an initial atmosphere of suspense provided by a packed courtroom of reporters, lawyers, ill-wishers and well-wishers, it would be difficult to claim that the proceedings made good theatre. For almost the only unknown ingredient in the drama was the length of the sentence. The other elements were a speech by the prosecution and a plea of mitigation by the defence; both were extremely long. Sitting in the dock, I could hardly believe that there was still so much to be said about charges to which I had pleaded guilty six months earlier and details which had been endlessly reported and commented on in the media for the past two years. But the law had to take its course. The counsel for the Crown, David Waters QC, was impeccably fair in his summary of the prosecution case. He seemed to be presenting it in as low-key a manner as possible. As the following day's newspapers were to demonstrate, it was extremely difficult to get a headline out of the Waters speech, for it contained no colourful or even censorious phrases. Instead it consisted of a dull but damning recital of the facts that told the story of my perjury over the payment of my 1992 Ritz Hotel bill in the libel case.

As I listened to the saga being retold, I felt once again the agonizing pains of remorse, particularly when parts of my own confession statement were read out dealing with the episode when I had drafted an unsworn witness statement for my daughter Victoria to sign in untrue corroboration of her mother's travel arrangements. Mr Waters seemed content to let the miserable facts speak for themselves, but the judge intervened to observe, 'It is a very grave feature of this case that the defendant should involve his daughter in this way.' I agreed with Mr Justice Scott-Baker, but his comment also sent any lingering hopes of judicial leniency flying out of the courtroom window.

One character witness was called. This was Sir Malcolm Rifkind, the former Foreign Secretary, who had been my immediate boss in the Ministry of Defence from 1992 to 1994, when he was Defence Secretary and I was Minister of State. I had neither expected nor asked Malcolm to come and give evidence in court for me. In an extraordinary act of kindness he had volunteered to do so one winter evening when he was taking me out to dinner at Simpson's-in-the-Strand several months earlier. At various times in my dramas, people have said to me, 'Well I suppose you've found out who your real friends are.' 'Yes,' I would reply and then sometimes recite a roll-call of gratitude, naming those who stood steadfastly by me in the darkest of days. Malcolm Rifkind has a pinnacle of his own in this pantheon of heroes.

The Rifkind evidence was important because it gave a completely different context to my relationship with members of the Saudi royal family than the one presented by some newspapers. Malcolm testified warmly about my well-known (in Whitehall) role as an interlocutor with the Saudi King, and the benefits to Britain that had flowed from that relationship in terms of jobs safeguarded and contracts won. 'I had no reason to believe that Mr Aitken had ever benefited personally from his ministerial contacts,' said Rifkind. 'I felt he was carrying out his work in a very responsible way.'

By now we had reached the lunch interval. Although still a free man I was not a hungry one. I could barely manage a couple of nibbles at half a sandwich as I sat in the Old Bailey cafeteria with my mother, sister and children. It was a difficult meal for many reasons. 'Now I know what zoo animals must feel like at feeding time,' I remarked as the crush of journalists trying to watch us eating and overhear what we were saying crowded around us. It was almost a relief to get back to the cavernous emptiness of the dock (built to accommodate whole gangs of criminal defendants) as my counsel, Sir John Nutting, developed his mitigation speech.

Like Malcolm Rifkind, Johnny Nutting was a wonderful friend. We had entered the same house in the same school on the same day as 13-year-old new boys, so we went back a long time. He refused to accept any fee for his brief, and delivered his speech with heartfelt passion. Apart from the predictable mitigation points about previous good character, long years of public service, and remorse, Nutting's tactics were to describe to the judge the pressures that had built up on me as a result of false journalistic accusations of arms dealing, pimping and ministerial corruption. 'It is difficult to imagine more serious allegations against a minister or ones more certain to question his fitness for office or more likely to undermine his role as an MP,' said my counsel. 'He was faced with a very genuine dilemma whether to say nothing and allow very serious allegations, the falsity of which he believed he could prove, to go unchallenged, or to sue knowing that in relation to the Ritz bill he would have to tell a lie.'

As an excuse this was pathetic. As an explanation it was true. Seeking to persuade the judge to have sympathy for the explanation was a high-risk strategy and one which initially seemed to irritate Mr Justice Scott-Baker. 'We can't retry the whole libel case, Sir John!' was one judicial intervention whose sharpness started me worrying that the mitigation plea could increase rather than decrease my sentence. But Nutting stood his ground. With old-fashioned but effective courtroom oratory, punctuated by expressions like 'perforce' and 'beyond peradventure', he insisted on taking the judge through the wilder allegations that had been made against me by the *Guardian* and Granada Television and subsequently withdrawn. In particular, Nutting made much of the little-noticed but vitally important statement in court by the *Guardian*'s and Granada's counsel, George Carman QC, withdrawing all his clients' defences of justification for their publication of arms-dealing allegations against me. Also withdrawn from the libel case pleadings was a serious allegation by my former secretary Valerie Scott that I had procured air hostesses to act as prostitutes for a Saudi prince. Nutting was scathing about that one and he also ridiculed the *Guardian*'s much repeated claim that my motivation for launching the libel case action was to make myself a fortune in libel damages. That was impossible, said my counsel, when under High Court rules the maximum libel damages awardable would have been around £150,000 less unrecoverable legal costs.

The trump card in Sir John Nutting's plea of mitigation was a letter to the judge, read out in open court, from Valerie Scott. Her allegations had formed the basis for much of the 1997 *World in Action* documentary, 'Jonathan of Arabia', and the *Guardian*'s articles based on the programme. But Valerie Scott had subsequently been filled with regret for what she had said. In her letter she acknowledged that her interview with *World in Action* journalists and her later witness statement for the libel case 'did contain many inaccuracies'. 'Some of these were misrepresentations,' Miss Scott's letter continued, 'others were mis-recollections, others were mistakes and others were caused by my words being taken out of context and used in a way which now makes me feel uncomfortable because I was manipulated into being unfair to Jonathan Aitken. I am deeply sorry for my part in this.' As Sir John Nutting read out this remarkable letter in its entirety, a hush fell over the courtroom. I noticed that the judge was leaning forward intently, following the text of the letter as it reached its conclusion: 'To set the record straight I wish to make it clear that Jonathan Aitken was never involved in pimping or procuring. He was never involved in corrupt business practices with Saudi Arabians or in corrupt dependency on Saudi Arabians.'

Valerie Scott's letter to the judge was a courageous attempt to unlock the prison door on the eve of the prisoner being bolted inside it. Only Mr Justice Scott-Baker will ever know whether her words had an impact on his sentencing. My hunch, based on his judicial body language which seemed to become more friendly to the plea of mitigation, was that Scott's letter cut at least six months off my time in prison.

Back in the courtroom, Sir John Nutting ended his two-and-a-half-hour speech with the peroration, 'Not since the days of Oscar Wilde has any public figure suffered so much public humiliation, so much media vilification and so much personalized vindictiveness from his enemies. His fall from grace is now complete. His marriage has ended in divorce. He has lost his home. He is one of only three people this century forced to resign from the Privy Council, he is bankrupt and his health has suffered. These are real and considerable punishments.'

Although I well knew that more punishment was coming to me, I was hugely grateful to Johnny Nutting for the painstaking work and passion that went into his speech. My instinct told me that his high-risk strategy had paid off and would result in greater judicial leniency than had seemed likely at the start of the day's proceedings. However, it was still anyone's guess as to how long my sentence might be. Perhaps even the judge had not yet made up his mind, for at 4.10 p.m. he adjourned the court until 4.30. As I stepped down from the dock, William came alongside me. 'Toughest 20-minute wait of your life I guess Daddy,' he said, giving me a loving filial squeeze of my shoulders. A woman journalist standing beside us who saw this filial gesture choked up.

We returned to the Old Bailey cafeteria for the last cuppa. Everyone in the family was rather quiet, but the mood was one of realism rather than foreboding. 'At least it's the end of the long nightmare,' I said rather too optimistically. 'It's all over now bar the sentencing.'

When I came back into the court, I was escorted by a green-uniformed lady jailer from Securicor, called Eileen, whose job it would be to take me down the spiral staircase at the back of the dock which led to the cells. She filled the remaining moments of waiting time with touching sympathy. 'Be brave. I know it's a terrible time for you and your family, but I can see you've got the strength to take it,' she said, offering me a mint. 'I just saw Lord Longford waving to you. The press have given him an awful time too.'

I looked up to the gallery, which seemed to be full of Aitken supporters. In the front row were Lord Longford, Father Norman Brown, Jim Pringle and Chuck Colson. They all had their eyes closed. As it was impossible for them to have fallen asleep in unison, I guessed that they must be praying. I thought of offering up a prayer myself, but decided against it on the grounds that the reporters would mock or at best misunderstand any visible sign of such activity. In any case, my friends were likely to be doing a much better job in prayer than I would. For some reason there floated into my mind an old adage, 'Let go and let God'. I decided to follow its advice. So I released all my fears in total trust and was rewarded with a feeling of total peace as I waited to know my fate.

At 4.37 p.m. the judge came back into court to pass sentence. He was stern, predictable and fair as he said, 'Jonathan Aitken, for nearly four years you wove a web of deceit in which you entangled yourself and from which there was no way out unless you were prepared to come clean and tell the truth. Unfortunately you were not … This was no passing error of judgement. It was calculated over a period of time … You swept others including members of your family into it, and most particularly one of your daughters who was only 16 at the time.' 'I was 17!' hissed Victoria with angry if irrelevant loyalty. Fortunately her interjection went unheard on the bench, where the judge was saying that he would take into account my 'considerable remorse'. He accepted that I had not brought the libel action to earn money and that I had already suffered other penalties. Finally he said the words that mattered most, 'The sentence of the court is that you will serve 18 months' imprisonment.'

My instant reaction was that the sentence was fair. Pessimists had predicted that I might get three years. Optimists had talked unrealistically about how I would receive the average High Court tariff for perjury offenders (six months) or even a suspended sentence. As my own forecast had been at the pessimistic end of the scale, I was genuinely relieved. I bowed to the judge and followed Eileen towards the steps down to the cells. I paused for a second at the top of the spiral staircase to blow a kiss to my children, my sister and my mother – all of whom were in tears. Then I vanished from the sight of the courtroom and descended into the bowels of the Old Bailey to start a new chapter in my life as a convicted criminal.

*   *   *

Tea, sympathy, form-filling, handcuffs and a first brush with prisoner violence were what I first encountered after descending from Court No. 1 to the cells of the Old Bailey. My jailer Eileen led me down three flights of dingy stairs encased on all sides with steel meshing. When we reached a corridor she said, 'I'm going to put you in this holding cell,' opening up a small, windowless room whose only features were a padded bench and a heavy door with an iron-barred viewing panel. 'I really do wish you good luck,' were her farewell words, locking me in with a noisy jangling of her keys as the mortice turned.

I was left alone in that cell for about 15 minutes. The solitude and the feeling of not being stared at were a welcome change from the high visibility of the dock. My thoughts were mainly for my family. I kept wondering how they were bearing up. For myself I felt peaceful. Extraordinary though it sounds, I began to count life's blessings. The 18-month sentence meant I would be out of jail in nine months' time because of the automatic 50 per cent remission on all prison terms of less than four years. The media feeding frenzy would soon die down. I could do my best to use the next 270 days in a positive way. Learning and changing would be my priorities. Nothing would be easy, I knew, but the worst was now over. I whispered the words 'thank you' to the ceiling of the cell three times. This was my way of expressing gratitude for what I had come to call my 'three F's' – faith, family and friends. On that strong tripod I knew I could start a new life, even a prison life.

These musings – some of them prematurely optimistic – were interrupted by two jailers. 'How about a nice cup of tea?' said one of them as he carried it in. The other had a sheaf of forms to be filled in. Before they did the bureaucracy, they did small talk, all of it friendly. One of these Securicor men had been on duty at Bow Street Magistrates' Court on the day when I was committed for trial at the Old Bailey. He commented amusingly on those proceedings. The other was full of compliments about my children. 'I feel for them, having teenagers myself,' he said. It was all rather unreal, very British, but genuinely kind.

The next kind person to arrive was a probation officer called Cathy Dixon. She too had forms to be filled in, but her main job seemed to be to assess my mood and mindset. She told me to stay calm and never to think of suicide. 'I won't,' I reassured her. 'I pleaded guilty, so I'm well prepared for this and think I'm in good shape both mentally and physically.'

I was moved to a larger cell 'for a legal'. This meant a short visit from John Nutting and my solicitor Bruce Streather. 'Well done Demosthenes!' was my greeting to Johnny Nutting. 'I reckon you shifted that old buzzard of a judge into cutting the sentence quite a bit with the power of the last 20 minutes of your speech.' With these two friends it was easy to be upbeat. Between them they raised my spirits with their good company and their good news. Bruce Streather told me he had already secured agreement for three 'police days' to come off my sentence. Under this arrangement an offender's prison term is reduced by the number of days previously spent in police custody or at preliminary court hearings. John Nutting was sure that I would qualify under the new Home Office rules for 'tagging' non-violent prisoners towards the end of their sentence. Thanks to this scheme, known as Home Detention Curfew, I would be released on an electronic tag two months early provided I agreed to stay at home between 7 p.m. and 7 a.m. throughout the tagging period. 'Hallelujah!' I said. Sixty-three days were coming off my sentence before I had even begun it.

'On the question of an appeal against sentence,' began Nutting, 'I would have advised you to appeal if you had got three years or more, but in these circumstances ....' I interrupted him to say, 'I wouldn't dream of appealing.' We agreed to issue a statement to this effect immediately. Our meeting ended in hugs, thanks and laughter. When Johnny Nutting returned to my children who were still in the main hall of the Old Bailey anxiously awaiting news of the prisoner in the cells, he told them, 'Your father's as brave as a lion.' Alas by the time he said this, it was an inaccurate statement

At about the same moment when Nutting's report was being delivered to my family, my courage was deserting me. I was having my first experience of a phenomenon that I was prey to many times in the coming months – sudden mood swings. Incarceration can be a psychological incubator which overheats good news into euphoria and chills negative news into despondency. My first mood swing came a few moments after Nutting and Streather had left me. The next visitors to my cell were another pair of jailers. One of them produced a pair of steel handcuffs. 'Sorry to have to do this to you, but its standard procedure,' he said. 'We're taking you to the cage and then after a short wait you'll go into the sweatbox.'

In the world of prisoners, there is no such thing as a short wait. For the best part of an hour I was in the cage. As its name suggests, this is an animalistic iron-barred enclosure, which holds the day's convicted and sentenced criminals from the 40 or so courtrooms of the Old Bailey while they wait to be transported to their designated jails. I do not think I will ever forget the scene in the cage on that afternoon of 8 June 1999. It was a panorama of anger and despair. One young black prisoner was in such a fury that he kept charging into the bars of the cage like a wild bull, battering himself over and over again until his head cut open and started to bleed. Elsewhere in the cage, three members of a gang were repeatedly kicking their fourth associate, apparently putting the blame on him for all their convictions as they were shouting, 'You got the script wrong! You effed up the effing script.' Another pair of villains, both built like huge refrigerators, were having a vigorous argument about which of them had annoyed the judge so much that he gave them the maximum sentence.

These scenes of aggression, furious though they were, somehow seemed sideshows in comparison with the overall atmosphere of the cage, which was one of catatonic gloom. Several heavily tattooed young men had their heads sunk into their hands. One or two of them were weeping. All seemed to be totally devastated. In these depths of despair no one took any notice of me. My notoriety, so prominent on the front pages of the morning newspapers, evidently meant little in the afternoon to those preoccupied with their own imprisonment. I got one or two curious glances from tear-stained eyes, but that was about all. Someone asked me rather aggressively 'Are you the Old Bill [a policeman]?' 'No I am not,' I quickly replied. The rest was silence. I thought it was the saddest environment I had ever been in during my life.

Eventually the Securicor guards came back with long chains which they clipped on to our handcuffs, and led us one by one down a long corridor until we reached an underground courtyard. There I clambered into one of the big prison vans which their regular customers call a sweatbox. Once inside, I was locked into a tiny white compartment resembling a toilet seat for a midget. It was claustrophobic but not quite as impossibly uncomfortable as it had first seemed once I had worked out a way of squeezing my long legs backwards into its corners.

As the sweatbox rumbled out of the Old Bailey to an explosion of photographers' flashbulbs, the prisoner in the cubicle immediately behind mine was violently sick. The odour of his vomit, the bumpiness of the sweatbox's progress, and its pursuit by paparazzi on motorcycles did not make for a comfortable journey. As we drove through the City of London, I recognized several landmarks which had once welcomed me in very different roles to my present one. Through the tiny porthole-sized window I caught a glimpse of two banks where I had once worked. One was the old office of

Aitken Hume Bank in City Road where I had been the group's Chairman. The other was the former headquarters of Slater Walker Securities where I had been Managing Director of the Middle East division. Close to the Slater Walker building stood St Paul's Cathedral. I had attended numerous services and ceremonies there over the years. Two of them came back to me. One was the memorial service for my great-uncle, Lord Beaverbrook, attended by a 2,000-strong congregation drawn from the worlds of politics and journalism in which he had been such a dominant figure. The other was the taking down of the banner of my maternal grandfather, Lord Rugby, in the Chapel of St Michael and St George, the patron saints of the order of which he had been a member as a GCMG and KCMG. I had loved and admired my grandfather and my great-uncle. Both of them had told me in my student days of their high hopes for my future career. Remembering these conversations, I came close to shedding a tear as remorse flooded over me for having let them and the whole family down.

I cheered up slightly as the sweatbox drove past the Mansion House. In my days as a minister I had attended many receptions, banquets and ceremonial state visits there, often pointlessly over-dressed in the flummery of white tie and tails. 'At least I'll never have to put on those silly clothes again,' I said to myself. It was probably a vain effort to look for a silver lining, but at the time my spirits lifted a little at the thought of saying goodbye to the pompous artificialities that characterize so much of British social life at the higher levels of official entertaining.

By now the sweatbox had crossed the river through the Blackwall Tunnel. We were chugging through the architectural wastelands of various south London suburbs. I began to wonder whether I could possibly find a way to be positive in prison. Probably not, was my conclusion. It would be a crossing of the desert, to be endured with stoicism. I would just have to try to grin and bear it – most of the time without the grin. But after prison? Here, the man I looked to as my unlikely role model was Richard Nixon. He had never actually gone to jail, thanks to receiving a pardon from his successor Gerald Ford. However, he had 'done time' as the most disgraced and vilified hate figure on the planet before eventually rebuilding his life and enjoying his Indian-summer years as a prolific author and respected elder statesman. In those years I had come to know Nixon well while writing his biography. Two memories of him resurfaced as I wrestled with leg cramp in my sweatbox compartment. The first was of Nixon telling me about what went on in his mind just after his helicopter took off from the south lawn of the White House on the day of his resignation as President of the United States. Amazingly he was pondering his future. He recited to himself some lines from 'The Ballad of Sir Andrew Barton':

> *I am hurt but I am not slain,*
> *So I'll lay me down and bleed awhile,*
> *Then I will rise and fight again.*

The second Nixonian reflection that tumbled out of the attic of my memory on that journey to prison was a remark he made to me some years after my biography of him was published. We were dining together in Marks Club in London, discussing why some people were resilient in the face of life's reverses and others were not. Nixon suddenly produced a gem. 'You have to remember that failure is not falling down,' he said. 'Failure is falling down and not getting up again to continue with life's race.' He added with a sardonic smile, 'And I sure know a thing or two about that.'

I had to break away from these historical memories as the sweatbox juddered to a halt. I realized we had arrived at our destination, HMP Belmarsh, because another round of flashbulb explosions was coming from a platoon of paparazzi. In order to avoid their attentions, I ducked my head below the window so I did not get a good view of my new abode except for a brief glimpse of its searchlights, watchtowers and high walls. All I saw clearly was the opening and closing of two forbiddingly huge doors as our van drove in. The only announcement came from a forward cubicle, as one of my fellow prisoners sang out at the top of his voice, 'Ere we are again. Welcome to 'ell.'

CHAPTER 2

First night in Belmarsh

Entering HMP Belmarsh was like landing on another planet. Everything about it seemed alien and antagonistic. My first few hours as a prisoner were thoroughly disorientating, for I had so many experiences of the unexpected. Some of my earliest encounters with both the officers and the inmates were marked by aggression and humiliation. Others were touched by humour and the warmth of human kindness. Yet despite the rough ride, which culminated in a terrifying chant of threats late at night, I somehow managed to come through it in a relatively calm state of mind. For I was learning, minute by minute, that the key to survival in Britain's highest-security prison was to go quietly with the flow of life as you found it.

As I stepped out of the sweatbox nervously clutching my small bag of personal belongings, the atmosphere of Belmarsh seemed powerfully oppressive. It was not just the massive concrete walls, the watchtowers, the glinting coils of barbed wire, the serried ranks of searchlights, the CCTV cameras pointing at you from all angles or the iron bars on every door and window. Nor was it the stern glares of the prison officers lining the courtyard or the barking of their Alsatians on leashes. These signs of institutional authority looked severe but they were not the source of the leaden heaviness hanging like an invisible pall over the entire establishment. That deeper oppression hit me the moment I walked into the reception building. I had an overwhelming feeling of entering a fortress contaminated by negative emotions and hostile tensions. Almost immediately I tuned into the bitterness, the resentment, the anger and the suppressed violence that ebbed and flowed like a river of darkness through the jail that night and every night of my incarceration there.

As I absorbed these atmospherics while standing in the queue of new arrivals waiting to be registered, I remembered some of the suggestions made to me by a couple of former Belmarsh inmates whom I had sought out during the weeks of self-preparation before being sentenced. 'Keep your head down.' 'Don't confide in anyone.' 'Blend into the background.' 'Put up with almost anything on your first day.' 'Don't play the tall poppy.' All these proved wise recommendations.

When my turn came to register as a new prisoner, I handed over the form given to me at the Old Bailey and stood at the reception point with my hands resting lightly on the surface in front of me. This was a mistake. 'Take your hands off the counter,' barked the officer in charge. These were the first words spoken to me, or rather shouted at me, by a member of the staff of Her Majesty's Prison Service. I jumped into a submissive schoolboy posture of hands clasped behind my back.

After more forms had been filled in and I was allocated my prison number, CB9298, I was put into the Belmarsh cage or communal cell. The scene was similar to that of the cage at the Old Bailey, only worse. New prisoners were steadily arriving from Crown Courts all over London and the south-east. Some were in a state of silent shock, others in a mood of noisy anger. Effing, blinding, shouting and kicking the bars of the cage seemed to be the tribal customs of the community I had now joined. However, I again saw quite a few tough-looking customers behaving in untough-looking ways such as burying their heads in their heavily tattooed arms and weeping.

Feeling horribly conspicuous in my suit and tie, I tried to melt away into one corner of the cage, keeping myself to myself. But one inmate came up to me and shook my hand.

'Sorry to see you in here,' he said. 'You once did a good turn to me brother when he was living in Ramsgate. What did the beak give you?' 'Eighteen months.' 'Oh well. That's politics I suppose.' 'Not really. It was my own fault.' 'There's not many who come in here saying that,' said my companion, astonished. 'Mind you, they generally change their tune when the time comes round for parole reports.'

19

To move the conversation away from myself, I asked, 'What did your beak give you?' 'I got a four. Easy gravy. Slim here got really weighed off with a fifteen, poor bugger.' 'What for?' I asked, immediately biting my lip for I had been warned that it was out of order to ask a fellow prisoner what his crime had been. 'Misunderstandin',' chipped in Slim with a hollow laugh. Before he could give further and better particulars of the misunderstanding that ended in a 15-year jail sentence, an officer came into the cage and announced that Induction would now begin. Induction is a word that survives in only two British institutions: the Church of England, which inducts new vicars into churches, and Her Majesty's Prison Service which inducts new convicts into jails. Their rituals are rather different, as I was about to discover.

'Aitken – property,' shouted an officer, gesturing me towards a room to the left of the cage. It was explained that all my property would be entered in my 'prop book' and divided into 'alloweds' and 'disalloweds'. I unzipped my small bag and put the contents on the table, confident that everything I had brought in would be allowed because it conformed to the list, published by the Home Office, of items a prisoner is permitted to bring into jail with him. Unfortunately, HMP Belmarsh had its own list and its own interpretations of it.

'Radio – disallowed,' announced the older of the two property officers, while, rather in the manner of a soft man/hard man routine, his younger colleague kept up a running commentary of explanation. 'Has a short waveband. Could be used to listen in to police or prison R/T.'

'Handkerchiefs – disallowed.' 'Larger than regulation size,' observed officer No. 2. 'Could be used as a noose.' He made a hangman-type gesture of a rope going around a neck.

'Notebook – disallowed.' 'Has a wire binding which could be used as a suicide weapon. We've had inmates top themselves by sticking wires up their noses and into their brains.' 'But I'm not in the least suicidal,' I muttered. 'All I wanted to do with the notebook was to write in it.' As if this explanation of my plans for using the notebook were an original new piece of evidence for the defence, the older officer sucked his teeth, saying 'Hmmm' in a pensive tone as he reached for a folder of prison rules. After thumbing through it, he found what he was looking for and pronounced a judgment of Solomon. 'You can keep the paper if you detach the pages from the binding,' he said. I painstakingly separated some one hundred pages from the wire spine of the binding only to discover that my hopes of putting pen to paper were going to be thwarted by another rule.

'Biros – disallowed.' The explanation was that all writing instruments in an A-category prison have to be transparent so that they can be held up to the light for inspection to see whether or not they contain illegal substances. This must-be-transparent rule resulted in most of the contents of my washbag being disallowed. By now over half my personal effects had been confiscated, and one or two items survived in the allowed category by the closest of calls. A sheet of postage stamps was handed back to me only after I had given an assurance that I would use them for sending out letters and not for selling to other prisoners. As for a pamphlet entitled *Praying the Psalms*, it was permitted after a debate between the two officers concluded with the decision that it was a religious book and therefore 'an allowed'.

The final indignity in Property came when I was asked to hand over my belt after the older officer had meticulously measured it. 'Disallowed,' he finally pronounced after reading various figures in centimetres off his tape measure and recording them in my prop book.

'I'm afraid you have one of those belts with a buckle that is larger than the belt buckles that are issued as standard uniform to members of the prison staff,' explained the younger warder, adopting the monotone of an 'I speak your weight' machine as he recited, 'A large belt buckle in the possession of an inmate could put an officer at a disadvantage in the event of an outbreak of fighting in which belts are used as offensive weapons.'

For a moment I thought my leg was being pulled. Did these men really think that I was going to start a fight with prison officers, flailing them with my belt buckle? The serious expression on their faces showed that they and the rule book thought it was a possibility. So my belt was confiscated too. Now I really knew that I was living on another planet. 'But how am I supposed to keep my trousers up?' I asked. 'Not our problem – and not yours either for the time being,' came the reply 'because now it's time for your strip search. Take your trousers off.'

A few seconds of nudity in male company did not bother me. However, the next question did: 'Are you carrying any illegal substances in your anus or in any other orifice of your body?' 'No I am not,' I replied nervously. 'I think we can take your word on that one can't we Fred?' Fred agreed. 'Thanks,' I said and got a couple of friendly smiles in return.

I was pulling on my shirt and reaching for my underpants when, all of a sudden, bells started to ring, walkie-talkies emitted a piercing screech, and the air was filled with noise, shouting, pounding of boots, as officers ran into the property department. 'Get him out of here! Get him out of here!' voices shouted. Apparently they meant me. I just had time to pull on my underpants before two burly officers shoved me into a tiny cubicle and slammed the door. The noises outside sounded rough, but totally confusing. It was all quiet again in a couple of minutes, but obviously there had been some sort of serious disturbance.

'What was that all about?' I asked when I was let out of the cubicle. 'Let's just call it party political activities,' said the officer called Fred. His younger colleague was more forthcoming. 'A con on induction took exception to being searched. So he tried to do a runner. As he was heading this way shouting your name, the SO thought you needed protection. But all's under control now. It's what we call an "incident" round here.'

The incident had the effect of bringing Governor Hewitson down to the property department. He was a young man in his thirties who seemed to be even more nervous than I was. In fact he was not *the* Governor of Belmarsh but Governor 5, the fifth official in the hierarchy of the prison's management. Mr Hewitson wanted to know whether I had been shaken by the incident and how I was getting on with my Induction.

'No problems,' I said. 'Any special requests?' 'No sir, none.' 'Well I think you're showing the right attitude,' he said. 'I don't think you need to be on the watch list, but I am putting you in a single cell for your own security.' I gave silent thanks to the prisoner who had tried to do a runner, and oral thanks to Governor Hewitson. He also decreed that I should not go over to the clothing department. Instead a clothing orderly brought a set of prison uniforms down to me. This was a mixed blessing, for the orderly took me for a 6 foot 6 inch overweight giant, with the result that all the clothes he produced were at least two sizes too big for me. The most embarrassing consequence was that my prison jeans were 42 inches round the waist compared to my normal waistline of 36 inches. As I had no belt, my concern about keeping my trousers up now became a crisis.

For the next hour or so I shambled around the various stages of Induction – fingerprinting, mug-shot photography, health and safety briefing – looking like a refugee dressed by Oxfam. My main preoccupation was how to make progress while hoisting up my trousers. This is a difficult operation when you are simultaneously having to hold several items of standard prison-issue kit such as sheets and plastic crockery. As I was shuffling my way along a corridor, hitching up my trousers every few yards, an inmate greeted me: 'Hello Jonathan. Just been watching you on the news. Can I do anything to help? I'm a Listener.'

A Listener, he explained, is a Samaritan – trained helper of prisoners whose mental states could make them suicide risks. My problem with the oversized trousers had not yet put me into this category, but perhaps my dishevelled appearance suggested otherwise. 'Can you help me find a belt?' I asked him. 'The property department confiscated mine because they thought its buckle was so big that I might use it to attack a prison officer.' The good Samaritan looked at me with renewed interest. Perhaps my mental state was now sounding bad enough to require his services as a Listener. 'Sit down right there,' he said. 'I'll see what I can do.' A few moments later he reappeared carrying a number of strong white laces of the kind used in trainers or football boots. 'These should fix you up,' he said. 'Thanks so much,' I replied, creating a makeshift belt from a double string of the laces. 'How did you get them?' 'Ssh!' replied the Listener, putting a finger to his lips. 'But if I were you I wouldn't go near the gym for a bit.'

Before I had time to worry about meeting fitness fanatics and weightlifters incommoded from their exertions by laceless shoes, I was summoned to see the prison psychiatrist. His job was to interview every new arrival to assess whether or not they were suicide risks. Barely looking up at me, the psychiatrist started reading out questions from a printed form. They began:

'Name?'

'Date of birth?'

'Prison number?'

'Next of kin?'

'Does your next of kin know you are in prison?'

The question after that on the form was, 'Does anyone other than your next of kin know you are in prison?'

I thought of the massed ranks of reporters and cameramen who had been outside the Old Bailey and Belmarsh. By now my sentence would not have gone unnoticed by the British public. However, it had gone unnoticed by the psychiatrist. 'I think perhaps 10 or 15 million people know I'm in prison,' was my answer to him, delivered with a wry smile. The psychiatrist did not smile back. His eyes narrowed. 'You think 10 or 15 million people know you're in prison do you?' he said slowly. Then after a pause he asked in a kinder tone, 'May I ask you, have you ever suffered from delusions?'

It took a few moments of explanation to unscramble that one. Then I was taken back to the cage, where we were given a cup of tea which smelt and tasted like dishwater, followed by a plastic container of rice and curry with a flavour almost indistinguishable from the tea. 'Not as good as the Ritz Hotel,' said one wag – a reference to my non-payment of a £900 bill at the Ritz in Paris which had been the cause of my perjury and imprisonment.

The banter that followed broke the ice. Someone asked whether I was a lawyer. No, I said, unwisely adding that I did have a degree in law. This rash boast unleashed a torrent of questions about appeals, introducing new evidence, complaints against solicitors, barristers or judges and so on. I fended off these enquiries, pleading ignorance. Then I found myself cornered by a young black prisoner holding an envelope. 'Can you do us a favour, mate?' he asked. 'I got a letter from me brief. But I got a problem. I can't read. Could you read it to me?' I duly obliged. The letter was from Lambeth Council in south London, threatening to evict the young prisoner, whose name was Milton Stokes, and his family from his council flat, for non-payment of rent.

Stokesy, as everyone called Milton Stokes, came up with a solution to his problem. He reckoned he could persuade his brother to pay off the rent arrears by instalments. I said he should let his lawyer and the council know this. 'But I got another problem,' muttered Stokesy. 'Me trouble is I can't do no readin' or no writin' neither. Could you do us another favour and write the letter for me?' 'Sure,' I said. With the benefit of 23 years' experience as an MP helping constituents with eviction notices at my weekly surgeries, I penned appropriate letters to Lambeth Council and to the lawyer. Stokesy signed them, saying cheerfully 'At least I knows how to do me moniker.' Then he put them in envelopes which I addressed for him. As the finale to our collaboration he held the letters aloft in the manner of a town crier, proclaiming to all and sundry, 'This MP geezer, he does fantastic joined-up writing!'

This plug for my graphological skills, which Stokesy broadcast over and over again during the next few days, fell on surprisingly receptive ears. For although I did not know it at the time, one-third of all prisoners in a big London jail like Belmarsh cannot read or write. So when it was advertised that I was willing to act as an amanuensis for my sub-literate fellow inmates, I was destined to become a useful member of the community.

Writing letters for Stokesy made me the last prisoner in the cage to eat supper and put the plastic meal container in the waste bin. This tardiness brought me a reprimand from authority. 'Hurry up Aitken – don't you realize you're going to be treated just like any other prisoner?' snapped an impatient officer. 'Stop pickin' on 'im, guv,' said one voice. 'Anyhow we're going to treat him just like any other Cabinet minister,' declared another. 'Oh please don't do that,' I interjected. 'It will make things much worse.' It was hardly the wittiest of ripostes but the cage audience found it funny. 'Quite the comedian are we?' said the officer with heavy sarcasm. 'Put that bowl in the waste bin – NOW!' Getting shouted at by the screws makes you one of the lads with the cons. Over the next hour or so I began to strike up some friendly relationships. I was surprised by how young so many of my fellow inmates seemed to be. Later I learned that the average age of a British prisoner is 23. This means that in a big London jail there are many teenagers floating around in the system. It looked and felt that way on my first evening in Belmarsh.

*   *   *

Eventually an officer carrying a clipboard approached me to say, 'Aitken – you're going to Beirut.' I had no idea what this meant. However, an older prisoner sitting a few feet away from me knew exactly what was being said. He came over and addressed me in tones of passionate urgency – although using a language which I did not understand. 'For Gawd's sake mate, don't let them send you to Beirut,' he began. 'That's where all the blaggers and the toolmen go. Now if you misspoke yourself and got a bit lairy with any of 'em – they could snooker yer 'amsteads, they could give you a servin' with claret. So take my word for it – don't let 'em send you to Beirut. What you have to do is take the cucumbers. It's a lot better than goin' to Beirut. Take the bloody cucumbers!'

I was completely mystified by this advice. It sounded well intentioned, but for all the sense it made it might as well have been addressed to me in Sanskrit or Hindustani. Once I learned how to translate prison slang, I discovered that what my helpful adviser had been trying to tell me was this: 'Don't let them send you to House Block 3. That's where all the armed robbers [blaggers] and toolmen [gunmen] go. If you get a bit uppity [lairy] with them they could use a snooker ball to knock out your teeth [Hampstead Heath] or they could beat you up so badly that you'll lose a lot of blood [a serving with claret].' Understanding the phrase 'take the cucumbers' required a journey into the more arcane realms of rhyming slang. In this argot, cucumbers = numbers. Numbers = rule 43. Rule 43 says that any prisoner may apply to be taken into solitary confinement on a Vulnerable Prisoners Unit for his own protection. Jailed police and prison officers usually apply to serve their sentences under rule 43, as do serious sex offenders. My helpful informant clearly thought that any passing Cabinet minister would be wise to take the same precaution.

26

Even if I had understood the real meaning of that horticultural advice about the cucumbers, I would not have taken it. For I had thought about this problem while waiting to be sentenced and had listened to many views (equally divided) about it. My instinct was to take my chances with the rank and file of ordinary prisoners in whatever jail I was sent to. Seeking protection on a special unit was not my style. I was after normality, not vulnerability. So although I initially gave those cucumbers a miss for reasons of incomprehension, I would have turned them down anyway for reasons of inclusion. My hope was to be included in the mainstream of prison life. I was willing to do what it took to achieve this.

If I had known what was going to happen during my first night as a resident of Beirut I think I would probably have chickened out and taken those cucumbers. First, I was escorted from the cage to House Block 3 by two rather jovial prison officers who led me along a labyrinth of brick corridors and iron-barred gates which all had to be unlocked and relocked every 60 yards or so along our route. By now it was after ten o'clock at night. The prisoners were locked in their cells, so the dimly lit landings of the darkened wings had an eerie feel of emptiness and spookiness about them. Almost the only sign of life came from a staffroom whose door was open. As I glanced into it I saw several officers gathered around a television set. My own picture was on the screen. 'That's the Channel 4 documentary, *The Real Jonathan Aitken*,' said one of my escorts. 'Makes you out to be quite interesting really. As soon as we've banged you up, we're going back to watch the last part of it.'

By now I was feeling like the unreal Jonathan Aitken, although the surreal part of the evening was yet to come. When we reached House Block 3 we began climbing three flights of iron steps from the ground floor of a wire-meshed enclosure. The ascent made me think I was in a structure that was a cross between a troop ship and a shed for battery hens. When we reached the third deck or landing we turned right along a high guard rail. After about 40 paces we reached a cell door which the officers unlocked and swung open with ponderous solemnity. 'Here you are, Aitken. Remember your cell number – 43 on the threes [third-floor wing landing].'

The first thing that hit me on entering the cell was its smell which was a mixture of stale tobacco odour, dodgy drains and fetid human sweat. The second was the graffiti which covered a lot of wall space and almost the entire ceiling. Then I took in the bulky iron bars across the window, and the furniture – one table, one chair, one clothes locker, one bed, one chipped washbasin and one toilet without a seat. Spartan, but nothing to whinge about. In a matter of seconds I was mentally acclimatizing to the constricted 12 ft by 10 ft space. The greatest blessing was that I was to be alone in it. So grateful was I for this privacy that the smells, drains, iron bars and other negatives seemed unimportant.

My evaluation of the cell was interrupted by a bizarre warning from one of the officers. 'It is an offence punishable by 28 days' loss of remission to feed the pigeons,' he declared in the voice of a magistrate reading the Riot Act. For a moment I wondered if he could be kidding me. Ever since reading the classic convict's autobiography, *The Bird Man of Alcatraz*, I had believed prisoners were encouraged to cultivate relationships with feathered friends. Evidently not in HMP Belmarsh. I waited to be warned of higher crimes and misdemeanours, but none were mentioned. The idea that pigeon-fancying should carry such a high tariff of punishment inside Belmarsh puzzled me. This was my first introduction to the illogicality factor that is the wild card in so many prison rules. I immediately wanted to know more about the reasons for the ban on feeding birds, but then I remembered one of my pre-prison advisers had said to me, 'For a new inmate a good motto is, "Ours not to reason why".' So I didn't.

Having delivered the prohibition against associating with pigeons, the officers departed. They pulled the cell door behind them with such force that its massive metallic clang immediately made me realize where the term 'the slammer' must come from. That particular slam and the noisy turning of the key in the door which followed it made me feel well and truly imprisoned. My sentence had begun.

*   *   *

For a few minutes I sat on the edge of the iron bedstead taking stock of my circumstances on the day that was now ending. 'Not as bad as I had expected' was my verdict. The sentence could have been heavier, the reception from my fellow prisoners could have been rougher, the screws could have been tougher, and my cell could have been crowded and more uncomfortable. 'For this relief much thanks,' I murmured to myself, borrowing a line from the opening scene of *Hamlet*. Making a mental resolution to reread this and other Shakespeare plays during my sentence, I shook out the dusty, threadbare mattress, made up the bed and prepared to sleep.

Alas, sleep soon proved difficult. The prisoners of Belmarsh, unlike the psychiatrist of Belmarsh, had been fully alerted by the media to my arrival in jail. Now they were being alerted to the exact location of my cell by my next-door neighbours who must have overheard the escort officers saying my name as they locked me in. When my ears became attuned to the acoustics of the prison, my blood froze, for what I was hearing was a chant of ferocious aggression echoing across the entire jail from cell block to cell block. Horrifyingly this chant was all about me.

The vocals in the chant were a stomach-churning mixture of the unthinkable and the unprintable. My cell neighbours seemed to have cast themselves in the role of conductors of a raucous choir. After announcing in their sing-song Caribbean voices the refrain, 'Aitken is here in 43 on the threes in HB3,' they would then ask a question: 'What shall we do to effing Aitken [or effing Aitken's private parts] tomorrow?' From the other three sides of the exercise yard came a thunder of obscene responses detailing in explicit terms what type of (expletive deleted) activity they would inflict on this or that (expletive deleted) organ of my body in order to demonstrate what they thought of (expletive deleted) Tory Cabinet ministers.

Although one or two newspaper columnists had suggested that I might have some difficult moments during my prison sentence, nothing had prepared me for the venom, the viciousness and the intended violence of this chant. I was terrified. During the rest of my time in Belmarsh I discovered that this high-decibel activity took place almost every night. It was known as 'doing a quizzy'. Heavily fuelled by drug-taking, the participants specialized in bellowing questions and answers quiz-style from one house block to another. The target of the quiz was often an unpopular prisoner, prison officer or even the Governor. It was a mean but meaningless exercise full of sound and fury signifying nothing. Unfortunately I knew none of this on the evening of 8 June 1999. The threats that night sounded realistic and I took them seriously. I do not think I have ever felt more lonely, more frightened or more vulnerable.

After half an hour or so of listening with mounting anguish to the chant or quizzy I took the only action which seemed likely to offer the slightest help to me. I knelt down and said a prayer. It would be more accurate to say, 'I tried to say a prayer,' for when I got down on my knees on the concrete flagstones of that cell floor, I found I was too scared to pray. I could not even articulate the words of the Lord's Prayer. My fear was overpowering and the hostile noises of the quizzy were overwhelming. The net result was a total failure of my prayer effort.

Resuming my seat on the edge of the bed, I felt a slight bulge in the pocket of my prison jeans. It was caused by the pamphlet *Praying the Psalms* that had been returned to me in the property department some hours earlier following a discussion between the two officers as to whether it was or was not religious material. Thumbing through its pages I saw that it was a calendar-style booklet of daily readings. For 8 June it recommended Psalm 130. I did not know what the title *Praying the Psalms* really meant, but as soon as I read Psalm 130 its words spoke to me. This is an ancient Hebrew poem composed for people going through the depths of trouble and despair. As I studied its eight short verses which begin,

> *Out of the depths I cry to you O Lord,*
> *O Lord hear my voice,*
> *Let your ears be attentive,*
> *To my cry for mercy*

a warm wave of reassurance flooded over me. Suddenly I realized that I was not as lonely, scared, helpless or vulnerable as I had thought. The author of the psalm had been there before me. Some three thousand years earlier he had experienced emotions of despair similar to mine. He had found a route to climb out of his depths with God's help and he had described that route in beautiful but realistic poetry.

The realism came from the psalm's recognition that a climb out of the depths is likely to be a long and tough haul. Only in the soft-option world of synthetic spirituality is the process of receiving God's forgiveness and entering into a new relationship with him a quick fix. For there can be no true penitence without pain, no real contrition without courage. After sinning against God, restoring fellowship with him can be a slow process. As if to emphasize this aspect of a penitential journey, the psalmist wrote two haunting verses about waiting for forgiveness:

> *I wait for the Lord, my soul waits,*
> *And in his word I put my hope,*
> *My soul waits for the Lord,*
> *More than the watchmen wait for the morning,*
> *More than the watchmen wait for the morning.*

As I read the lines, I had no problem in identifying with those watchmen. The months ahead were bound to be full of testing, watchful nights. I was going through one of them right now. Yet I sensed that how I waited was going to be important, for the final stanza of the psalm promised *unfailing love and full redemption.* They were worth waiting for.

Thinking about these two rewards drove away my terror and obliterated the obscenities of the quizzy. All of a sudden I was able to pray. With vanishing fearfulness my prayer followed the climb signposted in the psalm from out of the depths to the heights of God's unfailing love and full redemption. In a mood of preparatory acceptance for the journey I fell into a peaceful sleep which lasted seven hours.

CHAPTER 3

Early Days

My first full day as a prisoner was packed with incidents. I was busted for drugs, toasted in tea, tested for spelling, grassed up by an unknown enemy, asked for help by some new friends and blessed by a prison character known as the 'The Pie'. It soon emerged from these experiences that learning the ropes as a new boy in Belmarsh was going to be far more challenging than it had been in my previous seats of learning at Eton and Oxford.

I was woken by a pealing bell followed by two shouts that I heard every morning of my sentence. 'Unlock! Everybody out!' When the officers marched down the threes they threw open each cell door, repeating the second command at higher decibel levels to anyone still in bed. As I came out of my cell and joined the long line of prisoners parading on each level of the wing, unpleasant memories of the previous night's chanting flooded back. I became increasingly nervous as I remembered that the cell neighbours on my immediate left and right had been the noisiest vocalists in the chant's anatomical threats, so I trembled internally and kept looking over my shoulder, only to discover that the natives who had sounded so hostile the night before were now surprisingly friendly.

'G'morning,' said the man on my right, ''ope you slept well.' 'Sorry about last night,' chipped in the prisoner to my left. 'Nothing personal you understand.' I did my best to nod understandingly as he continued, 'We were just on the tackle [drugs]. Just lettin' off steam. Come and have a rosie [cup of tea]. We got Association for the next 15 minutes.'

Association was the Belmarsh word for tea-break time. Sometimes it lasted for an hour and took place twice a day. Sometimes it didn't happen at all because for unexplained reasons the prisoners were not allowed to 'associate' with one another at the expected times. To my amazement, several of the inmates made a point of being warm and friendly to me as we queued for what was dubiously called breakfast. 'Best of British, Jonofun,' said a guy with a heavy Italian accent, introducing himself as Zanzico. 'Welcome to hell,' said a cheerful Rastafarian as he shook my hand. 'Top o' the mornin' to ye,' declared an Irishman straight from central casting, adding in a sepulchral whisper that if I wanted any favours done, 'don't trust anyone in here except me'. I was trusting no one and watching everyone. The latter activity was mutual. I sensed that I was being sized up by many pairs of eyes, for a prison wing has the atmosphere of a closed community in which every newcomer is warily assessed for his weaknesses.

I was feeling weak from hunger. I hadn't eaten anything of substance since 'the last breakfast' in Lord North Street 24 hours earlier. The first breakfast in Belmarsh wasn't exactly tempting. It consisted of a small plastic bag of cornflakes, a packet of long-life milk, a teabag and a stale bread roll with jam. I devoured every morsel of it and felt better.

During my first Association I had several more greetings (all friendly) and handshakes (some bone-crushing). There was quite a bit of macho posturing. One bulky bruiser whose occupation I would have guessed was a professional weightlifter, came over and leered at me through broken teeth, 'All you need to know about Beirut is that it's got new boys, naughty boys and nasty boys. I'm one of the nasty ones.' 'Thanks for telling me,' I said, trying to keep my voice on an even keel as our eyes met. Whatever strange psychological test was being applied to me, I must have passed it, for the weightlifter stopped leering and started smiling. With a friendly thump on my shoulder he gave me his qualified seal of approval. 'You're a real man,' he said. 'You won't have no trouble. But best meet Razor – just to be sure.' Before I could find out anything about Razor, more bells pealed, more officers shouted and we were banged up in our cells for the next three and a half hours.

*   *   *

Being banged up was the dominant feature of the Belmarsh routine. On an average day we seemed to spend 17 or 18 hours out of the 24 locked in our cells. On a bad day (usually Saturdays and Sundays) the figure rose to 22 or 23 hours out of 24. We were supposed to be brought out of our cells every day for 'Association' (not always), for 'exercise' (often cancelled) and for 'work' (occasionally). The reason I have put these words in inverted commas is that in prison they signify something rather different to their meaning anywhere else. 'Association', for example, does not mean that all prisoners on a wing associate together. It is noticeable that many inmates come out of their cells as little as possible and talk to no one when they do. This may be because of fear, because of the nature of their offences, or because they are withdrawn, reclusive personalities. I always wanted to join in the human contact of Association even though my second experience of it gave me a bad scare.

The next Association period on the first full day of my sentence started at 11.45 a.m. There seemed to be around two hundred inmates on Beirut or HB3, and about half that number came down to the ground floor from the landings to fill their plastic mugs with teabags and hot water. As we mingled together I began to become accustomed to the sights and sounds of the wing. I noticed that over half my fellow inmates were Afro-Caribbean or Asian, that most were in their twenties or early thirties and that their accents ranged, domestically speaking, from posh Edinburgh to rough East End and, internationally, across every continent of the world. During that first morning I realized that prisoners in a big London jail are a polyglot community which is colour-blind and class-deaf. To many of my fellow inmates I was just another con with a funny accent. It was only among the British inmates who read newspapers that I had the doubtful privilege of that oxymoronic status 'a celebrity prisoner'.

It was that status, never claimed by me, which brought my first experience of trouble. Towards the end of Association someone shouted, 'Here come the ghostbusters.' This heralded the arrival of about 15 men in blue boiler suits bearing the large white letters DST on their backs. Among them were four or five dog handlers with Labradors. 'Stand still, everyone,' a voice commanded. This was my first encounter with the Dedicated Search Team of officers who act as the prison's specialist drug squad.

The Labradors sniffed their way around the milling population of Association tea drinkers on the ground floor of the wing without picking up a scent. Then the DST team headed for the landings, halting outside a cell on the third floor. One of the blue boiler suits shouted down, 'Aitken! Come up here.' 'They're spinning your peter,' said a man standing beside me.

Sure enough when I got to my cell (peter) I found that a full-scale search (spin) was under way. Three officers and two dogs had crammed themselves into the tiny room and were taking it apart. Bedclothes were being stripped, the mattress was being shaken like a rag doll, the contents of my locker were being emptied on the floor, and each and every one of my few possessions, including my Bible, was being sniffed by the dogs.

'Are you in possession of any drugs or illegal substances?' an officer asked. 'No,' I replied. As if to contradict me on cue, one of the Labradors chose this precise moment to let out a yelp, although I could see that this was caused by a DST officer treading on its foot. Nevertheless the yelp redoubled the search. For the next ten minutes the ghostbusters became even more hyperactive in turning my cell inside out. Even the blank pages of A4 paper that had been bound together in my notebook until the property officers confiscated its wire binding were individually sniffed and held up to the light, as were the pages of my address book. I was told to stand on the landing outside my cell. As I waited I began to experience feelings of paranoia – what if someone had planted drugs on me? Eventually the DST squad leader emerged to say, 'You're clean,' adding facetiously, 'The dogs don't seem to like the smell of an MP.'

Back on the ground floor, Association was still in progress. The search of my cell by the drug squad had been well observed. As I had not been arrested it was obvious that I was in the clear. So when I came down the stairs, somewhat shakily, from the third-floor landing, I was given a friendly reception. 'Here's to Jonno!' shouted someone raising his tea mug. Another 20 or 30 tea mugs were also held aloft. 'To Jonno!' was the toast. That was how my prison nickname started.

A few minutes later a friendly inmate I came to know as 'Big Red' approached me and said, 'Do you want to know why you got done over?' 'You bet I do – why?' 'One of the ghostbusters told me on the way out. You were grassed up.' 'Who by?' Big Red raised his eyebrows towards the roof as if to signify that he was talking to the village idiot. 'Never know, do you? – lots of grasses in here these days.' 'But why me?' The bushy red eyebrows rolled even higher with contempt for my imbecility. 'Because you're a celebrity, stupid.' 'Well this place couldn't be a better cure for that disease,' I replied.

*   *   *

The next dose of the cure came later that afternoon when I was taken to the prison education department to do a literacy test. The opening question of the first written paper was: *The fat cat sat on the m–t. Fill in the blank.* The later questions became a little harder, but not much. I passed. I also got through an oral spelling test, and read aloud an excerpt from a children's book without difficulty. 'I don't think you need attend one of our remedial classes,' said a lady teacher with earnest seriousness.

On the afternoon when I sat in the Belmarsh education department doing these tests, I was irritated and impatient with them. 'What a complete waste of time this is,' I kept thinking. But now, after more experience of prison life, I have come round to the view that the results of literacy testing offer some of the best insights into the causes of crime. The shocking statistics that this research produces show that one-third of all prisoners in Britain's jails cannot read or write; another third can read or write but only to the standard of an 11-year-old schoolchild. What an indictment of our educational system, particularly the truancy that affects so many inner-city schools! I am sure the high illiteracy rate in our prisons is linked to the high crime rate on our streets. From my later conversations with the many illiterate and sub-literate prisoners for whom I read and wrote letters, I formed the impression that many of these young criminals do not lack intelligence. They are street smart and accustomed to living by their wits, but their chances of earning an honest living in the world of legal employment are negligible. How can a young man who has no basic literacy skills hope to find a job? Basic literacy education and more skills training are two of the highest priorities needing attention in our prisons if the government wants to make better progress in the long-term war against crime by reducing the re-offending rate.

Some of these points came home to me when I returned to my wing landing after taking the literacy tests. For a small queue had formed outside my cell, consisting of three or four young men all of whom had been advised to contact me by Stokesy. His advertising campaign for my skills as a joined-up writer was clearly having an effect. One by one the guys in the queue came into my cell, and sat on my bed as I read them the letters they could not read for themselves. On that first evening I thought this activity was probably a one-off event. I was wrong. For the reading and writing of prisoners' letters, often on the most intimate subjects imaginable, became a routine feature of my daily life throughout my sentence. It was also the entry ticket which enabled me to become accepted as a 'regular guy', a fully fledged member of the prison community.

As I was finishing off the last letter of the evening for those who had been queuing, there was a knock on my door from a neighbour who said, 'The Pie's on the wing. He's asking for yer.'

The Pie was rhyming slang for the Chaplain (pie and liquor = Vicar), who arrived in my cell a few moments later. He was the Reverend David Powe, a blunt-speaking, no-nonsense, highly energetic pastor who greeted me with the evangelical exuberance which I came to recognize as his trademark.

'Wonderful to have you here,' he began. 'Praise the Lord for you. What you wrote in today's *Daily Mail* was absolutely fantastic. The Lord has great work for you in this prison.' I was thrown by the reference to the *Daily Mail*, for I had written nothing for the paper, nor had I seen a copy of it. What had happened was that the text of a lecture I had given at a private function for American leaders of the C.S. Lewis Foundation a year earlier had been published by the *Tablet*. The editor of this Catholic weekly had been in possession of the lecture for several months but had been persuaded by legal arguments not to publish excerpts from it until I had been sentenced. With perfect journalistic timing, the *Tablet* (which prints on a Wednesday night) ran a cover story on the lecture, which in turn was splashed by the *Mail* as a full-page feature.

The article was headlined 'JONATHAN AITKEN'S CONFESSION'. Allowing for a little journalistic licence, this was a fair description. To an audience of US theologians and lay ministers chaired by my friend Charles W. Colson in the summer of 1998, this lecture had described my journey of penitence in the context of a challenging chapter in C.S. Lewis' renowned book *Mere Christianity*. The chapter headed 'The Perfect Penitent' contained this arresting passage:

'It needs a good man to repent. And here comes the catch. Only a bad person needs to repent: only a good person can repent perfectly. The worse you are the more you need it and the less you can do it.'

In the lecture I had explored this paradox of penitence with personal illustrations of my own wrestlings with remorse and repentance. At the time when Chaplain David Powe informed me that these musings had hit the headlines, I was fearful that they would detonate an explosion of cynicism. Perhaps they did, but they also unleashed a counter-broadside of sympathetic correspondence. During the next 48 hours over 500 letters about my address to the C.S. Lewis Foundation arrived at the prison, virtually all of them from complete strangers and most ending with words to the effect of 'We are praying for you.' A prison officer who had to carry this mail up to my cell in a special sack because the entire post-room and censorship system was getting clogged up by it remarked, 'I don't know what you've done to deserve this lot.' Nor did I.

The combination of the chaplain, the letters and the promise of other people's prayers gave me the feeling that my prison journey was also going to be a spiritual journey. Like monks down the ages I soon discovered that a cell can be a great place for prayer. Although horrendously noisy by day and in the first few hours of the evening, when I awoke at around 5.30 every morning Belmarsh was as peaceful as a becalmed battleship. In that stillness I soon slipped into a disciplined routine of praying, Bible reading and meditation. These disciplines began soon after dawn and lasted usually for about an hour, occasionally much longer. Inevitably there were moments of distraction and days of dryness, yet the cumulative effects of making the steady daily effort to build a relationship with God through prayer brought me great and deep blessings. The most practical of these was that my early morning quiet times set me up with a framework of peace in which to endure the un-peaceful remainder of the prison day.

*　　*　　*

After the alarms and excitements of my first 36 hours in Belmarsh, the pace of prison life slowed down to a sluggish torpor. This was partly because of the rituals of Induction – a word which came to mean a lot of queuing for very little purpose. We new arrivals were interminably briefed, often with videos, on such matters as the Health and Safety at Work Act, the procedures to be followed if the fire alarms rang, the precautions to be taken if we were infected with HIV/Aids, where to find a Listener if we felt suicidal, how to plan our sentences with the Probation department and how to raise a grievance with the Board of Visitors. However, halfway through the Induction programme the prison seemed to shut down because it was the weekend. All briefings, classes, exercise times and Assoc-iation periods were cancelled. 'Lack of resources to pay staff overtime' was the explanation given over the tannoy. The officers on duty became noticeably fewer and the hours we prisoners spent in our cells were noticeably longer. On my first Saturday we were banged up around the clock apart from a one-and-a-half-hour Association period at 6 p.m. When we came out of our cells for this break I noticed several inmates circulating in the ground-floor area with strange jerky movements. Some of them looked as though they had permanent twitches or were suffering from St Vitus' dance. Others were swaying to and fro in slow motion as if respond-ing to the beat of inaudible rhythms.

'What's the matter with those guys?' I asked a fellow prisoner called Tony as we almost had our tea mugs knocked out of our hands by two lurching dancers. 'Clucking,' came the answer. 'What's that?' 'Clucking means running around like headless chickens.

They've been booting it.' 'Booting it?' 'Taking drugs. They mainly do it at weekends. No ghostbusters around. No MDTs. Screws don't care.' Tony sounded quite angry.

'What are MDTs?' 'Piss tests. Mandatory Drug Tests. From Friday afternoons to Monday mornings they don't happen, so that's when the druggies go on the tackle.' 'What sort of drugs are they taking?' I asked. 'Mainly horse and charlie, some crack, bit of puff here and there.' 'I think I can smell it,' I said as the recognizable aroma of marijuana (puff) wafted in our direction. 'Oh you can smell anything in here – and get anything in here,' declared Tony.

'But how do these drugs get into a high-security jail like Belmarsh?' 'Bottling it, gumming it, parcelling it. They're the three main ways.' 'You'll have to translate for me,' I said. 'Bottlin' it means sticking it up your arsehole. Lots of young guys are willing to do it,' explained Tony. 'They go in and out for court hearings or confiscation order hearings or whatever and the big guys sign them on as mules and arrange everything.' 'Don't they get searched?' 'Not many get a pull. Screws don't usually bother unless someone's been grassed up.' Tony seemed happy to talk about the workings of the drugs trade as I plied him with more questions.

'So what's gumming it then?' I asked him. 'You'll see it for yourself when you have a visit,' came the reply. 'Just as the SO calls out "Time's up!" a lot of heavy kissing goes on. Some is for real. Some is gumming it. There are plenty of professional toms who pass on a little package through their kisses into their guy's gums, then he carries it in.' 'Isn't gumming it rather obvious?' 'Yeah, it is,' agreed Tony, 'but mostly the screws just let it go. Sometimes they search a con who's got something in his mouth definite-like, but he just swallows it.' 'Isn't that dangerous?' 'It is if the package bursts. Then the gummer is brown bread [dead].' Tony gave a far from sorrowful guffaw. 'But usually it comes through nature's way. Sometimes you even see a guy washing his package in the washbasins outside the bog. Then he takes it off and sells it for phone cards.'

'I don't think I'll ever be a buyer from a gummer,' I laughed, but Tony took my attempt at humour rather seriously. 'Oh you'd be surprised how many people try the tackle when they're bored out of their minds. It's a cheap and easy way of making your bird [sentence] go fast.' I was learning fast.

'And what was the third thing you mentioned. Parcelling?'
'Parcel's just a word for a big delivery. How it gets delivered is the
secret. Maybe it's chucked over the wall at an exact place at an
exact time when a joey is waiting for it. Maybe it's brought in by a
bent member of staff. Maybe it's stuck between the pages of a copy
of the Koran or the Bible that's been heavily perfumed to put the
dogs off the scent. Maybe it's hidden in a box of eggs that the
kitchen orderlies know is coming. There's no limit to the ways
parcels get in, but most of them work. As you can see, this nick is
awash with the stuff.'

That Saturday evening Belmarsh smelt and felt more like a
Moroccan souk than an English jail. Yet having myself experienced
the tender touch of the DST team searching my cell two days earlier,
I found it hard to believe that the traffic in drugs flowed quite so
freely as I was being told. 'What about the ghostbusters?' I asked.
'They were pretty tough on me.' 'They look tough but they have it
easy,' Tony replied. 'They pick on the little guys who the big guys
grass up. If the ghostbusters were any good at their job, drugs
wouldn't be flowing through this nick like an effing river would
they now?'

At first hearing I was left unconvinced by Tony's diagnosis of the
prison drug business. Clearly there was a problem, but was it really
quite as bad as he said? I had one last question: 'How do drugs cir-
culate around the prison once they've got in here?' 'Oh you'll soon
find out,' replied Tony, 'because the dealers will offer you something. Look at that joe over there,' he nodded in the direction of a
prisoner with an acne-pitted face. 'He's called John Lewis because
he's never knowingly undersold. And there are other joeys called
Tesco's and Sainsbury's because they've got so many outlets.'

As I was absorbing all this amazing information, Tony had one
last surprise for me. 'Are you going down to the chapel tomorrow?
I read in the papers that you're kind of religious.' 'Kind of,' I said.
'Anyway I am going to chapel. The chaplain told me I had to put in
an application in writing to the SO by Friday evening, so I've done
that.' Tony laughed, 'Well don't expect to see godly people there,' he
said. 'Chapel's the one place where you can be sure of meeting the
guys who are from other house blocks, so that's where the barons

have their price-fixing meet every Sunday morning. They call it the boardroom. Nice name for a chapel eh?'

*   *   *

When I got to the chapel at ten the next morning, there were more uniforms in the room than you would see parading at your average city church on Remembrance Sunday. So many officers were lining the walls that trouble looked as though it might be afoot or at least suspected. As three-quarters of the chairs were occupied, I sat down at the end of a row and waited for the service to begin.

There was quite a lot of whispering along my row. It eventually resulted in a weird message being passed to me when my chapel neighbour leaned towards me and croaked into my ear, 'Greetings from Ronnie Kray. 'e says welcome to Belmarsh and 'e'll look after you.' I was startled in more ways than one. 'But Ronnie Kray's been dead for years,' I whispered back. Unless the Kray brothers had started up in the resurrection business, there was no way this message could be anything other than a hoax. 'You are so effing stupid,' growled an angry voice from further along the row. I was relieved to see that his contempt was directed at the neighbour who had whispered into my ear rather than at me. 'The message was from *Reggie* Kray,' continued the angry one. 'He's in effing Durham. He phoned through last night and sent you his best.' I thanked the growler politely but was unable to hide my astonishment. Why on earth Reggie Kray (whom I had never met) should be sending his fraternal greetings to me from one high-security prison to another was a total mystery.

Before I had time to ponder further on this strange communication from the surviving Kray brother, the organist struck up a hymn. It was the Methodists' turn to hold the Sunday service, but the methods of some members of the congregation soon caused confusion. The chapel attendees were divided between the noisily devout and the deviously noisy. The former were mainly Afro-Caribbean prisoners who sang loudly and enthusiastically expressed their approval of various parts of the service. 'Let's sing de last verse again, brothers,' was an unexpected exhortation from

42

the middle of the chapel as two of the hymns ended or rather were extended. The sermon was punctuated with cries of 'Right on, preacher!' and 'Dis is de Lord's truth!' while *hallelujahs* and *praise de Lords* were interjected at seemingly random points in the proceedings with great vigour.

Meanwhile all sorts of business was being transacted by the deviously noisy. The money changers in the temple had nothing on the phone card bargainers of Belmarsh chapel. Their green pieces of plastic worth £2 each (the real hard currency of prison since cash is forbidden) were passing to and fro amidst much horse trading. Sometimes an officer would try to stop it, but by the time he had moved from the wall to the seating rows the phone cards had vanished. A couple of prisoners were hauled out and frisked but with no apparent result. As they returned to their seats to a round of applause – easily confused with the applause that was intermittently being given to the preacher by the noisily devout – I could see that the service was teetering on the verge of chaos.

This view seemed to be shared by the Pie, or Chaplain, David Powe. Because he represented the Church of England, and the Methodists were (just) in control, he had removed himself to the back of the chapel. As a queue to take communion formed in the aisles with varying degrees of reverence, I found myself standing next to David who did not seem entirely happy with the prevailing atmosphere of order, counter-order and disorder. His anxiety proved well founded, for events up at the altar suddenly lurched out of control. Although the Methodist minister was dispensing the bread without any trouble, his ecumenical assistant, a Catholic nun, found herself having an unusual problem dispensing the wine. Being small of stature, she was no match in the wrestling stakes for a huge Jamaican communicant who wrenched the chalice out of her hands. In vain did the diminutive nun repeatedly leap into the air trying to regain possession of the wine. In vain did the Methodist celebrant try to come to her aid. In vain did David Powe, uttering one or two less than holy exclamations, sprint towards the altar rail to add his support to the chalice rescue party. Towering above all three of them, the Jamaican, with a look of beatific pleasure on his face, poured the entire contents of the large chalice down his throat, like a contestant in a yard-of-ale drinking competition. There was no stopping him. 'Dat was some great wine,' he announced to the congregation as a posse of officers escorted him out of the chapel. The rest of us had to live by bread alone.

* * *

Although some of the scenes at my first chapel service in prison had been extraordinary, nevertheless the experience as a whole was a profound one. Three conflicting emotions were stirred within me. The first was a strong sense of belonging to the body of Christ as manifested in Belmarsh prison. The second was an understanding of the spiritual warfare raging there. The third was some sort of urge to join in that warfare, accompanied by an opposing urge to turn completely away from it.

I had never before attended a church service where such joyful exuberance and commitment were shown by most of the worshippers. The irony of such a service taking place in Britain's highest-security prison with a congregation of convicts could not be missed. The black culture was as new to me as the prison culture, yet I felt swept along by the joyfulness and inclusiveness of my new brothers in Christ, who were so obviously sincere in their faith whatever their failings. In some ways I had failed more and fallen further than any of them, but failure, as the Methodist preacher had assured us, was no obstacle to making a fresh start. Some of my fellow prisoners were already doing it, I was trying to do it, so why not get going on the journey with *amens, hallelujahs* and *praise de Lords*? On that morning of chaotic rejoicings I felt a sense of real belonging to the body and family of Christ.

I also had a strong sense of being present on a spiritual battlefield. The conflict was not just between the well behaved and the badly behaved, between the over-the-top exuberants and the under–the-counter operators. Behind the rival scenes of evangelical singing and criminal dealing I saw a deeper divide. It was between the fallen sinners who wanted to repent and the arrogant incorrigibles who had no interest in personal or spiritual change.

Encouraging the first category is the sunny side of prison ministry.

Not giving up on the second is the more difficult side of the same vocation. As I watched the various chaplains and chaplaincy workers in action during and after the service, I vaguely wondered whether I would ever be the slightest use as a layman in prison ministry. Perhaps this was the first stirring towards a prison ministry vocation of my own. If it was, I promptly rejected it. For I had too much pride and too little patience to think of wasting my valuable time in such valleys of hopelessness. My mindset was still one of superiority towards my fellow prisoners. I did not particularly care what was happening in their lives, now or in the future. I was not sharing in their pain or brokenness. I had plans of my own for rebuilding my life. After five days in Belmarsh I had not learned very much nor travelled very far.

Perhaps this mindset began to crumble later that same Sunday. For when I returned from chapel to my cell at 11.30 a.m. and was then locked up for the next 20 hours until 7.30 the following morning, I had my first experience of what prisoners call 'a knockback'. This is a term meaning a depression, a downer or a black mood. It can be triggered by bad news or perhaps by a bout of homesickness, which was what suddenly hit me.

I found myself thinking about the Sunday lunch I imagined was about to begin at 8 Lord North Street. In my absence, my mother and sister would be presiding. All the children would be round the table. They might still be in a state of delayed shock from my sentencing and from the media barrage which I knew would still be going on, with more hard pounding from 'New Aitken revelations' in the Sunday papers. More importantly they would all be worrying about their own lives without a father, or to be more precise with a father who was in jail, in bankruptcy and in disgrace.

As these thoughts crashed over me I was buried in an avalanche of remorse. What could I do to dig myself out from it? What could I do to start a new life that would be of value in the eyes of those whom I loved? Thinking back to the sermon in the chapel and to my reading of Psalm 130, I realized that the climb out of the depths would be a long haul requiring spiritual as well as practical disciplines before progress was achieved. I needed to change. The first changes would have to come in the way I thought about prison and my fellow prisoners.

CHAPTER 4

Blaggers, Burglars and Screws

Monday 12 June was the beginning of my first full week as a prisoner. So far, life in Belmarsh had largely consisted of disjointed and disorientating one-off experiences. Gradually I settled down into a slower-paced routine whose main ingredients were work, exercise and blending into the community.

Work was a complete misnomer. I was one of about 30 prisoners sent to Workshop One, a factory floor space in the basement of the prison. It took the best part of an hour to get there because of the frequent head counts, recounts and body searches applied to our working party as we progressed at a snail's pace through numerous locked gates and checkpoints towards our destination. On arriving at Workshop One we were given a pep talk about the need to get into the practice of regular work as part of our rehabilitation process towards a life of good habits. It sounded admirable until the actual work started. This was so mind-numbingly boring that it quickly led us into bad habits.

There were two types of work. One was to fold large plastic bags down into small squares which we then stuffed into tiny plastic envelopes. 'To incentivize you, you are on piecework rates,' said the factory manager. This sounded admirable too until you learned the rate for the piece, which was 0.1p per bag folded. A really fast worker could get a bag into its envelope in 30 seconds which meant earning 12p an hour. Most of us were far slower than that because this pay incentivized talking and time-wasting much more than folding bags.

The other type of work consisted of putting 'fix-fast' roofing screws on to 'hold-fast' washers. I was all fingers and thumbs on this task, for these steel widgets were surprisingly tricky to unite together. However, the real turn-offs were once again the rate of pay (which worked out at about 15p per hour if you were quick at it) and the sheer monotony of the work. In any case, the civilian staff supervising us seemed uninterested in productivity or quality control. This was not real work, it was a time-filling exercise.

Despite the obvious flaws in such a programme, I enjoyed the gentle pace of life in Workshop One, and the conversation. Sitting round a factory bench together made for a good environment for talking, joking, and learning quite a lot about each other. The inmate I got to know best was Slim who had been introduced to me in the cage six days earlier. Then he had pretended that his 15-year sentence was due to 'a misunderstanding'. Now he was willing to tell the whole story.

Slim had been the leader of a three-man gang of robbers who carried out a daylight smash-and-grab raid at a well-known Mayfair jeweller's shop. Acting on 'good gen from our inside man', he and his fellow gangsters had disguised themselves as an Arabian princess accompanied by two lady sheikhas from Qatar – the oil-rich gulf state which had provided the jeweller's with many high-spending customers. Encased in flowing robes and burkha veils, the robbers entered the shop as a trio headed by 'The Princess'. She waddled in so slowly and regally that the commissionaire had to hold open both the shop entrance door and the inside security door simultaneously. This was all part of the plan, for as the last sheikha (aka Slim) brought up the rear of the entourage, he produced his shooter and pinned back the security door. In the next few seconds the two other raiders rushed forward to the front counter where under a reinforced glass case the inside man had laid out a treasure trove of diamonds, emeralds, rubies and sapphires in preparation for the expected arrival (arranged by a bogus telephone call) of the mythical Princess Al Thani of Qatar and her ladies-in-waiting. While Slim kept the exit door open, his right-hand man, appropriately called 'Smasher', produced a heavy lump of tungsten from beneath his robes and smashed it down on the top of the reinforced glass counter.

'Smasher done good,' said Slim as he relived the scene with gusto. 'There weren't no contest between that glass and that tungsten.

47

A couple of hits and all them diamonds were ours for the pickin'! It was help yerself time.' The third robber, whom Slim referred to disparagingly as 'effing Pee-Wee', was an experienced jewel thief. He did most of the work during the next 30 or 40 seconds of 'help yerself time', selecting or rather scooping the best of the jewels into a swag bag. 'And then we just scarpered,' continued Slim. 'It was the easiest getaway you've ever seen. We'd planned it well. It was no more than 70 or 80 yards to Bond Street tube station. We belted down there, hopped onto the next train which arrived within less than half a minute. Then we changed at Oxford Circus, changed again at Charing Cross, and changed again at somewhere else on the Circle Line. By this time we were laughin' because we knew the Old Bill couldn't have even got his skates on. They hadn't a prayer of catchin' us or so we thought.'

'Were you still dressed up as Arabs?' I asked. 'Not on your life,' said Slim. 'We dumped that gear as soon as we were down the stairs and out of the way of the cameras. Underneath them widow's weeds we were wearin' tracksuits so we travelled on the tube lookin' completely normal like.' 'So what happened?' someone asked as others gathered round the workbench to hear the story. Slim gave further details of the gang's tube journey which eventually took them out on the Central Line heading towards Epping where Pee-Wee lived, 'only in those days he weren't called Pee-Wee, he was still called Frank.'

Hearing the bitter edge in Slim's voice, I sensed there was something significant in the name change. I was right. 'So what happened when you got to Frank or Pee-Wee's home in Epping?' I asked. Slim went red in the face with anger. 'The important thing what happened, happened on the train before we got to Epping,' he continued. 'Train was practically empty. Just one little old lady at the far end of the compartment. We were foolin' around a bit, laughin', gettin' excited because we were all happy havin' pulled off a really big one. Of course we weren't so stupid as to talk about the job, but what we did keep talkin' about was Frank's problem. His problem was, he'd fortified himself too heavily before we did the business and now he badly wanted to go to the john. Problem was there isn't no johns on the tube, so Pee-Wee just had to keep holdin' himself in. Over and over again he kept saying, "I need to wee" or "I need to pee," and we kept laughin' at him.

'Well by this time the train was movin' real slow through them Central Line stations in Essex like South Woodford, and Woodford, and Buckhurst Hill. And Frank was havin' a terrible time holdin' himself in and we were takin' the mickey out of him like there was no tomorrow, callin' him Pee-Wee. We were takin' the piss out of him, you might say, except that he was havin' to hold his piss in him as he kept on sayin' over and over again, "I've got to wee," as the old lady on the train kept frownin' at him.'

Slim was telling the story like an actor, as he imitated Frank's discomfort and the old lady's frowns. He had his audience of workmates in stitches. No one was fixing any widgets or folding any bags as his tale unfolded. 'Well event-ually, the inev-it-able happens,' Slim continued, slowing down his raconteur's pace to raise the suspense level. 'By the time the train is approaching Epping, Frank just has to go. But instead of standin' up and doin' it on the train, which might at the worst have cost him a fiver in fines for urinatin', he does it inside his tracksuit – out of respect for the old lady, he says afterwards.' Slim gave a hollow laugh.

'But then Frank has another problem,' he continued. 'He's in a soddin' wet tracksuit and don't like it. And even less he don't like the idea of gettin' off the train and walkin' home in his soddin' wet tracksuit. So between Theydon Bois and Epping, Frank pulls off his tracksuit bottoms and just dumps them on the floor of the train. The little old lady frowns and purses her lips' (Slim put on another old lady imitation which made us all laugh), 'but she don't say nothin' to us, so we take no notice of her. When we got to Epping we got off the train like everyone else and Frank didn't look too bad without his trousers because his underpants were boxers. So we all walk to his place and have a jar or two and start divvying up them diamonds and other geegaws which are just unbelievable.'

'What were they worth?', someone asked. 'Hard to say. A *lot*,' replied Slim. 'Two million, three million, five million. Even after the fence had taken his cut I'd say we were going to get clean away with best part of a million each.' He raised his eyes to the roof and shook his head. 'But unfor-tu-nately we'd forgotten about the little old lady' (dramatic pause), 'while she *hadn't* forgotten about us.' A sigh went up from one or two listeners. 'I don't know exactly what happened,' resumed Slim, 'but she had to get off the train too because Epping's the end of the line. And there she reported us for vandalism by urination! Apparently the Old Bill took down the particulars and she gave them very good descriptions, saying we were suspicious characters who in her opinion were up to no good.'

'One old biddy's opinion don't mean nothing in law,' interjected one of our benchmates, showing off his professionally acquired legal knowledge. 'Well it meant somethin' to the Old Bill,' retorted Slim, 'because they were already lookin' for three suspicious characters last seen runnin' down the steps of Bond Street tube station in A-rab fancy dress. And to make matters worse for us they'd found the A-rab fancy dress and would you believe it they DNA'd it and it matched the DNA on Frank's or Pee-Wee's tracksuit bottoms.' 'I can see why you started calling him Pee-Wee,' said another listener. 'Pee-Wee or worse. Much worse,' snarled Slim with barely suppressed fury. 'Because it didn't take more than a week for the Old Bill to check out all the big jewel thieves with form. When they found one living 800 yards from Epping station, they knew they'd got their man, so they turned up at Pee-Wee's house with a search warrant and it was all over bar the nickin's. That's why I'm doing 15 effin' years. All because Pee-Wee couldn't hold his effin' drink in his effin' bladder until he got off the train.'

A sympathetic hush fell over our part of the factory. 'Caught by Miss Marple really,' I said.

Slim was unacquainted with Agatha Christie's heroine. 'Who's she? How the hell do you know her name?' he demanded aggressively. He seemed to suspect I was a personal friend of the old lady on the train to Epping. 'Miss Marple's a fictional detective in a famous author's crime novels,' I hastily explained. 'Oh I get it,' said Slim relaxing. Then he added with a touch of proprietorial pride, 'and I bet the story of Slim, Basher and Pee-Wee is better than any crime novel you ever read.'

* * *

Stories were the lifeblood of Belmarsh. I heard so many of them during my letter-writing sessions, over mugs of tea in Association, or in places like the exercise yard or Workshop One, that I found myself longing for the literary skills of a Samuel Pepys or a Jeffrey Archer to record them. In fact I did sometimes use the pages of my diary for this purpose. Yet the more I listened to even the most rattling of good yarns the less impressed I became with their (often heavily embellished) narratives. The real interest in hearing them moved to what could be learned about the mindsets and characters of contemporary criminals.

There were three main categories of prisoner's stories that came my way. They could respectively be headed, 'I am innocent', 'I am incredibly strong and tough' and 'I need your advice.' Tales that fell outside these categories (like the jewellery shop raid by Slim, Basher and Pee-Wee) were the most interesting, but, even with these more colourful anecdotes, the prevailing mood was one of sadness, although rarely linked to remorse. For all the drama and excitement that surges through the cast of characters in a crime when it is being committed, their mood, by the time they have all been caught and punished, becomes soured with depression and bitterness. Because of these characteristics, prisons are fundamentally sad and negative places. Overcoming that atmosphere and replacing it with acceptance, positive thinking and hope for the future is the greatest challenge of anyone's sentence.

The 'I am innocent club' was so huge that I soon came to the conclusion that a high proportion of my fellow inmates were fantasists. This impression was reinforced whenever a member of the club insisted on showing me his appeal case papers complete with prosecution statements. Early on in my Belmarsh days I was cornered in this way by a man called Milo serving four years for aggravated bodily harm. His uncorroborated version of what happened in a pub brawl was so different from the version given in the 22 independent witness statements he asked me to read that when Milo asked me what his chances were of getting his conviction overturned on appeal, I had to say, 'Virtually none.'

This set Milo off on a tirade of abuse about how I was a cozzer's nark, an establishment creep, a judge's arse-licker and so on. 'What was that all about?' asked a friendly old lag who overheard our exchanges. When I told him, he commented, 'Milo's crazy. Ever since he's been in here he's been a complete double Richard.' 'What's that?' I asked. 'Means he's serving his time twice over. Richard the Third/bird. Lots of 'em around. They get so angry with the judge, the jury, the verbals, the grass, the joe who left his finger-prints behind, and so on, that they forget they did the crime in the first place. So they get the hump and it grows and grows every day of their bird and as a result they do it double. Don't you ever start doing yer Richard twice mate. It'll kill you.'

The old lag's warning was more timely than he knew. For having started my sentence in a relatively peaceful mood of acceptance, after ten days in Belmarsh I was sliding into bitterness and resent-ment. These demons had nothing to do with what was happening to me inside the prison, for I was adjusting to the routine, learning how to cope with the pressures and making a friend or two. All my angry moments were being created by the latest wave of outside newspaper reports on my life in prison.

I was kept all too well supplied with the numerous newspaper articles on Prisoner CB9298 (me) by my fellow inmates and by well-meaning prison officers. Time and again, copies of virtually all the tabloids and broadsheets were shoved under my cell door, sometimes during the night hours when prisoners are banged up. These papers were often marked in biro with someone's comments such as 'See page 9 – untrue and unfair. You're doing fine.'

What prompted the above comment was a *Sun* headline, 'STINKER AITKEN WON'T COME OUT OF HIS CELL'. The report said that my arrogant ways had made me so many prison enemies that I was being threatened and bullied. As a result, I was 'a virtual recluse' cowering in my cell all day long, too frightened even to take a shower. The lack of washing had earned me the prison nick-name 'Stinker Aitken'.

Instead of laughing at this and other tabloid fictions, I allowed myself to get upset by them. I was also angry about other fictions regarding my past private life or business life which kept appearing in the more serious papers even though they were seriously wrong. Prison creates a fetid atmosphere in which small infections grow into big sores. I had somehow expected that the handful of journalists who had made my life such a misery in recent years would fold their tents and go away now that their quarry was behind bars. This was a vain hope. One or two reporters had virtually become 'Aitken correspondents'. I was their meal ticket, so no dish of rubbish was too exotic to be heated up in the flames of rumour and presented to the public. I took this fictional journalism personally, which was a mistake. It became a real problem to my psychological and emotional equilibrium until solved for me by some wise spiritual advice from a Franciscan monk.

The monk, whose name I have alas forgotten, was a frequent visitor to the prison exercise yard. He looked an incongruous figure in his brown habit and heavy cowl which caused him to sweat profusely in the midsummer sunshine. He was a member of the chaplaincy team, making himself available to any prisoner who wanted to seek his companionship or his counsel. As I was walking around the exercise yard on the twelfth day of my sentence, he came alongside me and asked how I was getting along. 'Pretty badly,' I told him. 'The trouble is my heart has become bitter and unforgiving. Of course I know what the Bible says about forgiving your enemies and those who hate or persecute you. Before I was sentenced I thought I'd done that. I really tried hard to forgive all of my media tormentors. But now my worst instincts are coming out in me all over again because my attackers are going for me all over again.'

Paraphrasing some of the nastiest articles, I tried to explain why it had become so difficult for me to forgive the journalists who wrote these calumnies. 'So what should I do?' I asked. The monk was loving, sympathetic and wise. 'I understand the problem,' he said. 'I've read some of those newspaper stories too. I would have great difficulty in praying to be able to forgive the people who wrote them if I'd been on the receiving end of such viciousness. So just for the moment, don't try.' I was startled. 'Well you can't forgive anyone by will alone,' said the monk, 'but what you could try is holding the whole problem up to God. You should ask him to give you the gift of a forgiving heart. You will receive it and when you have received it then use it to forgive others. You will find that passing on God's gift will come quite naturally and easily to you.'

Put like that it sounded worth trying, so I ceased the attempt to forgive specific individuals, and instead prayed for the more general gift of a forgiving heart. It was not granted the next day or for several days, but gradually it came just as the monk had said. After that, a great burden rolled away, my heart softened, I was willing to forgive any real or imagined adversary. From that time on I became free of bitterness, I have stayed that way ever since, with far greater inner peace. So I strongly recommend the monk's advice to anyone else who is troubled by an inability to forgive.

Other than the monk, I could not recommend anyone else as an adviser whom I met while on 'exercise'. This word was another prison misnomer. At what seemed to be random times of the day a bell would peal and an announcement would come over the tannoy. 'Anyone for exercise – report to the wing office.' After forming a queue we would be body-searched one by one and then allowed out into the exercise yard. This was a space about the size of two tennis courts. If you kept marching briskly round and round its perimeter for the whole of the 45-minute exercise period, you might get a decent three-mile walk, but at least two-thirds of the prisoners preferred other options such as sunbathing, 'having a burn' (cigarette), sitting around talking or 'putting the fright'ners on the nonces'. This last form of exercise was the choice of some 20 or 30 young men who spent the entire period standing at the far end of the yard bellowing insults at the inmates from the Vulnerable Prisoners Unit who were exercising in another wire-encased yard about 40 yards away from us. This was my first, but alas not my last, experience of the visceral hatred some 'straight' prisoners (i.e. murderers, arsonists, armed robbers and GBHers) feel towards sex offenders. The morality behind such attitudes is warped, but as I was to see with my own eyes a few days later, the violence it produces can be real.

Aggression and violence were never far below the surface at Belmarsh. Although I watched out for it, I soon saw that it was mostly the product of ancient feuds and young men's quarrels. So as soon as I felt anyone getting aggressive anywhere near me I walked away from him or let him push his way ahead of me in the areas for phones or food. 'If you avoid confrontation you avoid trouble' was one rule of survival in this jungle. As I wanted to survive, I obeyed it.

Towards the end of my first week, two prisoners tried to shake me down for protection money. They came alongside me during exercise and told me they'd heard talk among the hard men of 'serving up the Tory boy', so I needed to watch my back or better still I should let them watch my back – for a fee of five phonecards (£10) a week. This was such an unimpressive attempt at extortion that I deflected it without much difficulty. 'Thanks for the warning,' I said. 'I will watch my back, but I'm afraid I can't take you up on your offer. As you may have read in the newspapers, I've gone bankrupt.' 'Skint are you?' asked one of my would-be protectors in a tone of both scepticism and disappointment. 'Skint and bankrupt,' I replied. 'My Trustee in Bankruptcy even took away my watch and cufflinks.' 'Yeah I read that in the *Mirror*,' said the second man. It was the first and only example of the *Mirror*'s reports on my various dramas having a helpful impact. My two companions shook my hand sympathetically and melted away into the exercise yard throng.

One of the reasons why I was not unduly upset by this attempt to shake me down was that I was beginning to get an intuitive feel for the community in Belmarsh. Early on, someone had said to me, 'In here you have to work out who are the real men and who are the plastics.' It was good advice. For the plastics or flaky types were noisy nuisances but not much else. They were forever boasting, bragging, flexing their verbal or physical muscles and generally being a pain. Often they were all over me asking for my autograph, telling me they had met Margaret Thatcher several times, offering to do me favours and on one occasion solemnly offering me a loan of £1 million. I sensed that drug-taking often lay behind their erratic behaviour, but whatever the explanation for it these types were well summed up by the generic term 'plastics'.

When it comes to separating the real men from the plastics, a prison sentence can be compared to a voyage on a ship with a whole lot of passengers you would never have wanted to travel with in the first place. But before the ship has crossed the Bay of Biscay it is possible to work out simply by observation who are the passengers or prisoners who are unstable, unreliable and untrustworthy; who falls to pieces under pressure; who are 'the sensibles' and who is 'a man to go to the well with'. This Texan accolade is not easily bestowed, but one 'real man' who I thought deserved it was probably the worst and biggest villain in the whole of Belmarsh. His name was Razor Smith. To the surprise of everyone on the wing, Razor and Jonno (me) struck up a good relationship.

Razor Smith was as tough a professional criminal as you could find in a British prison. When I met him he was technically 'on remand' because he was in the middle of being tried at the Old Bailey on charges of committing 14 armed robberies, mostly on banks. His trial ended with a guilty verdict and eight consecutive life sentences – a judicial record. However, the only novelty in this saga was the judge's severity since Razor had 58 previous convictions. He had been doing robberies, raids, hold-ups, jail escapes, burglaries and violent assaults since the age of 15 – usually with a gun or a knife as his weapon. His nickname, an important part of his status as a hard man, came from a horrifying 1970s episode in a south London pub when the teenage Noel Smith went berserk over an insult and slashed the faces of a dozen or more victims. From then on he was known as Razor Smith and as a man to be feared.

I had heard the words 'Best meet Razor' on my first morning in Belmarsh, in a context which suggested that he was a powerful figure in the prisoner hierarchy whose seal of approval would be desirable. However, his name and the reputation it implied did not fill me with desire to make his acquaintance. If I could have avoided him I would have done so, but this was not an option since it turned out that we were occupying cells three doors away from each other on the third-floor spur or landing of HB3. So we were bound to run into each other and we did.

First introductions were formal: 'Razor Smith,' said a huge bear of a man lumbering towards me on the narrow strip of spur corridor that separated our cells. 'Jonathan Aitken. How do you do?' I responded shaking his outstretched hand. 'A friend of mine got shipped out of his cell to make room for you,' growled my new acquaintance. 'Sorry. Not my doing,' I said. The bear growled again but said nothing until we had gone down the stairs together. When we reached the ground floor he gave another throaty rumble of

ursine aggression and asked me, 'Do you know Michael Howard?'
'Yes I do.' 'He's an effing dog,' pronounced Razor. 'He is personally
responsible for most of the gratuitous hardships we face as prisoners
and I wish he was in your place because if he was I would be kicking
his face in. Tell him that the next time you see him!'

Although slightly shaken by this verbal aggression, I was more
intrigued than frightened by it, for I saw that Razor had shrewd
intelligent eyes and a voice to match. The phrase 'gratuitous hardships' made him sound more like a parliamentarian than a Belmar-
shian. What made this big guy tick? I wondered. So I took a chance
and replied, 'Actually, whatever you think of his politics, Michael is
a decent man with a good heart. He's been a friend of mine for over
20 years. He doesn't deserve the response you just mentioned.'

'Bollocks,' rumbled Razor, although in a noticeably less aggressive
tone than his opening salvo about his friend being turned out of his
cell to make room for me. 'Even his underling Doris Karloff, or Ann
Widdecombe as you'd call her, accused Howard of being the Anti-
christ,' he added. I grinned at this colourful exaggeration which I assumed was a reference to Ann's notorious description of Michael having
'something of the night about him'. 'Well that's Ann's opinion,' I said. 'I
have a better opinion of Michael. We're all entitled to our own opinions.'

I now know what was going on in Razor Smith's head while we
were having this conversation, because he later published his
thoughts on it in his autobiography *A Few Kind Words and a Loaded
Gun*.[1] 'Despite myself I was warming to Aitken,' he wrote. 'Here he
was, fresh into a very hostile and unfamiliar environment, confronted
by a sixteen stone tattooed monster and yet I sensed very little fear
in the man. It would have been easy for him to curry favour by
agreeing with my comments about Howard, but he didn't. He was
game and he had shown loyalty to his friend, two qualities that are
highly prized in prison. And that made him all right by me.'

At this time I had no idea that my new acquaintance was keen to
carve out a fresh career for himself with the pen rather than with
the sharp or loaded instruments of his customary profession. But
over the mugs of tea we drank together during that Association and

[1] *Viking 2004*

in several subsequent Associations I formed a good impression of Razor. This had nothing to do with his past record which was clearly an appalling one. In a jail environment I thought it would be absurd to become judgemental about a fellow inmate. You must take another prisoner as you find him and I found a lot to like in Razor Smith.

Razor's formal education was so inadequate that he could not read or write by the time he left school at the age of 15. However, he had made up for it since by formidable disciplines of self-education – mostly while in jail. He had a well-stocked mind, not just by prisoner standards but by anyone's standards. He knew more about philosophers (Kant and Nietzsche were his favourites) than I did. He was well versed in nineteenth- and twentieth-century fiction, quoting freely from Dickens, Steinbeck and Hemingway. Highly articulate at many levels of expression, he was an amusing conversationalist with acute perception and sharp (I could say razor-sharp) wit. In short, he was a lot of fun and a huge plus to my social life in Belmarsh no matter how much he deserved to be there.

One day I said to Razor, 'Have you ever thought of becoming a writer?' 'In a way I already am one,' he replied modestly, going on to explain that during his years in jail he had won the Koestler Award; the first prizes in both fiction and non-fiction categories in the prestigious *Prison Writing* annual competition; and an honours diploma awarded by the London School of Journalism. In addition, he had published articles in the *New Law Journal*, the *Guardian*, the *Independent* and the *New Statesman*. He showed me several of these pieces. I was impressed.

A day later, Razor said, 'I'm very keen to develop my career in journalism. Would you give me a hand and let me interview you?' I shook my head. At that moment I felt I'd had enough of interviews and profiles to last me almost as long as eight consecutive life sentences. 'Oh c'mon Jonno,' said Razor. 'You've read some of my stuff in *Prison Writing* and you said you liked it. Besides, I thought you Christians were into helping your neighbours. Who is your neighbour? On Spur 3, I am. So why not give my writing career a leg-up?'

It may have been this ingenious appeal to my Christian conscience that did the trick, but I think it was more a combination of not wanting to get on the wrong side of Razor Smith and enjoying being on the right side of him. So, reluctantly, I said yes. The interview took place the next day in an elaborately prepared corner of the ground floor of the wing. A small table had been set up there and we sat round it blocked off from the rest of the prison population by a giant associate of Razor's known as 'Mickey the Fridge'. 'He's called that because he's doing a three for nicking a fridge, not because he's built like one,' explained my interviewer.

Razor turned out to be a very competent journalist. When his piece eventually appeared, it read well and made headlines in many papers. This was not because of my answers to his questions. The real meat of the article came from Razor's observations of how I was bearing up in Belmarsh. On the whole, he was complimentary about me. As one paragraph put it,

'Jonathan works a few hours a day screwing nuts onto bolts at 1p for ten. He also goes to the gym where he does an aerobic workout and no he doesn't keep his underpants on when he has a shower afterwards. The big way he has won hearts and minds, though, is writing letters for people with problems. He has become an alternative social worker cum agony uncle. A few of the drug smugglers even badger him to write love letters to their girlfriends.'

This last activity was the subject of much humour. As Mickey the Fridge put it, 'Jonno – do yer realize the fantastic impact you is having on the girls of Brixton? They can't believe the sudden improvement in the quality of their love letters.' In the meantime, Razor was having a fantastic impact with the quality of his article. He posted his first piece to his old mate turned literary agent John McVicar. Within 24 hours McVicar had left a message with the wing office asking Razor to call back about a 'family emergency'. This turned out to be an offer from *Punch* magazine commissioning Razor to write two Aitken cover stories at £800 a time. McVicar was buzzing and Razor was flying. 'This was real journalism,' he said afterwards. 'I laughed all the way to the bank. Easier than robbing it too.' The two articles reached a far wider audience than the readership of *Punch*. They were quoted in most national newspapers and in many radio and TV broadcasts. As I thought they did no harm to me, and as Razor believed they would do a lot of good to him, everyone was happy.

Press articles about prisoners can easily become self-fulfilling prophecies. Razor's reflections in *Punch* soon became the prevailing wisdom of Belmarsh on Aitken. I lost count of the number of times fellow inmates came up to shake me by the hand with congratulations for 'having the guts not to go on the rule', 'not asking for favours', or 'doing your bird without whingeing'. All these compliments were down to Razor, as was the surge in the number of prisoners asking me to read or write their letters. Towards the end of June a queue was forming outside my cell every evening for this purpose. It was considerably longer than the queue that used to line up outside the office in my constituency when I held my regular MP's surgery. I hope I was helpful to people in both queues, but the big difference between the constituents and the prisoners was that the latter provided me with many insights into the minds of today's young criminals.

If I were to attempt a summary of those insights, I would say that far and away the most important discovery was the intensity of the connection between crime and drugs. This connection goes far wider and deeper than the crime figures suggest. Already some 20 per cent of the prison population are serving sentences for drug-related offences. This means that they have been caught pushing, supplying, distributing, growing or manufacturing drugs. However, this is only the tip of the real drug-related crime iceberg. I talked, with the intimacy of a fellow prisoner, to a cross-section of young burglars, muggers or thieves and when I got round to the $64,000 question, 'why did you do it?' I found that in about seven cases out of ten the answer was 'to get money to pay for my drug habit'. If this seven out of ten statistic is anywhere near correct, it means that over two-thirds of the prisoners in Britain's jails are there either directly or indirectly because of drugs.

Other impressions that emerged from my letter-writing sessions were no less depressing. I was astonished by the number of inmates who had spent most of their young lives in care; who had no idea who their father was; who had already done time in a Young Offenders Institution; who were illiterate; and who were dependent on or addicted to drugs. Another shock came when I gently asked the question, 'How did you start to form your drug habit?' The reply in an astoundingly high proportion of cases was 'In the nick.'

This extraordinary answer is often true. Prisons have been described as 'universities for crime', but this label is out of date. Today they are often initiators of drug addiction. This is largely to do with what is known as MDT – Mandatory Drug Testing – the principal method that is used throughout Britain's prisons for the testing and detection of drug users. An MDT – known to cons as a piss test – is a straightforward urine sample. I did eight of them during my seven months of imprisonment, which works out at about one MDT every three weeks. That is par for the course unless you are 'grassed up', 'busted', or come under suspicion more frequently.

The flaw in MDTs is that they detect cannabis, amphetamines or other soft drugs in the bloodstream for 28 days after use. However, an MDT can only detect hard drugs, such as heroin, cocaine or crack, for three days after use. It follows that a soft drug user has nine times more chance of being caught by an MDT than a hard drug user. This point is reiterated over and over again by the barons (big suppliers) and their joeys (small-time dealers) who run the drugs trade in jail. As a result, numerous young prisoners who start their sentences as occasional users of pills or pot are easily persuaded to start using hard drugs in order to reduce their chances of MDT detection. Once they go down the hard drugs route, their chances of becoming addicted are high. If that happens, they will leave prison with an expensive drug habit costing them between £200 and £500 a week. They have little or no chance of paying the bills for this habit except by returning to crime. This is one of the biggest reasons why eight out of ten young criminals who have served sentences in either Young Offenders Institutions or adult prisons are back behind bars within a year of their release. As 22-year-old Steve, one of my letter-writing customers who was serving four years for a string of burglaries, put it, 'It's become me way of life to do drugs, to go thieving, to get nicked, to do me bird, and to do more drugs while I'm doing me bird. The only good things about it are that I don't often get nicked and I do often get buzz.'

'Buzz' was a word which cropped up a lot in my prison conversations. It had two meanings. One was the buzz of excitement that comes from 'doing a job' – usually burglaries and robberies. The other is the buzz of energy produced by certain kinds of drugs such as cocaine or amphetamines. The two kinds of buzz are often combined. 'I almost always take a good snort of coover [cocaine] before doing a job,' said Steve.

The inescapable conclusion from listening to many such descriptions of young criminal lifestyles was that the prison culture, the drug culture and the reoffending rate are far more deeply and inextricably intertwined than most people realize. How to extricate young criminals from these self-created quicksands of repetitive drug-taking and wrongdoing was to become my greatest interest during the later stages of my prison journey.

During my early days in Belmarsh my greatest interest was survival. This was achieved by two mechanisms – inside acceptance and outside support. Getting accepted by my fellow prisoners was a gradual process, hugely helped on one level by the letters I was writing for the most vulnerable members of the community and on another level by the endorsements I was getting from the most influential prisoners. Razor Smith was one important figure whose support helped me, but he was not the only such backer. For example, I struck up a good rapport with the wing cleaner of HB3, a colourful Irishman from Limerick, Mick Clarke. Three years after my sentence ended, I talked with Mick when I visited Ford Prison. He told me, 'I liked you from the start because you were upfront without any airs and graces. I thought you needed a break, so I put the word round the wing, "Leave Aitken alone. He's all right."'

One influential inmate who did not think I was all right was Wolfie the laundryman. He was a former Nottinghamshire miner serving a six-year sentence for attempted murder. He took an instant dislike to me and kept pounding me with verbal aggression. Unfortunately I could not avoid him because the laundryman is a pivotal figure on the wing. I had to hand him my daily washing bag which invariably came back late, mixed up with other people's laundry, and on one occasion with every item of my clothing stained with a bright red dye.

Razor Smith tried to put in a good word for me, but Wolfie, a true hard man, refused to change his negative opinion, as a matter of political principle. 'I'm afraid he's got the hump with you,' said Razor. 'He's a card-carrying Communist.' 'I didn't realize there were any of them left,' I said. 'Wolfie's far left,' replied Razor. 'What he actually said to me was, "Aitken is a lying, bloodsucking, Tory parasite, not fit to clean a miner's boots. As far as I'm concerned, he's worse than a nonce. He can eff off and wash his own clothes."'

I was not quite as ill-equipped for this task as Wolfie probably expected. During my time as a TV reporter in the 1960s I had spent two weeks making a documentary on board an aircraft carrier where I had been taught the old Navy practice of 'dunking the smalls'. So I made quite a good job of DIY laundering in my wash-basin for the next few days, until one evening Wolfie came up to me on the wing and said in a gruff voice, 'You can put in your washing. I'll see you right.'

I took him at his word and he did see me right. For the rest of my time in Belmarsh I had no further problems with my laundry. In those days I had no idea why Wolfie's attitude towards me and my washbag had changed. But three years later I received the following letter from Wolfie which told me the story from his point of view:

> HMP The Mount
> Molyneux Ave
> Bovingdon
> Herts
> HP3 0NZ

Dear Jonathan,

My name is Robert _____. I hope you don't mind me dropping you a few lines, but I feel I must do so. I first met you, very soon after you had been sentenced and moved onto Houseblock 3 Spur 3 top floor cell in Belmarsh Prison, I must admit that at the time I didn't think too good of you, my image of you was somewhat clouded i.e. pompus Tory arshole, myself, a lifelong fly the red flag labour supporter, but you surprised me when on that very first day in the early afternoon exercise was called, and everyone including prisoners and officers alike expected you to stay in your cell. But (No) you did exactly the opposite and joined the queue and went out on exercise and actually interacted with several inmates, ignoring all the catcalls, name calling, insults. Well all through the period I quietly sat and observed all this, and thought well done John.

Well you probably don't recognise my name but I think you will remember me from the name everyone called me by which was Wolfie. I was the laundryman on Houseblock 3 you may recall it took you some time to get your clothing washed, and when you eventually did, I messed it up by dying all your white underwear pink, and all this after you putting 2 phonecards in an envelope and giving it to me, John I thank you for those cards but most of all I would like to apologise to you for deliberately making you wait so long to take your clothing, I wanted to see how far you could be pushed, not very nice of me. I apologise, I'm sorry. Today is the 12th of June 2002, I am being released in 9 days time on the 21st June after serving 4 years out of a 6 year sentence, and I thought it appropriate that I write and offer my apologies to a fellow prisoner whom I came to admire for the short period of time that I knew him and that is you Mr Jonathan Aitkin. Good luck with your studies and all the best for you and your family for the future.

Yours sincerely
Robert

*   *   *

Although it was a boost for my morale to be able to survive and even win over a few hard men like Wolfie inside Belmarsh, this was nothing in comparison to the strength I was gaining from supporters outside. Incoming letters were the greatest manifestation of such support. During my first two weeks in jail I received over 1,000 letters. Virtually all of these expressed sympathy and encouragement, and some promised prayers. Many enclosed pamphlets, books and bibles. This tidal wave of goodwill brought problems in its wake, for I was threatened with disciplinary action because of the mass of paper flowing into my cell. After one routine inspection a prison officer warned me, 'Aitken, if you don't get rid of that lot you'll be nicked and up before the Governor for breaking the volumetric control rule.'

'What's that?' I asked. The officer became as baffling as a bad maths teacher as he launched into an incomprehensible statement about the volume of cubic feet in a cell, the volume of cubic inches permitted for a prisoner's possessions, and my violation of the correct proportion between the two. 'That's the volumetric control rule and those books and papers of yours are breaking it,' he concluded, adding as an afterthought, 'and they could be a fire risk too.'

'But they are my mail. I can't stop people sending letters to me,' I protested. The officer looked bemused for a moment. Switching to autopilot he recited a second speech, this time about how under rule number something or other a prisoner is entitled to receive mail. Then, as if realizing that his two statements had contradicted each other, he declared firmly, 'Anyway it's your problem. I'll give you seven days to get it sorted.' 'But how? What do you suggest?' I asked. 'Your problem,' he reiterated, walking out of my cell and locking the door.

Life with the screws of Belmarsh had its ups and downs, but on the whole they were a fair and decent lot. They ran a tight ship but you usually knew where you were with them. I was noisily told off rather more than I perhaps deserved for peccadilloes such as not having my shirt properly tucked in, queuing on the right-hand side of the Senior Officer's desk when prisoners from Spurs 3 to 5 were supposed to be queuing on the other side of it, or being slow to respond when my name was called on the tannoy.

These rebukes were nothing to someone who over the years had been noisily told off countless times by grumpy schoolmasters, domineering bosses, irritated whips in the House of Commons or even by Margaret Thatcher. However, I noticed that many of the younger prisoners simply could not take the sound of a screw raising his voice in their direction. They became angry, resentful, sulky and on one occasion I saw a man burst into tears after being on the receiving end of a pretty mild version of a sergeant-major's bellow. The problem was that many of these youngsters had never been away from home until they were sent to prison and their immature vulnerability soon showed.

My worst bollocking in Belmarsh arose from my lighthearted answer to a question from a fellow inmate in the lunch queue, who asked me, 'Whaddya think of the food in 'ere, Jonno?' 'Unforgettable,' I replied. It was at best a feeble witticism, but the way my neighbours fell about laughing you would have thought it was comic repartee in the Billy Connolly class. An officer tried to silence the merriment and finished his diatribe by saying, 'And as you ought to know, as former Chief Secretary to the Treasury, the budgetary allowance for food is 40p per prisoner per meal. So no more lip from you Aitken.' Needless to say, this Treasury statistic was not in the forefront of my memory. If correct, it did much to explain the poor quality of the Belmarsh menus. For one anxious moment I thought the officer's linkage of my former Cabinet responsibilities with the inadequacy of prisoners' meals might cause me trouble. I needn't have worried. A few moments later a fellow inmate said to me, 'That screw was out of order dissin' you like that. You weren't no secretary, you was an effing minister weren't you?' Tempers frequently frayed in Belmarsh, but our officers' bark was far worse than their bite. I saw them using force to restrain prisoners on several occasions but it was never excessive force.

Queuing to use the phones was always a potential flashpoint. There were four phones on every wing (one of which was usually out of order), with some 250 inmates wanting to use them during the limited times of Association. So waiting in the queue to communicate with your loved ones often involved jostling and pushing, which sometimes flared into violence. On one occasion I was standing in line for the phone when the prisoner in possession of the receiver talked on and on as the clock ticked towards the hour when the bell would ring to end Association. His verbosity started to excite comment followed by verbal aggression, followed by physical aggression. Suddenly fists were flying and blood was flowing. Someone produced a knife and more blood flowed. It was a seriously nasty incident. The alarm sounded and screws rushed on to the wing by the dozen. Those of us who had been in the queue for the phone where the trouble started were detained for questioning. It was not the sort of orderly or cerebral investigation that would have pleased Miss Marple. Several of the detainees were in a state of such excitement that they all talked at once, offering completely contradictory accounts of what had happened. This blame game or grassing one another up game lasted for over an hour and produced nothing but confusion. Eventually it was my turn to be questioned.

'What did you see?' asked one of the screws. 'Nothing,' I replied, 'I was too far back in the queue.' The officer scribbled on his clipboard and then turned to the man next to me who was Razor's friend Mickey the Fridge. 'I didn't see nothing neither,' he volunteered. 'I was too far back in the queue, same as Jonno here.' 'All right, you two can go,' said the officer wearily.

As we walked back to our cells, Mickey the Fridge started to complain about the low moral tone of Belmarsh. 'Dunno what this nick's coming to,' he observed. 'All that gabblin' and grassin' – these effers don't know the old rules. Not even rule number one: don't grass.' I nodded sympathetically. As we reached our respective cells on Spur 3, Mickey the Fridge paid me a novel compliment, saying, 'Looks like the only ones who know how to behave in this nick are the old lags and the Old Etonians.'

CHAPTER 5

Blessings and Curses

Belmarsh was full of blessings and curses. Visits came top of the first category. Violence was the worst element in the second. In between came a range of experiences which involved an element of choice. Some prisoners choose to hate the officers. Others build reasonably good relationships with those in authority. Some men rail against the long hours of bang-up. Others find ways of using them constructively. There are fighters against the system and those who go with the flow of it. The list of these choices is a long one in which personal chemistry and mental attitude play a big part. I was helped by my determination to find ways of serving my sentence positively. Even so I was fortunate to have good visitors, a loving family, a mind which found riches in solitude, and relatively few encounters with the dark sides of Belmarsh life.

Most prisoners live for visits. They are the connecting point between the gloom of incarceration and the hope of freedom; the bridge between the inmate and his family; a link with friends; and a window to the outside world. Because the Prison Service understands the importance of visits to the well-being of an inmate, the visiting regime is fair and generous. It works on the simple principle that good behaviour earns extra visits. At the beginning of a sentence the flow of personal visitors seems slow. However, this was not my experience, for reasons which were nothing to do with me.

Like every new prisoner, I was entitled to approximately one personal or family visit every ten days during the early part of my sentence. That was it – or so I thought. In fact I had seven visits in my first fortnight, six of which were a surprise to me. This flow of surprises began with an unexpected commotion at the gates of Belmarsh, where a man whom the officers initially described as 'an unknown vagrant' staged a sit-down strike, declaring, 'I'm not going to move until you let me in to see Jonathan Aitken.'

The first I heard about this incident was when a Senior Officer (SO) unlocked my cell door and said, 'Aitken you've got a visit. Come with me.' 'Oh sorry, I didn't see it up on the noticeboard,' I said, hastily pulling on a clean shirt and sweater. I assumed that my children had somehow managed to book a slot in the visiting hall far sooner than expected. 'No it wasn't up on the board,' said the SO. 'In fact your visitor's been making a bit of a nuisance of himself at the gate. He's been camping there for the last two hours. I only just managed to stop the gate officers from calling the police to remove him as an unknown vagrant.'

My mind reeled. I needed this sort of trouble like a hole in the head. 'Who on earth is he?' I asked. 'Lord Longford,' said the SO, 'and I've decided to use my discretion to allow him in as a special visitor. Mind you I'm not doing this as a favour to you, and don't you forget it. I'm doing it because I've got a lot of respect for the old boy. When I was a young officer starting at Strangeways, he used to come all the way up to Manchester to visit the worst of the worst and the lowest of the low if you get my meaning. Then when I was in Gartree, same again. Same again in the Scrubs.'

By now I was being escorted through long corridors and several locked gates towards the visiting hall. The SO was one of that wise, humane and experienced breed of ex-military prison officers of whom I met many during my sentence. 'If you've been in this job for as long as I have,' he was saying, 'you know that even the untouchables – perhaps especially the untouchables – need to feel the warmth of human kindness. And that's what Lord Longford's been doing for the last 40 years or so to my certain knowledge, so he's the last man on earth I'm going to turn away. He's in his nineties now and he looks it, but he's still going strong. A very special gentleman in my book.'

Unfortunately some of the officers on duty at the visiting hall were not reading from the same book as the SO when it came to their handling of the Earl of Longford. He had made himself a nuisance, he had beaten the system, so both he and the prisoner he was visiting were going to be given a hard time – that seemed to be their attitude. The hard time they gave me was marginal. I was searched much more aggressively than on any subsequent visit, issued with a bright orange bib to tie around my neck and brusquely directed to a numbered seat behind a wooden barrier on the far left of the visiting hall. After waiting in this aircraft-hangar-sized room for several minutes, watching some 250 other prisoners enjoying their visits, I became aware of an altercation somewhere behind the entrance doors. As they swung open, above the hubbub I heard the familiar voice of Frank Longford protesting, 'But unless I have my sticks I really can't walk that far.'

This protest evidently failed, because when Frank slowly shuffled his way into the visitors arena he was without his sticks. They had been confiscated, he explained later, 'by a rather officious young man who had the curious idea in his head that you could use them as an offensive weapon.' This idea was not on my agenda, but rules are rules in Belmarsh. So Frank had to wobble his stickless way towards me, teetering and tottering in unsupported lurches of such fragility that his progress was agonizing to watch. He advanced about halfway across the hall before his 94-year-old legs gave way. As he crashed to the ground, four or five officers stationed at strategic points of vigilance around the perimeter rushed to his rescue. The scene put me in mind of Humpty Dumpty, particularly when Frank's bald head had to be propped up by all the Queen's men as they lifted him off the floor. For a moment I was worried about injuries to my visitor, but I realized he was unharmed when I heard that piercing Longford voice telling the officers, 'I warned you I'd be more trouble without my sticks!'

Having been gently escorted to the seat in front of me, Frank opened the conversation on an idiosyncratic note. 'How wonderful to see you,' he began. 'It gives me just as much pleasure to be here as it did to be in Windsor yesterday afternoon for the Garter ceremony. By the way, I told the Queen Mother that I was coming to see you and she seemed very interested.' This was beyond parody even for a Longford dialogue with a prisoner. But Frank had higher things in mind for our discussion than tea with the Royals at

Windsor Castle. 'You know I almost envy you,' he said. 'To be humbled by God is painful, but it is a sure sign of his love for you and perhaps of his call to you. That was the way I interpreted my worst time of humiliation.'

Longford's humiliation had happened in the 1940s soon after being called up into the army. Coming from a military family, he was expected to 'do his bit' with courage and distinction. Instead he fell to bits with a nervous breakdown and had to be invalided out of his regiment as unfit for service. In those days his upper-class contemporaries saw his medical condition as a disgrace or even as cowardice. One of them presented him with a white feather. Yet out of his ordeals of misery and psychological darkness came a rebuilding of Longford's spiritual life, his self-confidence and his political career.

'It's often the way that God works,' said Frank as he told me his whole story. 'He breaks us down, remoulds us, and builds us up again so that we can go out and serve him in different ways from anything we had ever imagined.' This was food for thought at this time of my own searchings. Over the next few months, I had several more conversations on this theme with Frank Longford in prison; he had a major influence on my life's journey for which I shall always be grateful.

I was also grateful for two other early and unscheduled visits to Belmarsh, both of them by spiritual emissaries. I heard about the first one from a prisoner who had the job of chapel orderly. He was sent to my cell to deliver the mixed-up message, 'Hey man, get your ass up to de chapel real fast. De Speaker of de House of Commons is comin' to see you.' 'Shurely shome mishtake,' I retorted in *Private Eye*-speak – and it was, but not completely so. In fact my visitor was Canon Robert Wright, Rector of St Margaret's Westminster, Canon of Westminster Abbey and Chaplain to the Speaker of the House of Commons.

I had heard that chaplaincy visits were occasionally granted to prisoners on compassionate grounds, in addition to their allocation of visiting orders (V/Os) for scheduled visits. However, at my first meeting with the Chaplain of Belmarsh, David Powe, he had told me, 'I've had all the world and his wife calling up, trying to get in to see you. I'm afraid I'm saying no to all of them. I can't do you any special favours.' 'Fine. I understand,' I replied.

Against that background I was not expecting any chaplaincy visitors. However, Robert Wright had been exempted from this 'no favours' edict because he had been despatched to Belmarsh on the orders of the Speaker, Betty Boothroyd. The warmth of her private message to me and her kindness in sending her chaplain to deliver it touched me deeply. As he was leaving at the end of our talk, Robert Wright invited David Powe to preach on his work in Belmarsh from the pulpit of Westminster Abbey. This delighted David, for prison ministry does not always get the attention it deserves in the highest echelons of the Church of England. Perhaps this invitation caused a further relaxation of the 'no favours' rule, for a day or two later I was allowed a second chaplaincy visit, this time from the Reverend Nicky Gumbel of Holy Trinity, Brompton (HTB).

Nicky's standard dress for delivering Alpha talks, officiating at HTB services and filming Alpha course videos is invariably jeans and an open-necked shirt. I had never seen him wear anything formal, let alone clerical. But under some curious Belmarsh rule, all ordained ministers entering the prison were required to dress like Victorian vicars. The sight of Nicky in this unaccustomed garb amused me. 'Wearing a dog collar! Now I really believe in miracles,' I said, as we exchanged hugs and greetings. I was delighted to see him because he had been such an influential mentor in my pre-prison spiritual journey. My reluctance to do the Alpha course back in 1997 had quickly been overcome by the excellence of the talks by Nicky and other speakers. The Holy Spirit weekend, despite even more reluctance on my part to go on it, had been a major turning point towards repentance and a commitment to a new life. I tried to thank Nicky for all he and the Alpha course had meant to me, but he brushed aside my words of gratitude. 'God changes lives not me,' he quietly insisted.

Nicky asked if I realized what an impression had been made by the *Daily Mail*'s reprinting of my lecture on repentance to the C.S. Lewis Society. He told me I must speak more on this theme when I came out of prison. 'You could have a powerful impact as a witness for Christ,' he said. 'But I can't think who would want to listen to me,' I replied. This was not false modesty. When you are ten days into a jail sentence you don't see the paths ahead which may be so clear to other people. Nicky politely disagreed with my low opinion of my future potential as a Christian speaker. Six years later I have to admit he was right, for since my release I have addressed well over four hundred audiences, many of them at Alpha suppers and events.

With no further legal events in my life as a criminal defendant since I was not going to appeal, I was not expecting any legal visits in Belmarsh, but I underestimated the loyalty of my two lawyers, Sir John Nutting QC and Bruce Streather, who both came separately to see me. Our conversations were far more personal than legal, but each of them proffered interesting perspectives on events at the Old Bailey. Johnny Nutting believed that the judge had spoken, and interrupted him, severely in order to sentence leniently. Bruce Streather reckoned that the Valerie Scott letter and the Nutting peroration had made a great impact on everyone in court, and that the large file of other letters read by the judge were an important factor.

My sixth friend who ingeniously arranged his own entry into Belmarsh was Alan Duncan MP. He appeared in the previously unknown capacity of Parliamentary Visitor, bringing many messages of good cheer from former colleagues in the House. All these friends who made visits or sent messages did wonders for my morale. However, the greatest blessing of all was the first visit from three of my children, Alexandra, Victoria and William, driven to prison and accompanied there by my brother-in-law, Patrick McGrath.

'Balzac would have paid to get in here,' he remarked after his novelist's eye had surveyed the cast of characters in the visiting hall. Balzac might also have written a good description of the Aitken family's first reunion since my sentencing. Anyone who visits a high-security jail for the first time experiences a culture shock. For one thing, there is all the noise – slamming doors, jangling keys, barking dogs and shouting officers. Then there are the orders, searches and ominous warnings given to visitors – my daughters, undergoing these procedures, were understandably startled to have their mouths searched for drugs. But the biggest shock of all was the first sight of their father in a prison uniform.

The last time William, Victoria and Alexandra had seen me I was dressed in a Savile Row suit, Turnbull and Asser shirt and Hermès tie. I was the centre of journalistic attention, the focal point of the packed Old Bailey courtroom. Now I was a complete nobody, one of a herd of prisoner-animals corralled into the zoo-like setting of the Belmarsh visiting hall, all identically clad in orange bibs, striped shirts and green overalls. How would my children react to me?

The trio, escorted by Patrick, entered the cavernous hall uncertainly, walking nervously as if half-shuffling, half tiptoeing. They stared in all directions as they came through the entrance doors rather like tourists at Whipsnade peering into the long grass, attempting to identify the Dad-animal they had come to see. With my heart in my throat, I gave a sedentary wave in their direction. I was behind a wooden barrier in position No. 67, blending anonymously into the grey-green horizons of the Belmarsh landscape. For a second I was filled with absurd fears that they wouldn't recognize me at all and would go away again. Then William spotted me, gave me a shy wave back, and broke into a loping stride towards me.

A moment later we were hugging and kissing with the primeval instincts of parent–children bonding and love. Tears were in some eyes, including mine, brought on by mixed emotions of joy at the reunion and sadness at the situation. William greeted me in tones of surprised relief, 'So you haven't had your head shaved!' Apparently a different prisoner's shaved head, misidentified as mine by the *Daily Express* in its front-page photograph of the wrong sweatbox leaving the Old Bailey on the afternoon of my sentencing, had been causing my son sleepless nights. It was one of a dozen examples that emerged in the next hour or so of how inaccurate press stories had caused family heartaches.

Mutual reassurance was at the heart of this first visit; I wanted to be sure that everyone was coping and surviving back at home; they wanted to be sure that I was not having a terrible time. Although I had written to them in good spirits every day since being sentenced, the contrast between my positive letters and the negative media reports had caused great worry. My nearest and dearest had imagined that I was trying to keep their morale up by feigning an artificial cheerfulness on paper. Now that they saw me being genuinely cheerful in the flesh, those fears receded.

Long before the visit ended, we all relaxed into a good mood. Love, loyalty and laughter seemed to be uniting us. Were we putting on an act to strengthen each other? I don't think so. Family visits to prisoners are often bittersweet encounters, but for most of this one the sweet side was in the ascendant. However, our parting was a different matter. None of us actually broke down in the visiting hall when the officers called 'Time's up!' but we were close to it. The pain of this poignant moment increased after we parted. When I got back to my cell I lay on my bed and shed tears of remorse for all I had put my family through. I now know that within seconds of waving goodbye to me as they left the visiting hall, Ally, Victoria and William shed their own tears, as did my sister Maria who was waiting for them in the car.

One of the reasons why the word 'passion' is used in the title of this book is that it has the additional and older meaning of suffering. This emotion was a painful reality to me every day of my sentence, but I always knew that the sufferings of a prisoner's family are greater than those of the prisoner himself. So whenever I shed tears, they were usually for my four children, my mother, my sister, my ex-wife and other immediate relatives.

Whenever I felt overwhelmed by such emotions, at least I could release them in the privacy of my single cell. This privacy was such a bonus that I soon came to see the long hours of bang-up not as a curse but as a blessing. Like every prisoner, I had my times of frustration. Yet I learned how to count my blessings as I worked out a way of maximizing the gains of solitude and minimizing its pains.

Solitude and loneliness are two completely different experiences. Not for one single moment of my prison sentence did I feel lonely. Even when at weekends we were banged up for 22 or 23 hours in the day, I filled almost every minute with journeys of the mind, pen and spirit. Rarely did I take a nap during the day. Charles Colson had warned me of the depressing effects he had noticed on prisoners, during his time in jail, if they tried to 'sleep away their sentences'. I took his advice seriously. Indeed I was so determined not to squander the advantages of solitude that I drew up a daily schedule of in-cell activities. They were apportioned by hours into four main sections: QT, GT, RT and LWT.

QT stood for quiet time which meant prayer, Bible reading and occasional meditation. In later chapters I will return to some of the disciplines I used in these hours which usually filled the early morning time before our cells were unlocked, and the last hours at night before falling asleep.

GT was Greek Time – the hours I spent learning New Testament Greek. I had made a commitment to master this ancient language because I had been accepted by Wycliffe Hall, Oxford, to read theology after I came out of prison. I knew that satisfying the Oxford University examiners in a Greek paper would be a tough call for someone who had never opened a Greek textbook in his schooldays. So now I studied Wenham's *The Elements of New Testament Greek* every day for at least two hours, constantly testing myself on the book's exercises in grammar, vocabulary, and verb conjugation.

RT was reading time. I divided it between reading for pleasure and reading for spiritual study. While in Belmarsh the authors I enjoyed for pleasure included John Le Carré, Tony Parsons, Rudyard Kipling and Paul Johnson. Some of my favourite authors on spiritual subjects were Philip Yancey, John Stott, Richard Forster, Evelyn Underhill and Thomas à Kempis.

As for LWT, or letter-writing time, this could easily have filled every minute of the day, for by the time I had spent two weeks in Belmarsh I had received well over a thousand letters. I answered most of them by handwritten postcards each about 50–100 words in length. I sent these out at the rate of around 40 a day. In addition, I wrote three or four much longer letters every day to close friends or family members. On top of that I helped at least half a dozen of my fellow prisoners by reading and writing letters for them. This sounds a heavy load, but I have always enjoyed the art of correspondence and I loved answering my old friends or new well-wishers who had been kind enough to keep my spirits up by writing to me. If writer's cramp or brain fatigue crept in, I would sometimes take inspiration from George Nathaniel Curzon who, even when Viceroy of India, was in the habit of writing a hundred letters a day in his own hand. *Curzon and his Circle* by Kenneth Rose (from which I gleaned these facts) was another marvellous book I reread while in Belmarsh. It occasionally made me say as my mantra, 'Come on Curzon,' when I sat down to tackle yet another pile of incoming mail with postcard replies.

The four disciplines I have summarized – QT, GT, RT and LWT – kept me busy and also surprisingly fulfilled. By changing them around and even adding more activities to them, such as learning poetry and keeping up my diary, I was never bored. One way and another I made the best of the long hours of solitary bang-up and turned its curses into a blessing.

Cursing was literally what many of my fellow prisoners did the moment they came out of bang-up. As soon as our cells were unlocked for meals or for Association I saw a lot of men tumbling out on to their spurs effing and blinding in rage, which was often a reaction to their claustrophobia, drug-taking, boredom or stir-craziness. I felt particularly sorry for the guys who were unable to read or had no discernible intellectual resources, because they found long hours of incarceration a form of torture. Sometimes I would ask my neighbours standing alongside me in the queue for food what they had been doing in their cells for the past few hours.

'Just starin' at the effin' ceiling mate',
'Booting it [taking drugs]',
'Sleeping it off',
'Playing kaluki [a prison card game of interminable length]',
'Dreaming of beautiful women',

were typical responses. Prison reformers of the future must find better ways of replacing the mindless boredom of bang-up with properly organized regimes of skills training, education, and real work if our society is seriously interested in reducing the reoffending rate.

One or two of the younger offenders, usually in their early twenties, came to look on me as something of a father figure on account of my Methuselah-like age of 56. I was not much use in the paternal role but I did sometimes dispense help and advice to them in addition to writing letters. I remember doing a small favour for a slim young Afro-Caribbean lad called Jude who asked if he could talk to me one evening.

'You don't know what I'm in here for, do you?' he began. 'Yes, you told me yesterday. GBH.' 'That's not the truth. Don't tell a living soul, but I'm doing a four for rape.' This story poured out of him. Jude was another member of the 'I am innocent' club. However, there were possible reasons for believing he might be one of those rare ones who had been handed the wrong verdict by a jury. For this was a complicated tale of consensual sex in a relationship which went sour, that suddenly became the source of a rape allegation by the jilted girlfriend. Her story was backed up by her allegedly vengeful sister with whom Jude had also had a relationship.

'I know they were lying, but that's not what's bothering me right now. I'm scared, real scared,' he said. 'Why are you scared?' I asked. Jude had seemed a confident character. 'Because there's one con on the wing who knows me and knows Doreen [the rape victim].' Jude pointed in the direction of a heavily built prisoner who looked twice his own size. 'I've heard him talking to his mates and I think they may be scheming to give me a jugging. So I'm real scared.' 'What's a jugging?' I asked. He told me. I was shocked. I would have been even more horrified if I had known that I was going to witness a jugging at first hand in a few hours' time.

'Do you really think they might do that to you?' I asked. 'Yes I do. I'm real scared, Jonno.' He began to cry. As his tears flowed, a nun who was a member of the chaplaincy team came on to the wing. Her name was Sister Campion. 'Anything I can do to help?' she asked, seeing Jude's obvious distress. I explained the problem. Sister Campion was evidently a miracle-worker. For within 48 hours Jude had been shipped out to the Verne Prison in Dorset. For him, the immediate threat of a jugging was over.

Prisoner-to-prisoner violence was one of Belmarsh's biggest curses. I came to recognize this more clearly when I was moved to House Block One. The hard men of HB1 seemed to be noticeably harder than the gentle souls like Razor Smith and Mickey the

Fridge whom I had left behind on HB3. There were more fights on my new wing. It also took much longer to use the phones, largely because a third of them were out of order, having been smashed by prisoners losing their tempers, so the jostling in the queues to use them was much rougher.

Far and away my roughest experience in Belmarsh, although I was not the target of it, was to be an involuntary spectator at the jugging of a nonce, or sex offender. This was exactly the sort of violent attack that Jude had feared. I had a ringside seat at this event because I was taking a shower a few yards away when the attack happened. The washing facilities at the end of my spur were pretty basic. They consisted of four shower cubicles separated from each other by bikini-style partitions which cut off just above the waist. In these showers, privacy was minimal, water temperature erratic, flow from the nozzles sporadic and the floor area was permanently awash with dirty soapsuds which gurgled away sluggishly through inadequate drains. At the best of times, taking a shower under these conditions was no pleasure. This one was to end in terrible pain for the victim of an unexpected jugging attack.

When I entered the showers I hardly noticed the only other occupant of them. He was a wiry, nondescript middle-aged man of average build. As his head and face were covered with shampoo lather, it was difficult to make out his features. Two shower cubicles away from him, I was soon preoccupied with my own ablutions which were awkward because of the temperamental surges in the water pressure, so I did not catch sight of my neighbour's two attackers until they were halfway across the room. Fully dressed, walking on tiptoe and with towels covering most of their faces, they looked like stage baddies impersonating Arab terrorists. But instead of a bomb, one of them was carrying a large plastic jug of the type normally used during Association for pouring out tea.

'Where are ya Izzy?' they called out, like hounds baying for a fox. Izzy did not regard their inquiries as the prelude to a pleasant social encounter. With a wail of terror, he dived underneath the shower partition to try to hide himself. This set the assailants off in full cry. 'Effing nonce! ... Come out of there you effing Izzy! You effing front wheeler! ... You effing, effing nonce!' they bawled.

The man carrying the jug took off its lid and hurled the steaming contents towards Izzy's naked body which the second man was trying to pull out from under the partition. As all three participants in the fracas were slithering around in the soapsuds, they collided with each other, and a lot of the dark liquid from the jug was spilt on the floor, but some of the hot brown stuff did hit its target – Izzy's private parts. It stuck to them like toffee-coloured tar, making him scream. In an attempt to escape from his agony, he jack-knifed backwards into the shower, writhing under it in frenzied efforts to wash away whatever was sticking to his loins and scalding them.

Having inflicted their torture on Izzy, his attackers splashed their way to the exit with whoops of sadistic delight. They were on such a high that they did not seem to notice there was anyone else in the showers. One of them paused in the doorway to deliver his parting bellow, 'That'll learn you, you effing nonce!' After that, I was alone in the washroom with Izzy whose cries of pain subsided into moans and sobs as he stumbled out of the shower and tried to pour cold water from a basin on to his genitals. The whole horrible scene had lasted no more than 20 seconds.

I was shaken myself, but Izzy was in traumatic shock of the kind I had only seen before in road accident victims. I helped him put on his shorts and flip-flops. 'Bastards,' I said. 'Are you badly hurt? Do you want to see a doctor?' 'I'll live,' he said through white lips and chattering teeth, 'and I don't want no doctor. Don't say a word to anyone. I'm not a nonce. I swear it.'

Further inquiries into the damage to Izzy revealed that he had been scalded but not badly burned. The pain he had suffered from the mixture of hot water and sugar that had been thrown at him was serious, but it was more psychological than physical. The vicious and unprovoked attack had been partly anti-Semitic, for as he explained to me, the racist term 'front wheeler' comes from front-wheel skid = Yid. However, the real cause of it was the loathing some so-called straight offenders feel towards sex offenders. The worst effect was the fear that would last long after his sore body had healed.

Whatever crime Izzy had or had not committed, I felt sympathy for him as the victim of a jugging. I asked him whether he wanted to report the incident, with me as a witness. Even though he knew who his attackers were he would not hear of it. 'Don't even think of it – please,' he said piteously. 'It would make it far worse for me, and for you too.' I had learned enough about the culture of Belmarsh to know he was right. So that was the end of the jugging. I walked the still-whimpering Izzy back to his cell, advised him to apply for a transfer to the Vulnerable Prisoners Unit and wished him goodnight with a heartfelt handshake. Having seen at first hand the curse of Belmarsh violence, I wanted to move to another prison as soon as possible.

CHAPTER 6

On the Move

About two and a half weeks after arriving in Belmarsh I was summoned over the tannoy and told to report to the Allocation Officer. 'I've got good news and bad news for you,' he said with a sphinx-like smile. 'The good news is that you've got your D-cat status. The bad news is that no D-cat prison is willing to take you.' By this time I was getting quite used to the curious inconsistencies of Her Majesty's Prison Service, so I said nothing. My continuing classification as an A-cat prisoner had already been the subject of much comment among knowledgeable old lags on the wing.

'Do yer think someone high up has got it in for yer, Jonno?' inquired one fellow inmate. 'Sticks out a mile that you're a D-cat. Normally geezers like you get shipped out after a couple of days. Maybe a week at the most. It don't make no sense keepin' you banged up in here with all us A-cat hard men.'

This was a logical observation. Belmarsh is Britain's highest-security jail. All its prisoners are automatically classified as A-category (high risk) on arrival. The only exceptions are a handful of terrorists, E-list men (potential escapers) and dangerously violent villains who are held in a special fortress-like enclave within the jail and given the super-high-risk status of AA-cat. However, Belmarsh is also a dispersal prison, which means that it operates as a Grand Central Station for all prisoners sentenced by the courts in and around London. So once a new prisoner has been processed, unless he is confirmed in the A-cat classification, he is usually quite quickly dispersed, or 'shipped out' as cons call it, to a jail with the security classification appropriate for his crime and circumstances.

As a first offender serving a short sentence with no history of violence or bad behaviour, I was a prime candidate for being moved to a low-security or D-cat jail. However, the Allocation Officer's announcement suggested that this might not be going to happen.

Eventually I asked the obvious question, 'Why isn't any D-cat prison willing to take me?' The officer consulted the notes on his clipboard. 'Medical reasons,' he replied. 'What medical reasons?' I asked. 'I've only been to the surgery twice since arriving here. Once was to collect my asthma puffer which I've hardly had to use. The other time was to get my toenails clipped.' It was an anti-suicide rule at Belmarsh that no inmate is allowed access to nail clippers. The officer frowned and made a further perusal of my case notes. 'Sorry. Couldn't read the SO's handwriting,' he said. 'As you were on medical reasons. It should have been media reasons.'

The media had reported many fictions about my impending move from Belmarsh. One BBC bulletin told the nation that I had already arrived at HMP Ford in Sussex. Another 'authoritative source' said I was going to serve the rest of my sentence in HMP North Sea Camp in Lincolnshire. Other headlines confidently reported that I was destined for HMP Spring Hill in Oxfordshire. However, according to the information on the clipboard the governors of all these D-cat jails, and others, had refused to accept me on the grounds that I would cause media stake-outs and intrusions which they could not handle. 'So it's a problem,' said the Allocation Officer. 'Governor Hewitson wants to see you about it.'

Governor Hewitson was apologetic. 'This will have to be sorted by Headquarters,' he told me, 'but that may take some time. So I'm afraid you're not going anywhere for the foreseeable future. I'm going to have to put you on House Block One.' This was a blow. I was getting on well in HB3 with a good network of friendly faces around me. Being moved to another part of the prison would mean a new beginning in a new community. But of course I had to do it. Starting life on a different wing made me unhappy, restless and sleepless. My initial insomnia had a lot to do with the location of my new cell on HB1. It was situated directly above the kennels housing the Belmarsh pack of Alsatians. Their nocturnal disputes were so noisy that I asked my wing officer whether there was any chance of getting moved to another cell. 'You don't by any chance think you're still staying in the Ritz Hotel do you?' he retorted.

*　　*　　*

I forgot about moving and continued not sleeping. On the night of the violent jugging in the showers I could not sleep at all. The memory of Izzy's screams kept me tossing and turning for hours. If I did drift off, the sound of barking Alsatians soon woke me up again. I tried to pray, but ineffectively. At about 4 a.m. I got out of bed and watched the dawn breaking over Belmarsh. The grim prison architecture was softened by the sounds of birds singing as the matinal rays of sunlight touched the plane trees, lawns and flowers which were planted round the edge of the perimeter walls. This contrast between the beauty of nature and the beastliness of incarceration set me off on a train of theological and poetic thought. Eventually I picked up my pen and began scribbling in verse. By the time my muse was interrupted by the now familiar cry of 'Unlock. Everybody out!' at 7.30 a.m., I had composed a 44-line poem about God, nature and repentance. I gave it a title, 'Ballad of Belmarsh Gaol', and posted it to a friend, asking him if he thought any poetry magazine would be interested in publishing it. This was an error of judgement. Whether it was caused by an excess of sleeplessness, literary pride or emotional anguish I do not know. But it was a mistake which brought me plenty of problems.

The first I heard about the furore created by the 'Ballad of Belmarsh Gaol' was three days later when my next-door cell neighbour greeted me on our spur with the words, ''ave you been writing a poem, Jonno? The bleedin' radio's been readin' it every 20 minutes since six o'clock, slaggin' you orf.' The prison officer supervising early morning Association was more complimentary. 'How's our poet laureate then?' he asked with a friendly smile. 'I read it on the bus. Very impressive.'

Unfortunately his verdict was not shared by the leading critics in the national press. The actual Poet Laureate, Andrew Motion, panned it in *The Times*. Several journalists made unfavourable comparisons between the artistic abilities of J. Aitken and O. Wilde,

84

whose rather more famous composition, *The Ballad of Reading Gaol*, came off far better. The *Daily Telegraph*, in a delicate exercise in the literary technique known as praising with faint damn, gave the poem a half-page spread under the headline, 'AITKEN'S VERSE COULD BE WORSE'. Almost the only friendly commentators were Auberon Waugh, Editor of the *Literary Review*, who said, 'Jonathan might have spent more time on it. But I still think it is rather touching'; while Frank Johnson, Editor of the *Spectator*, said, 'I think it's better than Andrew Motion. It scans and rhymes.'

It was Frank Johnson who brought the poem to national attention by publishing it in the *Spectator* complete with a colourful cartoon on the magazine's cover depicting me scribbling away in a cell, wearing a ball and chain. He also dropped dark hints that his magazine had obtained the verses by a clandestine operation. This started the rumour mills grinding away. It was speculated that the poem had been smuggled out by an accomplice on the staff of the prison. This set off an official investigation inside Belmarsh. Two or three civilian employees were interviewed. Eventually the investigating officer got round to interviewing me. 'The Governor is not considering any disciplinary action against you. You can go on writing all the poetry you like. However, I'd like to ask for your co-operation over these newspaper reports that a member of the South London Probation Service smuggled it out. We have to take that seriously as a breach of security.' 'No breach of security by anyone,' I assured him. 'I simply put the poem in an envelope, put a stamp on it and posted it to an old friend of mine, Bruce Anderson c/o The Travellers Club. He works for the *Spectator*.' 'Oh that's good,' said the officer. 'My investigation is over. I can close the file.'

In retrospect I wished I had never opened the file on the 'Ballad of Belmarsh Gaol'. I kicked myself for being a self-indulgent poet and a self-promoting fool. I had completely underestimated the levels of media excitement and hostility which I was still capable of provoking. To this day, I think Frank Johnson was wrong to make such a meal of the poem, but the fundamental mistake was mine.

The only lingering effect of this episode was that it unleashed a new torrent of letters. Most of them were much kinder about the poem than the press had been. My correspondents seemed to understand that the point of my verses was that they reflected the deep valley I was passing through in terms of pain and penitence. Although I still think that the quality of my poetry in the 'Ballad of Belmarsh Gaol' strains towards the average, nevertheless it gives an accurate snapshot of my spiritual and personal emotions in the fourth week of my sentence. For that reason I now reprint it:

Ballad of Belmarsh Gaol

The guard dogs bark, the barbed wire glints
As russet dawn unveils each day
To towers of steel and walls of flint
Weathered and worn to drabness grey.

Small sights and sounds relieve the pain:
Dew-caressed grass, blackbirds in song
Like cantors, chanting the refrain
That nature's prisoners do no wrong.

Plane trees like sentries guard the flowers
By gentle breezes brushed and kissed,
Unlocking growth in those still hours
Of silence, peace, and wraith-like mist.

This garden knows no handcuffs, chains,
No wardens' shouts, no orders, powers
Only God's beauty lives and reigns,
Seen through the prism of cell bars.

Bars sharpen senses; tune the ear
To whispered cadences of truth
Whose gentle message casts out fear,
Rekindles fire and faith of youth.

Four bars, whom do you represent?
Are you mere gaolers, cold and stern?

Or are you sowers with intent
New seeds to plant, old chaff to burn?

Some dawns I hear you call with names
Of children loved, yet far away.
Or friends whose loyalty proclaims
Bonds that will hold till Judgement Day.

Judge not, speak not, nor verdict give.
For life's strange road has paths unseen
High peaks unmapped, strong years to live
Unleashed from fear, from sin made clean.

Four bars, what say you? Do I hear
The call of Matthew? Sheep or goats?
Or is it John's High Priestly prayer?
Or Peter's nets cast out from boats?

These gospel stories, sinners' bread,
Strike chords. So, Father, who did run
With outstretched arms to greet from dead
A wayward but returning son.

Stretch out again your arms in love
To prisoners one, to prisoners all
To show us, and to doubters prove
That You will hold us when we fall.

*   *   *

Whatever the poem's literary flaws, it did reflect some of the turmoil
I was feeling towards the end of the first month of my prison sentence.
My pain, specifically mentioned in the second verse, was one raw
emotion. Love of family and gratitude to friends, the subjects of verse
seven, were two more passionate feelings that were welling up inside
me almost continuously. The last three verses give some insights into
the journey of prayer and repentance that I was struggling to make.

I soon discovered that repentance in its fullest meaning is not a quick fix. My early flounderings with New Testament Greek had taught me that the word for repentance in the original language of the Gospels was *metanoia* (*meta* = a change; *noia* = of mind). Changing your mindset is a tough call, but if you believe it is God's call, you get going on the journey in spite of the obstacles and setbacks. That is what I was trying to do in my prison cell, often failing, but at least I was acknowledging those failures in prayer. On that basis, perhaps my journey was going slightly better than I recognized at the time.

One practical prayer I remember saying in this period was along the lines of 'Lord, please move me to a D-cat prison as quickly as possible.' Contrary to the forecast made a few days earlier by Governor Hewitson, my move came unexpectedly soon, when on 29 June the Allocation Officer told me, 'We're shipping you out tomorrow to Standford Hill.' 'Where's that?' I asked. 'Kent,' he said. I was surprised. I had been a Kent MP for 23 years and thought I knew most of the prisons in the county. 'Whereabouts in Kent?' I asked. 'Sittingbourne way,' he replied. 'What's it like?' 'Well it's a D-cat but in some ways it's more like a C-cat,' was his enigmatic answer, which left me little the wiser.

I was ordered to be waiting in my cell with my bags packed by 5.30 a.m. Although I was up and ready to move at that hour, when the duty officer unlocked my cell door my actual moving turned out to be a big problem. My possessions, which three weeks earlier had easily been contained in a small bag, had by now grown to fill three enormous bin-liners weighing about 20 pounds apiece. The reason for this expansion was my well-wishers' generosity. Not only had they written me over a thousand letters; many had also sent in gifts, articles of clothing, and enough books to start a library. Even though I had distributed many of these well-meaning presents around the prison, carrying even the residue of them was heavy lifting.

The holding cells for inmates being moved to court hearings or new prisons were located about half a mile away from my cell in HB1. Transporting my three bin-liners along the deserted corridors for this distance was almost too much for me. As well as the bulk that I had to carry, on that particular morning I was suffering from an asthma attack. At first it was a mild one, but every time I tried to move my three huge bags along a corridor the lifting made me even more breathless so I had to rest. Repeated applications of my Ventolin puffer failed to solve the problem. By 6 a.m. I had only struggled about halfway to my destination. I was beginning to wonder whether I would make it in time to catch the van for Standford Hill.

Suddenly a friendly face appeared in the corridor. It belonged to Razor Smith who was also on the early call list because he had to travel each morning to the Old Bailey where his trial for 14 armed robberies was still in progress. 'Hiya mate,' he said, 'everything all right?' 'No, I'm having an asthma attack,' I wheezed, explaining that carrying my bin-liners was partly the cause of it. 'No problem at all,' said Razor. 'You carry these photographs and I'll carry your bags.' He handed me a sheet of about a dozen pictures of a big man in a balaclava holding up a bank with a sawn-off shotgun. In return he picked up my bags as if they were packets of crisps and strode with giant steps towards the holding cells. When I caught up with him, we swapped our cargoes. After thanking him warmly for his help, I said, 'I don't see how anyone could identify you as the guy with the balaclava over his face in these photographs.' 'Ssh,' said Razor putting a finger to his lips, 'let's hope the jury thinks the same way.'

Evidently the jury thought differently, for Razor Smith received a heavy sentence and this was the last time I saw him. However we have been corresponding regularly for the last six years. He is now about a third of the way towards his release date. I think he is unlikely to return to crime, for he has now become a successful author and has gone through some life-changing courses at HMP Grendon Underwood, the prison which specializes in therapeutic and psychiatric treatment for violent criminals. The tragic death of his teenage son was a turning point in Razor Smith's life which sent him on his own journey of remorse and rehabilitation.

Being back in the cage or communal holding cell at HMP Belmarsh was almost as bad an experience on the morning of my departure as it had been on the evening of my arrival three weeks earlier. So oppressive was the tension that it felt like being in a tropical heatwave just before the monsoon rains. Everyone looked apprehensive, including me, although my level of anxiety at going to a new prison was nothing compared to what defendants like Razor Smith must have been feeling like as they set off to their courtrooms. I sat next to a man who told me that the jury in his case had already been out for two days. 'If they give me a guilty I think I'll top myself,' he muttered, rubbing his eyes with his fists. 'It's never worth topping yourself,' I muttered back. I hope he believed me.

The last prisoners to be brought down to the cage were the E-list men, and a gang of AA-catters. Both lots were double-cuffed and had chains around their feet and waist. The E- (for escape) list inmates were taken into cubicles to be stripped and reclothed in bright yellow-and-green jumpsuits stamped in huge letters HM PRISON SERVICE. Similar strippings and re-handcuffing, but without the jumpsuits, were given to the AA-cat men. One of them started a fight and had to be held down and rechained. As I watched his flying fists and noisily obscene gestures, my sympathies were with the screws who managed to restrain him with the minimum physical force. It was an incident which confirmed my general impression of the prison officers at Belmarsh. I thought the over-whelming majority of them were professional, fair and decent, often in the face of extraordinarily difficult pressures.

We were given toast, coffee and a banana for our in-transit break-fast in the cage. It seemed no worse than the food in many an airport departure lounge, although I knew that the sweatbox cubicles in which we would soon be travelling were far more uncomfortable than the narrowest of economy class seats. The airline analogy could be extended still further, as destinations were announced, names checked against passenger lists, last calls declared and strag-glers rounded up. I was evidently on a 'delayed flight', because at 10.30 a.m., five hours after I had left my cell, there was no sign of any transport to HMP Standford Hill. Only a dozen of us were still in the cage which at 7 a.m. had held ten times that number.

Eventually a burly, moustachioed prison officer carrying a list came over to me. 'The Right Honourable Jonathan Aitken MP,' he began. I thought I could do without this sarcasm, having lost both titles over two years earlier, but it became apparent that his agenda was unexpectedly different: 'I am addressing you like this because in my opinion you are still an honourable gentleman sir,' he continued. 'In my opinion, you should not be in prison at all for your errors of judgement. But at least it is now my pleasure to accompany you to your conveyance and to wish you good luck.'

I felt I had walked into a pantomime performance, but this character in uniform was indeed a genuine prison officer. He paid me further compliments in this Dickensian style as we walked across a courtyard until reaching not the expected Prison Service sweatbox but a civilian minivan. 'Your property has already been loaded into the boot sir,' said my uniformed admirer. If I had been carrying any money, I think I might have thanked him for his good service and given him a tip. Instead we shook hands and he wished me 'the best of British'. It was an odd way to say goodbye after experiencing the worst of Belmarsh.

There were five of us in the van for Standford Hill. One of my fellow travellers was another larger-than-life Belmarsh character. 'Oh I do like to be beside the seaside!' he carolled as we swung out of the gates. 'Not that the Isle of Sheppey's quite the seaside, but it has got sea views and sea air that blows you off in your stride in winter.' 'Been there before have you?' asked someone. 'This will be my third visit to the establishment as a guest of Her Majesty,' was the reply. 'What's it like?' I asked. 'Without doubt the worst D-cat in Britain,' declared the old lag. He looked at me with interest. 'Seen you before haven't I? Are you a solicitor?' 'C'mon Biggsie,' said another voice. 'He's Jonathan Aitken.' My name obviously meant nothing to Biggsie, but he wanted to be friendly. 'John Biggs,' he said, extending his hand. I shook it. Handshakes followed all round. We exchanged names like strangers meeting at a cocktail party. I almost expected someone to say, 'And what do you do for a living?'

Sure enough Biggsie asked me, 'So what are you in for, Jonathan?' 'Perjury.' 'Perjury. Good God! If they sent all the perjurers in the police to jail they'd have to build new prisons all the way from Land's End to John o'Groats.' I had heard many variations on this theme in Belmarsh often accompanied by examples of allegedly fabricated verbals. I changed the subject.

'So what are you in for?' I asked. 'Aha! Have you got three hours,' he replied. 'He's a kiter,' said Ernie, the one man on the minibus who already knew Biggsie. 'What's that?' I asked. 'It means he doesn't just pass the odd dud cheque,' explained Ernie. 'He bounces so many of them that they fly around like kites.'

By now we were driving down the M2. It had been the route to my South Thanet constituency for nearly a quarter of a century. I knew the various motorway signs and exits as well as I knew the milestones of my political career. It felt weird and rather sad to be on the same road to prison. As the miles flew by, the words on the Monopoly card 'GO DIRECTLY TO JAIL. DO NOT PASS GO' came into my mind. I had certainly managed to play my cards stupidly in the game of real life.

We stopped for petrol at a service station. Our escorting prison officers seemed to be deliberately casual about our security arrangements, having left the minivan doors unlocked. 'It would be jolly easy to escape, wouldn't it?' said Ahmed who was doing three years for embezzlement and VAT fraud. 'You're a D-cat prisoner now,' drawled Biggsie. 'That means they trust you.' 'But only as far as they can see you,' chipped in Ernie.

At first sight, Standford Hill was almost as forbidding a fortress as Belmarsh, but this was a case of mistaken identity, for on the windswept Isle of Sheppey three prisons coexist within a quarter of a mile of each other. They are HMP Elmley (B-cat), HMP Swaleside (B- and C-cat), and HMP Standford Hill (D-cat). Because their boundary walls and wire fences are so close, it is easy to mix them up from a distance. As we drove up to the entrance of Standford Hill, which had no more than an electronically operated traffic barrier to stop cars passing through, there could be no doubt that I had arrived in an open prison. This was where I would serve the remainder of my sentence – unless there were unpleasant surprises in store for me.

CHAPTER 7

Difficult Days at Standford Hill

'This is an 1850s boarding school run by a 1950s trade union,' was how I described HMP Standford Hill in a letter to my daughter Alexandra soon after I had arrived there. Perhaps I was being a little ungracious. For it was a huge improvement on Belmarsh and I now look back on the six months I spent there as one of the most enriching periods of my life.

However, in my early days of imprisonment at Standford Hill I chafed and fretted a great deal about the absurdities, indignities and pressures which I encountered. Many of these were produced by the tabloid press which throughout my sentence invented situations and stories worthy of a *Carry On* film. Others were produced by a weak governor unable to control a strong branch of the Prison Officers' Association (POA) trades union, whose antics created scenes worthy of the movie *I'm All Right Jack*. As both film scripts lurched out of control, I, the anti-hero of them, had many a fretful moment. However, the arrival of a new governor, the building of some good friendships, and the relationships that grew out of an inmate-led prayer group were forces that calmed the early turmoil and gradually changed me into a prisoner with different and better attitudes.

I realized that Standford Hill was on another planet from Belmarsh as soon as I went through the reception formalities in the property department. The Standford Hill officers were models of courtesy, helpfulness and humour. 'Never in the field of human endeavour', joked one of them, 'has so much had to be written in one prisoner's prop book by so few.' During the Battle of Britain Standford Hill had been a famous RAF base, and the original Winston Churchill quote was actually painted on a nearby wall. The prison officer's version of it sprang from a rule which required every single item in my three big bin-liners to be recorded in a property book. This process took over two hours, but whereas in Belmarsh most items were confiscated, in Standford Hill almost everything seemed to be permitted. However, there was an *Alice in Wonderland* moment when out of my third bin-liner came two sheets of unused postage stamps.

'Ah, now we have a little problem,' said one of the officers, 'because these violate rule 76 under which no prisoner may have any stamps in his possession in this prison.' I gasped. How on earth was I supposed to answer my enormous postbag without postage stamps? But before I could protest, the property officer continued, 'On the other hand, under rule 77 a prisoner may keep in his possession any stamps he brought into this prison from another prison. Therefore you may keep them.'

As he passed the sheets of stamps back to me I tried to under-stand the implications of these contradictory regulations. 'What happens when I've used up these stamps?' I asked. 'You see I have to write about 30 letters every day.' The officer looked at me incredulously as though William Caxton were standing in front of him. 'Well if you run out of stamps, you can get more by buying a book of them out of your wages,' he said. 'But you have to buy stamps which have been officially authorized by your wing officer. He has to enter them in his register in the wing office and put his signature on the back of them. Unless you do that, all stamps are illegal here – except the ones you brought in from another prison.'

'But I could have all the stamps I wanted in Belmarsh,' I said. 'Lots of people sent them in to me without any difficulty.' 'Well this isn't Belmarsh is it?' said the officer. 'The rules are different in every establishment.' I was learning fast. Later I discovered that Standford Hill was the only prison in the country to have a no-stamps rule. Manoeuvring around this particular absurdity used up a lot of effort and ingenuity later in my sentence.

The big plus of Standford Hill was that it was a relatively modern D-cat prison. Every one of its four hundred inmates had a cell to himself. It had a farm, a market garden, a gym and a playing field. Its 1970s cell blocks were well designed and the plumbing worked. This was intolerable luxury in the opinion of the tabloids, who dubbed the jail 'The Savoy' and added many imaginary facilities such as a TV in every cell, mobile phones for every prisoner, a Turkish bath and a cinema. Another imaginative tabloid touch was that I was known as 'the prodigal son' because my job on the farm was swilling out the pigs. Actually the farm had no pigs and I did not work on it anyway. These were minor fictions compared to later instalments of the media's *Carry On* circus.

I was allocated a cell, No. 39, on the second-floor landing of A wing. It was slightly smaller than my Belmarsh accommodation but with a far better view across green fields to the Thames Estuary. The décor consisted of breeze blocks painted a bilious green and pockmarked with the detritus of previous occupants. The walls, right up to the eaves of the cell, were scratched and splattered with holes, carvings, glue-stains, cigarette burns, toothpaste marks and chocolate brown splodges which I hoped originated from coffee. There was no washbasin or toilet in the cell. All of us 'on the twos' shared communally in these facilities which were located at the end of each spur.

After settling into my cell, I was put on the briefing course for new arrivals. It was called Induction and was carried out in slow motion, lasting for 11 days. For sheer tedium this was the low point of my sentence. The purpose of it, explained Mr Rook the Induction Officer, was to introduce new inmates to all aspects of life in the prison. We would learn the ropes and be allocated our jobs at the end of the course.

Patience is not one of my greatest virtues, and it was tested to the full by some 50 hours' worth of interminably boring Induction briefings about every nook, cranny and activity of HMP Standford Hill. Each talk was accompanied by reams of bumf which invariably drew our attention to more and more rules. The rules on postage stamps were no isolated example of pointless bureaucracy. Almost worse were the rules governing 'movement slips'.

Although it was a small prison, in theory 'open', with all its important buildings located within 150 yards of each other, nevertheless a prisoner needed to queue up for a movement slip in order to be permitted to walk to, say, the chapel, the library or the education department from his wing. Another stamped movement slip was needed to walk back again. There was no rhyme or reason in these elaborate arrangements. Our lives were monitored by six roll-calls a day, and any prisoner wanting to abscond faced no serious difficulty, with or without movement slips, since there were no high walls around the prison.

'Why do they have to make life so damn complicated?' someone on the Induction course asked following a bewildering briefing on the rules about the times of day when red shirts and green trousers must be worn, the times of day when blue shirts and grey trousers must be worn and the times of day when own clothes could be worn. 'Because it's jobs for the POA boys of course,' said a sharp-tongued solicitor who was doing four years for embezzling his clients' money.

The POA branch at Standford Hill was a strong one. During my sentence its militancy surfaced in several incidents, of which the rudeness to Michael Howard was the worst (see pages 124–7). I had few difficulties, however, with the individual prison officers, who were a good lot. Their collective views as a union were not so good, as I soon discovered.

When the Induction course came to an end, all new prisoners (about 30 of us) were invited to apply for jobs or for educational courses. After detailed discussions with the Standford Hill education department, I applied to continue my New Testament Greek studies there. My application was strongly encouraged and approved by the head of the prison's education department, Mr Colin Morris. He corresponded with Professor Alister McGrath, the Principal of Wycliffe Hall, Oxford, who supplied the necessary confirmation from the University that I had been accepted for a theology degree course which required Greek.

With all this support, it seemed certain that I would be assigned to my approved education course at the end of Induction. Not so. When the Induction Officer read out the list of assignments for new prisoners, my name was omitted from the education list. Instead I was assigned to a manual labouring job in the market garden. Baffled by this turn of events, I asked Mr Rook, the head of Induction, why my application had been rejected. 'The officers feel that you should not be seen to get special treatment,' he said. 'You must qualify to do education by doing a proper job first. You can reapply for an education course in a few weeks' time.'

Although I wondered how manual labour in the gardens could provide qualifications for studying New Testament Greek, I accepted the umpire's decision. The education department, however, did not. Colin Morris, became incandescent. 'This is an outrage,' he told me. 'You are a victim of discrimination. This is typical of the mindset of the POA. You must appeal to the Governor.' So I took his advice, applied for an appointment to see the Governor, and waited.

My waiting took place mainly in the market garden, where I was not a great success. On my first day there I was given a strange reprimand. 'Aitken, stop weeding so fast!' It was an early indication that work at Standford Hill, like work at Belmarsh, was primarily an exercise in time-filling. Further evidence of this culture was the amazing length and number of our break times in the working day. During the five hours when we were theoretically engaged in outdoor manual labour at the market garden, we were actually indoors for two tea breaks of 45 minutes each; four smoking breaks (equally available to non-smokers) of 15 minutes each; a ten-minute break after clocking in and a ten-minute break before clocking out. In the remaining two hours and ten minutes when we were not busy with these breaks, our labouring duties were undemanding.

On my first day as a market gardener I was told to weed a small flower-bed. Having received one reprimand for doing too much too quickly, I assumed a sedentary position, only to get a second bollocking for doing too little too slowly. 'But I've pulled up all the weeds in this flower-bed,' I replied. 'Pull up the flowers and replant them,' snapped the supervisor.

On my second day in the market garden our group spent all morning moving empty rhubarb boxes to one side of a courtyard and all afternoon moving them back again. 'Makes a change from talking rhubarb in the House of Commons I expect,' said one of my fellow labourers.

On the third day I joined a working party pouring concrete into empty holes that had been dug for this purpose the previous week. In the afternoon session, the only prisoner who had building work experience went off sick. In his absence, I was ordered to take charge of the concrete mixer. I had never operated any such machine before and was a stranger to the technology. At a crucial moment in the mixing process I pulled the wrong handle. The gentle churns of the machine roared up to high-speed revolutions, the bowl tilted, and 20 pounds of liquid cement shot into the air.

The first victim of my mistake was a nearby prisoner who had been leaning peacefully on his shovel until the contents of the mixer buried his ankles and knocked him over. I apologized profusely. 'No need to keep on sayin' sorry, mate,' was his cheerful response as he struggled to his feet. 'You done me a big favour. I'll be off work for weeks. And I'll be able to sue the Home Office for violating the Health and Safety at Work Act, causing me injury and stress.' He gave a theatrical laugh and began practising an even more theatrical crippled walk.

My other victims were two shire horses who had been ambling past the mixer when the accident happened. They were a magnificent pair of Suffolk Punches whose duties on the prison farm were as light as those of the prisoners. Until the moment when I pulled the wrong handle, these handsome animals had never been seen to move at a pace faster than a stately plod. The sight of the flying concrete made them rear up, snort, and shoot off like cruise missiles in the general direction of the Thames Estuary.

For the next hour or so, Hengis and Horsa, as the shire horses were called, galloped and cantered all round the prison farm. Their handlers and several officers tried in vain to recapture them. That job was eventually done by a prisoner called 'Gipsy Dave' Jones who had a special expertise in calming down horses by whistling and speaking Romany to them. Had the Suffolk Punches been very upset by the incident? I asked him afterwards. 'Oh no, don't trouble yourself. They've never had so much fun in years as they did when they were on the loose this afternoon,' he replied. Nobody seemed to be upset with me either. The only faintly negative comment came from the manager of the market garden who said, 'After all this fuss I think I'd better transfer you to work in the greenhouse.'

The tale of my exploits with the concrete mixer and the Suffolk Punches never made it into the newspapers. It must have been too boring for them, for they were busy inventing much more exciting stories of their own. On 11 July the *Sunday Mirror* published a full page story under the headline, 'JAILBIRD'S FURY AT AITKEN'S DAY OUT. HIS CELL IS WRECKED IN ROW OVER FUNERAL'. The accompanying story under the byline 'Tim Luckett, Crime Correspondent', reported my harrowing ordeals from death threats, cell trashings, attempted stabbings and the appointment of special bodyguards to protect me. I did not see this article until two days after its publication. It was brought to my attention by a prisoner who physically attacked me as a result of reading it. His were the only punches thrown at me during my entire prison sentence. It was all a dotty misunderstanding.

I was walking along my spur on A wing when this prisoner approached me saying, 'Can I tell you something? Me Nan [my grandmother] died last Friday. She brought me up 'cos I'm an orphan. But the effing Governor refused me application to go to her funeral.' 'I'm so sorry ...' I began. Before I got any further with my expressions of sympathy, a flurry of punches flew in my direction. 'He's an effing friend of yours, that effing Governor,' shouted my assailant.

For a moment his attack was alarming but his barks were much worse than his blows. He was striking me rather feebly, lashing out in tearful frustration rather than violent anger. I grabbed his wrists and tried to calm him down. 'Steady on,' I said. 'I've never met the Governor. He's not my friend.' 'That's not what it says in the paper,' said the bereaved man, pulling a crumpled copy of the *Sunday Mirror* out of his pocket. As I read Tim Luckett's article it dawned on me what the trouble was.

According to Mr Luckett, I was on first name terms with the Governor of HMP Standford Hill, Keith Naisbitt. He had responded generously to my request to be granted special leave to attend the funeral of my former parliamentary colleague William Whitelaw. The article implied that I had attended the funeral; as a result, furious fellow prisoners had wrecked my cell, threatened to cut me up and issued death threats. Not a single word of this nonsense was true. Before any part of it became a self-fulfilling prophecy I set the record straight.

'This is all lies,' I said. 'I never went to Willie Whitelaw's funeral, I never asked to go to it. I have never met the Governor.' The man dropped his arms to his side. 'Sorry,' he said in a quavering voice. His head rolled from one side to another. I noticed that his pupils were dilated which may have been a sign that he was taking drugs. 'I'm sorry,' he repeated, 'I'm upset.' We talked for a few moments about the loss of his grandmother. I suggested that he should go and see the Chaplain to ask if he might be willing to get the funeral leave decision reviewed. My attacker and I parted company on calm and amicable terms.

The incident just described was by any standards a minor one. It was seen only by a couple of other prisoners, but one of them wrote it up in lurid terms and put it in the 'grass box'. This was a small wooden postbox nailed to the wall beneath an archway on the ground floor of our wing. Some inmates called the archway 'Traitors' Gate' because grasses had to pass through it to deliver their information. During my first week at Standford Hill, three anonymous notes arrived in the grass box about me. All reported that I was being bullied.

I learned this when I was summoned to see Governor 4, Mr Elliott. He was a kindly man who sounded almost tearful as he spoke of his horror of prison bullying and his deep regret that I was a victim of it. I looked at him in amazement. 'But I haven't been bullied,' I said. A Senior Officer alongside Governor 4 read out a garbled version of the incident with the bereaved prisoner. Other grass notes reported two more 'bullying' episodes. One consisted of a loudmouth shouting mildly offensive comments about press pictures of my daughters. The other, involving the same loudmouth, consisted of some noisy teasing of me about 'the fancy food' I selected in the prison eating hall. This second incident sprang from yet another *Mirror* exclusive in their new column called

'Aitken Watch'. The paper had acquired a copy of the weekly form all prisoners had to fill in with their meal choices. Someone had forged my signature on the form and marked up their meal selections – which were considerably more elaborate than my preferences. The *Mirror* devoted a full page to reprinting 'my' meal choice form, with much comment about how I was wining and dining in the lap of luxury. All the loudmouth had done was to chant out the paper's headline, 'Chilli con carne, Madras curry and smoked mackerel. It's tough inside for Mr Aitken.'

I said I didn't regard any of these incidents as bullying. The first was a misunderstanding by a deeply upset man. The second and third were just lighthearted heckling. 'After 23 years in the House of Commons I think I can cope with a bit of heckling,' I said. So that was the end of the Aitken bullying investigation. However, I took my chance to ask Governor 4 if there could be an investigation into why my application to do an education course had been refused. 'We're looking into it,' said Mr Elliott, sounding rather defensive. 'I believe Governor 1 is going to discuss it with you tomorrow.'

Governor 1, Mr Keith Naisbitt, had the prison nickname Dino, which stood for Dinosaur. He lived up to it at his meeting with me the following day. He began by complaining that the *Sunday Mirror* had described the two of us as 'being on first-name terms', making it sound as though I was somehow to blame for this and other pieces of misreporting. I said that I too was upset by the steady stream of newspaper fictions. They were making my life difficult, as were the intrusions (at this point still unsuccessful) of the paparazzi into the prison grounds. Only yesterday two of them had been chased away by fellow prisoners from the greenhouse where I was working.

'Well yes that's bad,' said the Governor. 'We'll have to think what to do about it, but it will really be a problem for my successor. I'm retiring in three weeks' time.' I suggested that one thing he could do about it was to allow me to start an education course. That would put me inside a building away from paparazzi lenses. I would be taking up the place that had been offered to me by the education department. The head of the department had said that it was my legal right to take it and that the refusal to let me take it amounted to discrimination against me.

'Oh no, there's no discrimination in this prison,' said Mr Naisbitt. 'I'm afraid there is, sir,' I replied. 'As you know, 20 out of 24 inmates were dismissed from their jobs in the kitchen three days ago on suspicion of theft. The problem is that the 20 who were dismissed were all black. The four who were not dismissed were all white. I think any outside body might look on that as discrimination.' The Governor shifted uneasily in his chair. 'Oh dear, oh dear,' he said. 'I don't know anything about this. I'll have to look into it.' As I had already been involved behind the scenes in a prisoner-led protest about this episode, I took my chance to brief Mr Naisbitt on it. 'A petition complaining about this discrimination was signed by all 20 of the dismissed prisoners and delivered to your office yesterday,' I continued. I was sure of what I was saying since the leaders of the aggrieved job-losers had asked for my help in drafting their petition. I had thought their grievance was justified, so I had taken a lot of trouble with the wording of the petition to the Governor. Apparently he had not yet read it. 'Oh dear, oh dear,' repeated Mr Naisbitt.

The conversation returned to my application to do an education course. The Governor agreed that I had a right to do it. The question was one of timing. 'My officers feel you should work at a job in the market garden first. That qualifies you to do education. You can reapply for a transfer to the education department in a few weeks' time.' I realized that Mr Naisbitt was singing from the same hymn sheet as the Induction Officer Mr Rook, whose words and music were written by the POA, I strongly suspected. I made one last try to introduce a new line of argument.

'Sir, do you think you could consider speeding up my transfer to education in order to get me out of the line of fire from the paparazzi?' I asked. 'It's only going to be a matter of time before they take pictures of me on the farm or in the market garden. That would be a breach of the Prisons Act, a violation of my privacy and a violation of the privacy of any inmates photographed with me. But if I was indoors in the education department it could not happen.'

The Governor hummed and hawed. 'Well yes, I think I could consider it,' he said. 'Mind you, I can see the difficulties. But there are difficulties everywhere. It may have to be a matter for my successor, as I'm on the verge of retirement. But I will go away and think about it.'

On that note, a clear indication that the Governor's indecision would be final, my interview ended. That evening I wrote in my diary, 'What a third rate old fuddy duddy this man is. He hasn't a clue what is going on here. He had no idea that I felt vulnerable to the media's onslaught and intrusions. I despair.'

There were other reasons for my growing despondency at this time. In addition to being stalked from the outside by the paparazzi, I found myself being stalked on the inside by an ardent homosexual suitor. His wooing methods were not subtle. One night a note was pushed under my cell door. It read: 'You really have the most beautiful legs I have ever seen. I really fancy you. Let's meet in the 2 spur showers 8 p.m. Saturday. We'll have a ball!'

On that Saturday evening, and for a good many more evenings, I took care to give the showers the widest possible berth. As the note proposing this assignation had been unsigned I had no idea who was making these overtures. However, a day or two later, the identity of my admirer became known. 'I hear you've been gettin' a love letter, Jonno,' said an affable old lag in the dining hall queue. I looked at him suspiciously. 'Was it from you?' I asked. 'Not in a million years. I ain't no ginger,' he replied in mock umbrage. 'It were from Mad Frankie. He's been telling all the world and his wife.' 'Who's Mad Frankie?' I asked. 'Big Luco. Big Stoker. The lads call him the African Queen.' I was becoming sufficiently fluent in rhyming slang[1] to get the picture. It was completed a few hours later when I was watching the test match in the communal TV room. A burly 6 foot 6 inch Afro-Caribbean inmate came and sat down beside me, asking, 'Like cricket do yer?' On getting an affirmative reply, his next inquiry, delivered with a throaty chuckle, was: 'And do you like to bat and bowl?'

I was slow on the uptake. In the context of watching the test match I took the question at face value. I did not know that in the argot of the prison gay community 'to bat and bowl' meant to swing both ways. Fortunately some cricketing angel must have been watching over me. For instead of replying, 'Yes I enjoy being an all-rounder,' which would have been an accurate answer in the days when I turned out for the Lords and Commons XI, I said: 'No, I haven't played for years.' Even this dead bat response started to produce some strange body language from my interrogator. Suddenly realizing that he must be the African Queen, I made my excuses and left. The idea that at the advanced age of 57, my legs or any other portion of my out-of-shape anatomy could possibly be an object of desire to a fellow prisoner was a disturbing discovery. Although Mad Frankie's leerings never developed into anything worse than a mild embarrassment, they were a worry to me in my early days at Standford Hill.

A greater worry came from a different kind of letter which arrived through the conventional mail from my Trustee in Bankruptcy, Mr Colin Haig of Baker Tilly. He wrote to inform me that he had decided to make two aggressive moves against me. Their first move would be to take legal action to seize my parliamentary pension for the benefit of my creditors. The second would be to take legal action to seize all my files of personal papers and correspondence in order to sell them as an 'asset' at an auction to the highest bidder. Both these actions were unprecedented in the history and law of bankruptcy. I knew I would have to fight them, but the prospect of doing so in court, combined with the prospects I seemed to be facing in prison, filled me with gloom. At the end of my first three weeks at HMP Standford Hill, I was an unhappy prisoner.

[1] Ginger Beer = queer; Lucozade = spade; Stoke-on-Trent = bent.

CHAPTER 8

Settling Down

It may say something about my state of tension in mid-July 1999 that I regarded my sudden appointment to the job of junior toilet cleaner on A wing as promotion, liberation and the dawning of a new opportunity. I was told I was being changed from a market gardener into a toilet cleaner for 'medical reasons', although in actuality it was once again more a case of 'media reasons'. In the press, a spokesman for the Prison Service was quoted as saying that I was having trouble with my asthma because of the high pollen count and needed to be moved to indoor work. This explanation was greeted with much scepticism in high places. *The Times*, calling me a 'delicate flower', declared that I had, like Ernest Saunders, 'pulled off a nice one' to secure this 'cushy job' of cleaning, and wished me 'a happy and speedy recovery upon release'. The 'Aitken Watch' column in the *Mirror* reported that the skiving Aitken had complained 'that he couldn't push a wheelbarrow around outside because of his asthma'.

Although I was on the side of the sceptics since I had complained neither of asthmatic nor wheelbarrow-pushing difficulties, I was grateful for the change in my prison job which I guessed was due to the Governor's acceptance of my argument that the market garden offered far too easy access to the paparazzi. However, before I was allowed to start work I had to go through a morning's Induction into loo-cleaning. Inevitably, HMP Standford Hill had a rulebook on this subject. It was the size of a church Bible, with large laminated pages complete with diagrams. 'Wing Cleaners Manual', said the front cover. Inside it, after pages listing various items of the required clothing and technical equipment such as rubber gloves, plunger, mop, scrubbing brush, etc., there was a section headed 'How to clean a toilet bowl'. It began, 'Take Harpic in left hand, long handled scrubbing brush in right hand. Sprinkle Harpic at four points of compass. Scour bowl with four circular movements of brush in clockwise direction. Repeat in anti-clockwise direction. flush toilet.'

To give him his due, the Induction Officer, Joe Rook, burst out laughing as he read such passages from the Wing Cleaners Manual aloud to me. 'Anyone who gets a photograph of you cleaning the bogs with this lot will make his fortune,' he chuckled, as he handed me my plunger and rubber gloves. Never was a truer word spoken.

My job as junior wing cleaner on Spur 2 of A wing required me to clean 12 toilets, 12 urinals, 12 showers, 18 washbasins and the surrounding area of floorspace and corridors. I had to do it twice a day in the space of six hours. 'Morning session will take you twenty minutes, afternoon ten minutes,' advised my boss, the senior wing cleaner, a diminutive Scotsman know as 'wee John'. On my first day I took about 45 minutes to do the afternoon clean.

'Very thorough, aye very thorough indeed,' said wee John. 'Before the end of the week they'll be movin' ye up to my job.' He knew what he was talking about. Four days later, wee John made a carefully planned nocturnal escape. Due to his unavoidable absence I became the senior wing cleaner. It was a fast-track promotion, and with it my prison wages rose from £4.80 to £5.60 a week.

Although the toilet cleaners' trades union might have said something about the rate of pay, I was delighted with my assignment for several reasons. First, it was a job with a point to it. Hygiene is important in a prison washroom, where verrucas, athlete's foot and other infections spread easily, so I did my cleaning rounds thoroughly.

Secondly, my thoroughness was noticed. Not only did I get glowing written reports, I was paid bonuses. 'Cleanest bogs in the gaff again, Aitken. I've added £1.20 to your wages,' said my wing officer Joe Johnston. He rewarded me in this way almost every week. The inmates seemed appreciative too. The head honcho of the jail, Les, also known as The Big Face, was a lifer coming to the end of a 30-year tariff for multiple gangland murders he had committed in the 1960s. He had a prized corner cell on the ground floor of B wing, but accompanied by his minders he regularly patronized the A wing toilets. 'I come over to piss in your bogs, Jonno,' he solemnly told me, 'because they're so much effing cleaner than they are on my wing.' Such commendation in prison was the equivalent of getting a knighthood in politics.

Thirdly, the small print of the rulebook stated that once the wing cleaner had completed his duties he must remain 'on call' in his cell in case of unspecified emergencies – which never seemed to occur. Since my cleaning rounds took me less than a couple of hours, I had at least four hours a day available to study New Testament Greek in my cell. It was a roundabout way of doing education but it worked.

Finally, the wing cleaner has a certain status in prison. He often becomes the concierge of his block, the passer of messages, the repository of confidences, a mentor to the new arrivals, and 'a man of respect' in the community. Acquiring some of these qualities by osmosis, I found a steady trickle of interesting inmates dropping in to chat with me during the day. I enjoyed their company as well as the job.

Inevitably the media, once they got to hear about it, saw my role in a more negative light. I had to endure several headlines about the terrible humiliation of being reduced to the rank of lavatory cleaner. 'Aitken becomes a Privy Councillor again', was one of the better ones.

In addition to my enjoyment of the job there were other features which helped to stabilize me after my rocky start at Standford Hill. The most important of these were my prayer life and the daily services in the prison chapel.

In that hot summer of 1999 I woke every morning at dawn and settled into a disciplined routine. The more relaxed rules of a D-cat prison allowed an inmate to move out of his cell in the early morning to get hot water from the Heatrex machine at the end of the spur, so at the start of each new day I would brew myself a cup or two of Nescafé and settle down for a longish period which I came to call 'coffee with God'. This started with an hour or so of reading the Bible with the help of a commentary. This was followed by a second hour of prayer, often using the structure recommended by the Alpha course, the ACTS formula – Adoration, Confession, Thanksgiving, Supplication. I also worked my way through a three-volume masterpiece on the Psalms, *The Treasury of David* by C.H. Spurgeon, gradually falling in love with the extraordinary riches of these ancient songs of experience written by Israelite poets some three thousand years ago. The fruits of my 'coffee with God' quiet time have subsequently been harvested in two books, *Psalms for People under Pressure* (2004) and *Prayers for People under Pressure* (2005), both of which were written on the basis of annotations originally jotted down in my prayer journal.

The official day began with a 7.45 a.m. roll-call followed by breakfast in the dining hall which I rarely ate. However, I was a regular attendee at an 8.30 a.m. service of Morning Prayer held in the chapel. Although no more than seven or eight prisoners usually attended, it was to me and others a beautiful and communal form of worship, led by the Chaplain, the Reverend Clinton Davis, who gradually became a close friend. It must sound as though I was in the grip of excessive religiosity to be spending the best part of three hours every morning before nine o'clock in devotions in my cell or in the chapel. Yet that was what I felt like doing and it set me up in a peaceful frame of mind to get through the less peaceful parts of the rest of each day.

Work, tea breaks, meals, roll-calls and other minor duties filled the hours from 9 a.m. to 5 p.m. After that there was plenty of time for Association, taking exercise, going to the library, eating supper or walking round the prison on certain designated paths. No one could call the regime at Standford Hill harsh or oppressive. But it was a fussy and over-regulated one in which the loss of liberty always made itself keenly felt.

There was a period every evening from eight until the ten o'clock roll-call when prisoners had to be on their own wings but were free to visit each other in their cells. Most inmates seemed to spend this time playing cards, especially kaluki, or listening to pop music. I did quite a lot of correspondence in this period, usually on behalf of those who wanted letters or applications written for them, but I always found time for evening conversation with the prisoner who had the next-door cell to mine. He was called Mickey Aguda and he soon became my 'best mate'.

Mickey Aguda was a professional criminal. Italian by ancestry, he had grown up in Clerkenwell in north London. As a schoolboy his role models were a local 'firm' of gangsters known as The Orsinis. After some teenage sporting successes as an ABA bantamweight boxer and as a professional footballer on the ground staff of Fulham FC, Mickey turned to crime. He was good at it, creating The Agudas, a family firm comprised mainly of his own relatives. The firm's business was armed robberies, bank raids, hold-ups and heists. They never did burglaries, regarding them as 'against the code'. As Mickey explained, 'Robbing commercial premises was fair game in our book, but breaking into ordinary people's homes to steal their personal possessions was wrong. We thought of burglary as one step behind rape. So we didn't touch it!'

The code of the Agudas included minimum violence ('I often carried a shooter but never used it') and maximum discretion. Loving 'the buzz' and the rewards of big-time crime, they had some spectacular successes including pulling off Britain's largest silver bullion raid of the 1960s. However, most of its £20 million proceeds had to be returned to the insurers in a clandestine deal with the Flying Squad which kept Mickey out of jail.

Although Mickey, also known as Spider in some circles, had been arrested many times and had served two short prison sentences, for most of his 46 years he had stayed one step ahead of the sheriff. This was sometimes due to the cosy relationships he enjoyed with individual CID officers, but it was mainly due to his skills as a professional blagger, particularly those of a wheel man (getaway driver).

Mickey's luck as a professional criminal ran out in the late 1990s, when he turned his hand to white-collar crime. For him this meant robbing banks by non-violent methods of embezzling money from dormant accounts with the help of an inside accomplice. Mickey and his associates siphoned away the best part of £1 million before their plot was uncovered. So it was for the crime of embezzlement that he was doing a four in Standford Hill. His sentence would have been 12 months if he had been willing to turn Queen's Evidence against the senior bank manager who was his inside man. It said something for the code of the Agudas that Mickey turned down the deal offered to him by the Crown Prosecution Service. He refused to be a grass and accepted the longer sentence.

I met Mickey on the afternoon of my arrival at Standford Hill from Belmarsh. He helped me to carry my three giant bin-liners up to my cell which was one away from his cell on the second-floor landing. 'When you've got yourself settled, come and have a cup of tea with me,' he said. I accepted. Ten minutes later we were having the first of our one-on-one conversations which continue to this day, six years after that first encounter.

It is difficult to explain why Mickey and I bonded. Physical proximity first brought us together, but in no time we were travelling at much deeper levels of intimacy than that of good neighbours. Naturally I drew heavily on Mickey's well of knowledge about prison and criminal life, but if I had to identify where the bonding started I would say that it was in our shared sense of humour.

Although all prisons are sad places, life there also has its lighter side, for it is full of situations and characters that are unusual, entertaining and often highly amusing. In my weeks at Belmarsh I had met several personalities who seemed to have stepped straight from the cast of a pantomime. The same phenomenon soon became apparent at Standford Hill. To enjoy it to the full you needed a raconteur to tell you the stories, the perception to understand them, the humour to laugh at everything including the jokes at your own expense, and a kindred spirit with whom to share the show. Mickey Aguda fulfilled all these roles.

As we drank our first cuppa together, Mickey started by giving me a series of thumbnail sketches of the prisoners in the adjoining cells to ours. 'X is doing a three for drug dealing. Since he arrived here his business has never been better,' he began. 'His cell is known as Arkwright's after the shop in the TV series that's open all hours. You can get knocked over in the rush of his customers coming to buy from him.' That gave me a chuckle, as did his sharp portraits of various prison officers whom he divided into dogs and diamonds.

'Fortunately the ones on A wing are mostly diamonds,' said Mickey, 'but I'll bet my life they won't be able to cope with the sort of media attention you've been getting at Belmarsh. You watch out.' It was a prescient comment, for within 48 hours I was under a media siege which was far from well handled by the Governor and his officers.

Against the background of constant leaks, inventions and intrusions by journalists, I needed a friend I could trust: someone who could keep confidences, share laughs, offer advice and occasionally provide a shoulder to weep on. Mickey became that trusted friend or, in prison parlance, 'best mate'. I told him funny stories (like the concrete-mixer episode) and expressed my frustrations (such as not being allowed to do education), completely confident that he would never pass anything on. He was a sympathetic listener, a humorous commentator and a wise counsellor. Because we were so often in each other's company, some people began calling him 'Aitken's minder'. This was a misleading label.

Until a much later stage in my sentence, I had no worries about my personal safety at Standford Hill and no need of a physical minder. However, Mickey did perform two helpful minding services. First, he minded or rather managed the evening queue of inmates wanting advice or letters written for them. In this role he was much more of a receptionist than a bodyguard, but he did it well. Secondly, he was often warning me to 'mind out' for this or that fellow prisoner who was trying to find out information about me in order to sell it to the newspapers or to manoeuvre me into part of the prison grounds on which the long-distance paparazzi lenses were focused. So well informed was the Aguda intelligence service on these matters that for several weeks I managed to remain un-photographed by the tabloids despite the amazing skulduggery that went into securing the 'exclusive first pictures' of Aitken in jail.

A variety of sources kept me well briefed on paparazzi activities. One photographer fell out of a tree on the edge of the prison grounds, breaking his arm. Another suffered severe sunburn and nettle rash after concealing himself in a patch of long grass all day. No less than eight cameras were intercepted as they were being smuggled into the prison through various means and intermediaries. As the Principal Officer in charge of security, Mr Peck, told me later, 'We were pretty chuffed by the success we were having in detecting the cameras, but we knew we couldn't keep them out indefinitely. The money being offered for your picture was just too much.'

The 'first picture' race was soon won by a horse from the Murdoch stable. 'Today the *News of the World* offers you an exclusive *Hello!*-style photo-shoot of disgraced tycoon Aitken's new life behind bars,' proclaimed the paper under the headline 'ELLO, 'ELLO, 'ELLO.

The *Mirror* came a close second with a feature on 'EX MINISTER'S CUSHY LIFE'. The photographs illustrating these articles were taken by inmates equipped with specially provided cameras. One of the photographers, disappointed that he had only obtained one grainy shot of me carrying my wing cleaner's bag of equipment, offered me half his fee if I would cooperate with him by posing for other shots. Although I could have done with the £12,500 that would have been my cut of the proceeds, I made my excuses and left. Not that it made much difference. For various reasons it was strongly suspected that members of the prison staff had co-operated with these photographic enterprises, possibly by smuggling in the cameras and smuggling out the negatives. As those suspicions grew, two senior Prison Service officials descended on Standford Hill to conduct a leak inquiry. From the vague nature of my interview with them it was clear that their investigation, like so many Whitehall leak inquiries, was destined to end in failure. So it proved. The leaks and the photography increased, as did the daring of the tactics used.

Over the years, Her Majesty's Prisons have seen their fair share of escapes and break-outs, but it took my presence at Standford Hill to achieve a unique event: the first recorded example of a prison break-in. This event began on a quiet Friday morning just before lunch. I was walking towards the dining hall when I was approached by a prisoner I knew as Dwight Gabbard who said, 'Hey Jonathan, I need to speak to you very urgently.' Dwight Gabbard was an American citizen who was in Standford Hill awaiting deportation and extradition hearings. I knew about his case because he had come to ask my advice on it at one of my regular evening letter-writing sessions in my cell. I had helped him draft a briefing note to his lawyer. This had happened about a month or so earlier.

'Hi Dwight,' I said. 'Haven't seen you around lately. Have you got new problems about your deportation order?' Dwight looked and sounded extremely nervous. He was as white as a sheet and words tumbled out of him in jerky, neurotic bursts. 'Yeah, deportation, sure. I've been back in Brixton – that's why you haven't seen me. But we must talk right now. Can we go somewhere on our own?' I suggested that we should talk over lunch. Dwight was curiously resistant to this idea and asked if we could talk outside, waving vaguely in the direction of a tree. I said no, I wanted to eat lunch; we could find a quiet corner in the dining hall and then go back and talk in my cell afterwards. Dwight reluctantly agreed, and we queued up at the food counter together and found an empty table. He sat down opposite me and began asking rather strange questions.

'How are you Jonathan?' he began. 'Are you having a hard time here?' 'No I'm absolutely fine. How about you? What's the news on your deportation?' Dwight did not seem to want to talk about his legal problems. 'How are your beautiful daughters?' he asked. 'Have they been visiting you?' 'Oh they're fine too.' 'And your mother Lady Aitken. I hear she's been visiting.' 'Yes, she's been three or four times. But what's up with you Dwight?'

'And Margaret Thatcher?' he persisted. 'I read in the paper that she's coming to visit you. Has she booked in yet?' I was beginning to wonder whether Dwight was slightly unhinged. He was shifting around in his seat as though he had a twitch. He looked increasingly pale and nervous. I noticed that in addition to his green prison overalls and red shirt he was wearing a black woolly hat and a heavy prison windcheater even though it was a warm day. I was in a T-shirt like most of the other prisoners.

'Dwight, are you OK?' I asked. 'You haven't touched your food. What's on your mind? What did you want to talk to me about?' The response was an incoherent ramble. He said his lawyer had managed to get him released but he had been sent back to prison again to make him decide whether or not to comply with the deportation order. He wasn't making much sense.

Suddenly he leant forward and said, 'Jonathan I must talk to you completely privately. Can we go somewhere else?' This seemed an odd request since the dining hall had largely emptied, the nearest prisoner being four tables away from us, but as I finished my lunch I said, 'OK, let's go over to my cell.'

So Dwight and I walked back together to A wing. His behaviour was peculiar. 'He walked like a cat on hot bricks,' I said afterwards, 'moving away from me, then back towards me, then going around me. I wondered whether he had been taking drugs.' Although these suspicions were forming in my mind, they did not cause me much concern in a jail where large numbers of prisoners were on drugs. So Gabbard and I climbed the staircase to the second-floor landing and moved along the spur corridor. Just as we were about to enter my cell, the faithful Mickey Aguda sprinted up to us. 'Watch out, Jonathan,' he said in a breathless voice of high urgency, 'I think we have a problem.'

Behind Mickey came Paddy and Alan, two Irish prisoners with whom I had become friendly. 'Jonno, mind your back!' shouted Paddy, 'this bastard's setting you up.' 'He's wired up for sound!' cried Alan. From the other side of the wing on the spur opposite me, an old lag known as Big Jim called out, 'The bastard's got cameras stuffed up his front and wires trailing out of his back.'

'What the hell is all this about, Dwight?' I demanded. Dwight did not stay to give me an answer. He turned tail and ran back along the spur corridor. Then he hurtled up the staircase towards the third-floor landing. 'He's got friends on the threes,' announced Alan.

Mickey Aguda and I walked down to the ground floor. I was shocked and bewildered. 'What on earth am I supposed to do about this?' I asked. Mickey was muttering furiously along the lines of, 'I'd like to shoot the effing bastard. He's completely out of order setting you up like that.' Then he saw the formidable figure of Officer Rook emerge from the wing office. 'Tell Rookie! Tell him now!' he advised. I had considerable respect for Mr Joe Rook. So I told him. 'Do you have a description?' he asked me sharply. 'He's about 5 foot 10 inches – in a black hat' was my instant reply.

After that the action did become like a *Carry On* film. Rookie dived into the wing office; alarm bells pealed; officers came running from other parts of the prison; the wing was sealed off; radios crackled. Due to a mishearing in the Aitken–Rook dialogue, a lot of energy was expended on seizing the wrong suspects: Mr Rook thought I had said, 'He's as black as your hat,' so various 5 foot 10 inch Afro-Caribbean inmates were strong-armed in error. Meanwhile, still wearing his black hat, Dwight Gabbard was being lowered out of a window by his accomplices. My Irish friends blew the whistle on his exit, but not quickly enough. A posse of some- what overweight officers set off in hot pursuit, but Dwight Gabbard was fitter and faster than they were. He reached the perimeter fence well ahead of those chasing him, climbed nimbly over and sped away in a waiting car.

Amidst continuing pandemonium, the whole prison had an emergency roll-call, only to discover that no one was missing. So who on earth was the escapee? 'Of course I know who he was,' I told the SO in charge of the investigation. 'He's called Dwight Gabbard and he's on B wing.' Various computers were consulted and records checked. 'Gabbard was released three weeks ago,' said the SO. 'He's not on bail – he's a completely free man. He must have broken into the prison, borrowed a set of prison uniforms and then broken out again.'

The first recorded example of an ex-prisoner climbing back into jail disguised as a current prisoner went curiously unreported in the national press. A team of Prison Service investigators called the Chaucer Group, headed by an outside governor, descended on Standford Hill to conduct an inquiry. I was questioned at length, as were several others, but no progress was made. The accomplices could not be identified. The getaway car, although well photographed by the CCTV cameras, turned out to have false number plates. 'Mr Gabbard has vanished off the face of the earth,' the visiting governor in charge of the inquiry told me. 'It's a mystery.'

It did not take too long before the mystery was solved. Within a few days of Gabbard's adventurous break-in, the *Mirror* was sharing yet another 'Aitken exclusive' with its readers. 'SECRET FOOTAGE OBTAINED BY THE MIRROR REVEALS TODAY WHAT LIFE BEHIND BARS IS REALLY LIKE FOR EX CABINET MINISTER JONATHAN AITKEN', trumpeted the paper. It published some rather grainy snapshots of me eating a bowl of soup in the prison canteen, queuing at the food counter, collecting my mail and opening the door of my cell. So Gabbard the photographer had done quite well. However, as an interviewer he had failed completely, for not a single quote from my conversations with him appeared in the *Mirror*. I don't know whether this was due to some malfunction of the tape recorder or whether my anodyne answers to Gabbard's rather feeble questioning over the lunch table were too boring to be worth printing. So the page was filled up with more creative reporting, mainly about my eating habits. The topics covered included the cutlery I used – 'white plastic plate, knife, fork and spoon', evidently another *Mirror* world exclusive – the clothes I wore, my preference for brown bread over white, and my new prison nickname, 'Oliver Twist', which my fellow cons gave me because I was always asking for second helpings. Both the nickname and my enthusiasm for the Standford Hill cuisine were news to me. It was a case of another day, another tabloid story, although the methods for getting the story had indeed been original.

After the Gabbard scoop had been splashed across the centre pages of the *Mirror*, many fellow inmates expressed their sympathy to me. By this time I was becoming almost immune to such journalistic goings-on. My earlier sense of outrage about the media had become a 'what next?' sense of amused resignation, so I was surprised by the vehemence of the emotions felt about the episode by my fellow prisoners. None were more upset than the contingent of Irish travellers (gypsies) headed by Paddy and Alan, the two inmates who had first spotted what Dwight Gabbard had been up to.

Although I do not think of myself as one of nature's Irishmen, I do have one or two qualifications for that role. I was born in Dublin. My third Christian name is Patrick, given to me because I was christened in St Patrick's Cathedral in front of a congregation that included the then Prime Minister of Eire, Eamon de Valera. Some of my earliest years were spent in Ireland, at the official residence of my maternal grandfather, Lord Rugby, who was British Ambassador there in the 1940s. Then I spent three years immobilized on a 'frame' (a forerunner of an iron lung) as an in-patient at Cappagh hospital in Dublin suffering from TB. I was nursed through the disease by a wonderful nun, Sister Mary Finbar, whom I dearly loved. As a result of these earliest experiences, I have great affection for the Irish, whose touches of humour and blarney rarely fail to amuse me.

Against this background it was easy for me to find common ground with the dozen or so Irish prisoners at HMP Standford Hill. The leader of the pack was a young burglar of enormous charm and energy, called Paddy. He and I shared many a laugh and a story. One evening he invited me into his cell for coffee. This cup of coffee with Paddy was one of the turning points of my prison journey. Our conversation began with jokes and pleasantries, moved on to a lot of talk about each other's families, with showings of photographs, and culminated in the usual chatter about the day-to-day life of the prison. Towards the end of our relaxed dialogue, Paddy became surprisingly formal. Switching into the traveller equivalent of a vote of thanks, he cleared his throat and began delivering what was obviously something of a prepared speech: 'Jonno, there's something I'd like to say to you,' he started. 'On behalf of all the lads, I'd really like to thank you for all you've done for us since you came into this prison, specially the letter writing. So I'd like to give you a present to say how much we appreciate it. The present is that you can have anything you like – free of charge – from me library.'

My immediate reactions were to feel rather moved, and then rather surprised as Paddy dived under his bed and began rummaging around in his 'library', a cache of cardboard boxes on the floor of his cell. Eventually he emerged not with some learned tome or presentational volume but with a remarkable selection of hardcore porn magazines. As he fanned them out in front of me I felt a twinge of temptation but said, 'Thanks, but no thanks Paddy.'

Unfortunately the tone of my refusal must have put him in mind of my old persona as a pompous politician because Paddy took umbrage. 'Not good enough for you, eh?' he said with a bitter edge to his voice. Before I had time to reply, Paddy's fertile mind thought up an alternative explanation for my refusal. 'Ooh, if it's boys you're after,' he said, now diving under the right-hand side of the bed, coming up with an alternative selection of hard porn pictures. 'No, no,' I said hurriedly. 'I used to like the first sort of magazines you showed me, but these days I'm trying a different path in life.'

'So what kind of path would that be?' asked Paddy. 'Well, if you really want to know, it's the path of praying to Jesus and obeying his teachings,' I replied. 'It's a path that has changed my life.'

A long silence spread over us in that cell. It was eventually broken by Paddy. In a slow voice he said the unexpected words, 'You know, I'd really like to try that path myself.' Before I could respond, the floodgates opened and he poured out a litany of woes describing all that was wrong with his present path in life. Much of his misery came from the kinds of complaints that are often heard in the world of freedom. 'There's no meaning to my life ... my wife doesn't understand me ... all I care about is money and, when I've got it, there's no point to it ... my relationships keep going wrong ... my life's just empty... totally unfulfilled.' After much more in this vein, Paddy ended by saying, 'Me nan [grandmother] used to believe in Jesus and she really had something. I can see that you've got something, so I'd like to try that path myself. I really would.'

One of my self-imposed survival rules in prison was that I had resolved never to talk about religion. Before I went inside, an ex-prisoner had warned me that 'Jesus freaks sometimes get served up [beaten up]', so I had kept my prayers for the privacy of my own cell until this moment. Now I realized that I had to respond to Paddy, it was my turn to create a long pause between us. Finally I said, 'Well Paddy if you feel that way why don't we say a prayer together?' Although my lips said these words firmly, my head was telling me to go slowly. I was a novice in the practice of shared oral prayer. For most of my adult life I had belonged to the church-reticent wing of Anglicanism. In 1997 when a Baptist friend of mine, Mervyn Thomas, had first suggested that I should try praying together with him *out loud*, I would have preferred, at that moment, to have my teeth pulled without an anaesthetic. In the ensuing months of membership of a weekly group founded by Michael Alison MP to support me through my legal dramas, I had participated more regularly in shared prayers, but always as a learner rather than as a mentor. Now I suddenly found myself with a much younger man offering in effect to lead him in prayer. So I was nervous.

Paddy, however, liked the idea of praying together with me. Soon he became enthusiastic about it. On our first evening I started by praying for the various members of Paddy's family he had just been talking about. He reciprocated by praying for my family with far greater fervour and eloquence. Although a long-lapsed Catholic, he knew the Hail Mary and the Lord's Prayer, so we said those. I remembered the *Book of Common Prayer*'s second collect for evening prayer which goes:

'Lighten our darkness we beseech thee O Lord and by thy great mercy defend us from all perils and dangers of this night, for the love of thine only son our Lord Saviour Jesus Christ Amen.'

Paddy was impressed. 'Oh Jonno, you has the words, you really do,' he said, apparently under the impression that I was the author of the collect. I confessed my plagiarism, which led us to talk about more serious matters of confession. Paddy said he would be up for that tomorrow night, so we were off and running as prayer partners. For about a week we met for an hour every evening. Both of us felt we were participants in a very special experience. After a while, Paddy started saying that it was so special that we should not keep it selfishly to ourselves. He wanted to expand our two-man prayer partnership. Reluctantly I agreed that we might look around for a third partner.

Paddy, who had in him the qualities of a good recruiting sergeant, had bigger and better ideas, so he went off recruiting and came back with two of his friends, then two more, and then still more. Before we knew where we were, we had gathered together about 12 young men in a rather unusual prayer group – so unusual that it gave a new meaning to the Christian term 'a cell group'.

Far from being the leader of this group, I was its greatest learner and beneficiary. Until my time in prison I had prayed from my lips. It was my fellow prisoners who taught me how to pray from the heart. Their examples showed me how little prayer has to do with the human activity of polishing up words and phrases which we think are appropriate for addressing God. What my prison prayer partners instinctively knew was that prayer is a supernatural activity in which we rely on God to enter our hearts and let our feelings rise up to him in words, occasionally in silences, which he inspires. In retrospect, it seems extraordinary that I should have had to get into a prison cell to learn these facts of prayer life.

Our disparate group contained a multiplicity of races, backgrounds and types of offender. The regular membership included a couple of lifers (murderers), two drug smugglers, a dipper (pickpocket), a penman (forger), a blower (safe cracksman), three fraudsters, a burglar (Paddy) and a perjurer (me). We were interdenominational and interfaith, for at various stages we had two or three Muslim participants. What united us were four words which coincidentally began with the letter P. The first was Pain, a combination of the suffering we were going through ourselves and a remorseful sense of the sufferings we had inflicted on our victims, families and friends. The second was Penitence, bound up with its linguistic first cousin Repentance. We translated this key word with the help of my New Testament Greek primer as 'a change of heart and mind', which is what, in the original language of the Gospels, *metanoia* literally means. The third was Perseverance by which we meant perseverance in prayer, repentance and our spiritual searchings. The fourth was Power, by which we meant that force of divine empowerment which we needed to clean up our lives, change direction and make the commitment to a living faith.

Inevitably there were different degrees of commitment, but we were all engaged with these four P words, perhaps especially the last one – Power. Whose power? God's, or in the case of the Muslims, Allah's power of course. But there were interesting variations on our understanding of his divinity and the purposes for which his power was asked in prayer.

When, two years after I was released from prison, I was at Oxford reading theology, my tutors set me an essay on the doctrine of the Trinity. I made a bad job of it. I had difficulty in explaining the concept of a three-personned God in intellectual terms. However, in those meetings of our prison prayer group I grasped the concept of the Trinity with real understanding. For as I listened to the prayers of my fellow prisoners, I heard some of them praying to God the Father. That was because they longed for a father figure in their lives. Many of them had no idea who their father was, and virtually all of them came from broken homes with absentee fathers. So their yearning for a rock of paternal love, stability and even discipline in their lives was more than understandable.

Other prisoners prayed mainly to God the Son. That was because they longed for the blessings that Jesus personified: compassion, healing, mercy, forgiveness and a love of sinners.

And others prayed to God the Holy Spirit who would empower them to break bad habits such as drug dependency, greed, dishonesty or lying. The Holy Spirit would also be their guide, comforter and the one who came alongside them. Such amateur theology in a cell often made a lot more sense than academic theology in a classroom.

In a later chapter I will say more about the prayer group and its results. In its early days we met once a week, squeezing into Paddy's cell and later into a cleaning alcove on the wing. We were entirely a prisoner-led gathering, but we kept the Chaplain informed and soon we had to ask him if we could borrow a room in the chapel. The Reverend Clinton Davis was delighted, if initially surprised, when 18 or so inmates turned up to pray. He encouraged us with enthusiasm and joined in with sensitivity. The first time he attended he peeled off his clerical collar, saying, 'Please think of me not as the Chaplain but as just another member of your group, for I am a sinner too.'

Calling ourselves the PFG, which stood for the Prayer and Fellowship Group, we were allowed to advertise on the prison noticeboards. The resultant growth meant that we soon had to split into two groups. Then there was a third spin-off of our members who wanted to do Bible studies, led by the prison's nonconformist pastor Phil Cain. His teachings on the Book of Job and Luke's Gospel were immensely illuminating to me and several others.

The PFG attracted both cynicism and curiosity within the Standford Hill community. I realized we must be making an impression when one of the officers said to me, 'I don't know what you lot are doing in these meetings of yours on Thursdays but you certainly seem to have changed X and Y into having a different attitude.'

The only time when our group made the wrong kind of impression was when we inadvertently started a fight between two prisoners in the middle of the night. Spiritual in its origins, this episode was the stuff of which soap operas are made. Paul, a young and highly impressionable car thief on my spur, became a regular attender at the PFG. At one of our meetings he had a charismatic experience in the course of which he publicly confessed his sins (a long list even by prison standards) and began speaking in tongues. He was so much ablaze with his new-found faith that there was a moment when it looked as though the fire extinguishers might be needed! Eventually he calmed down. I walked him back to the wing and almost had to put him into bed, so exhausted was he by his spiritual exertions. As I said goodnight to Paul I lent him a spare Bible and suggested he might try reading 1 Corinthians 13, the famous chapter on love.

At 10.30 p.m. the prison shut down but Paul could not sleep. After reading and rereading 1 Corinthians 13 he became on fire all over again. He thought he heard voices giving him a divine message. Even though it was now 3 a.m., an hour when it was strictly forbidden to enter another inmate's cell, Paul felt a powerful urge to pass on the message to me, so he tiptoed along the spur and tapped on what he thought was my cell door, calling out my name.

I slept through this summons for a very good reason: Paul was knocking on the door of the wrong cell. In the semi-darkness of the early morning hours he had lost his bearings, so he ended up tapping on a cell four places away from mine on the spur. It was occupied by a rather irascible character known as Big John. He also answered to the name of 'Jonno' which is a common from of prison address to the numerous Jons, Johns, Johnnies and Jonathans in any jail. This misunderstanding was the cause of the hilarious dialogue which now followed. It went something like this:

Knock knock.

'Jonno! Jonno!'

'Who's there?'

'Paul.'

'Eff off Paul. Don't yer realize it's three o'clock in the effing morning,' said the sleepy voice of the other Jonno, aka Big John.

Paul was not going to be so easily deterred from his religious zeal.

'Jonno, I've got to talk to you.'

'What the effing hell about?'

'I got a message for you.'

'Who the effing hell from?'

'It's a message from God.'

This announcement was given a rough response in forthright language. Paul was upset.

'Jonno I think you're a effing hypocrite,' he complained. 'Earlier tonight you said you loved God. Now you don't want to hear his message. A hypocrite, that's what you are, a effing hypocrite.'

Big John did not like being accused of hypocrisy. By now thoroughly awakened, he pulled open the door of his cell and punched Paul on the nose. Paul punched him back. Then he realized he was hitting the wrong Jonno. His apologies did not receive instant forgiveness. The ensuing bout of fisticuffs apparently lasted some little while, but I slept through them. The first I heard of the misunderstanding was the following morning when Big John moved menacingly along the spur in my direction. 'You 'ave some very peculiar friends,' he growled. It took quite a few minutes of explanation and counter-explanation before Paul's celestial telephone lines were uncrossed.

Despite this difficult start at the wrong door, Paul became a good friend and a good believer. Although I have not heard from him for some time, I know he was a regular attendee, for at least a year after his release, at St Luke's Church in Redcliffe Gardens, Fulham, where Bruce Streather and others mentored him.

Several participants in the PFG were inspired by our shared prayers and Bible readings. As our numbers grew, Paddy must have said to me at least a dozen times, 'We really started something, didn't we?' After one particularly special meeting of the group, at which two inmates had said the prayer of commitment, I remember saying to Geoff, another PFG friend, 'I've done many interesting things in my not uncrowded life, but none of them has given me so much satisfaction as helping some of these young guys get to know the Lord.' 'I think you're getting to know the Lord rather better yourself,' responded Geoff. 'You look a lot more peaceful than when you came in here.' 'Yes,' I said, 'I think I am settling down.'

CHAPTER 9

Visits and Exits

Visits helped me to settle down too. D-cat Standford Hill had a relaxed regime compared to A-cat Belmarsh. Security was minimal, access was easy and, with the passage of time, I was allowed one ordinary visit each week plus additional LVs, CVs and PVs – Legal, Chaplaincy and Parliamentary visits. As I had many friends in the last three categories, my cup was soon overflowing. All these visitors especially my immediate family who were wonderful in their love and loyalty, strengthened my morale.

One of my earliest visitors was Michael Howard. It was marvellous to see him, but he must have been as surprised as we prisoners were by the antics of the Prison Officers' Association who put on a classic *I'm All Right Jack* performance on the afternoon of his arrival. In the eyes of the Standford Hill branch of the POA, Michael Howard was bad news. He was well known to have been tough on crime during his years as Home Secretary. What was less well known was that he had been tough with the POA, bringing an end to some of their old Spanish customs. Apparently his ministerial rulings on certain POA practices relating to overtime claims were still much resented by some of the officers at Standford Hill. When they heard he had booked in for a visit, they decided to make life as difficult as possible for him.

Michael Howard did not ask for any favours or privileges when he came to Standford Hill. But as an ex-Home Secretary still protected around the clock by police officers from Special Branch he was entitled to certain minimum standards of courtesy and security when entering a prison. The Standford Hill officers on duty in and around the visiting hall on the afternoon of Tuesday 15 July 1999 did not think so. In fact they treated him worse than any other visitor.

Michael arrived with his son Nick at about 2.30 p.m. To the incredulity of his Special Branch minders, he was rudely greeted with the words 'Who are you?' by a woman prison officer who pretended not to know him. He was then aggressively searched by another officer keeping up the same pretence. After that, both Howards were sent to the back of a large queue of prisoner friends and relatives. They were kept waiting there longer than anyone else, before eventually being let into the visiting hall where I was sitting at a table towards the back of the room.

When Michael's Special Branch detail saw these arrangements, they hit the roof. The main point of giving former Home Secretaries police protection is to prevent the possibility of revenge attacks on them from the most dangerous potential source – prisoners or ex-prisoners with a grievance. But now the most controversial Home Secretary of recent times, in the eyes of many prisoners, was walking completely unprotected through a room full of incarcerated criminals, some of whom were serving long sentences for murder and other crimes of violence.

The body language of the two Special Branch protection officers revealed their agitation clearly. Their actual language, overheard by the prisoners at the front of the visiting hall, spelt it out vehemently. All I could see, as Nick and Michael Howard threaded their unescorted way through the line of tables to get to me, was that a lot of aggressive finger-wagging and argument was going on at the front of the hall between the policemen and the prison officers.

'Oh it were a sight for sore eyes,' was how an old lag sitting close to the action described it afterwards. 'The Old Bill were going hammer and tongs at the screws, and the screws were getting the hump with the Old Bill, saying things like, "We are solely responsible for security in this prison and don't you forget it." It was big-time aggro on both sides.'

When Michael Howard arrived at the table where I was waiting for him, he maintained an amused air of detachment from these squabbles. 'Oh I'm not bothered by this nonsense,' he said. 'I've come to see you.' Two of Michael's most attractive qualities are his kindness and his sense of humour. Both were on display in abundance as he, his son Nick and I talked together for the next hour. Michael brought me messages of good cheer from many mutual friends including Henry Kissinger. He said how much he was enjoying his new freedom on the backbenches. 'You won't be there long,' I said. 'The party will need you as a big gun.'

Michael talked of the big causes he wanted to champion. In particular he was trying to set up a foundation which would promote the cause of European–American cooperation. He had just come back from a visit to Washington where he had talked with many foreign policy specialists like Henry Kissinger who were worried about the growing rift between the EU and the US. As Michael described his talks in Washington (my home from home for many years), I felt a rare pang of wistfulness for the life of politics. He was involved with exactly the same interests, issues and influential people that I would have liked to be associated with on the international stage if my life had not gone pear-shaped and prison-shaped. These were not envious thoughts. I was simply being realistic. For as I listened to Michael and looked down at my prison uniform which on that afternoon consisted of a bright orange bib, red shirt and green trousers, our conversation brought home to me he was talking about a way of life which had slipped away from me forever.

As if to reinforce these reflections, there was a shout from the prison officer presiding over the visiting hall: 'Aitken – keep facing the front.' This was another childish POA reminder (probably directed at Michael Howard more than me) of where the power resided in this prison. One of the rules about visits is that a prisoner must sit with his face towards the front so that the officers can see if any wrongful activity such as drug-smuggling is taking place. I had not moved my face more than an inch or two out of line, making this almost imperceptible shift to engage in the conversation with Nick and Michael, so the rebuke was pointless and silly – except to make another silly point.

The row between the screws and the Special Branch officers continued for most of the visit, thereby alerting everyone in the room to this public spat between two traditional enemies: the police and the Prison Service. As a consequence, several prisoners decided to demonstrate their support for the Howard firm. As the visiting session ended with each inmate being called out by name, a dozen or so prisoners put on little demonstrations of respect towards the former Home Secretary. 'Good afternoon, Mr Howard,' 'Nice to see you at Standford Hill, Mr Howard,' 'Good to 'ave you with us sir,' and 'Thanks for coming to show yer loyalty to yer old friend, Mr Howard', were some of the bouquets tossed in Michael's direction by inmates passing our table as they left the visiting hall. The point they were making was if the screws were going to be rude then the cons were going to be polite. It was a rather better point than any made that afternoon by the POA.

Michael Howard was not my only political or prominent visitor. Hard on his heels came Michael Portillo followed by Malcolm Rifkind and Norman Lamont. Four ex-Cabinet colleagues seemed a good score. Other parliamentarians included MPs John Bercow, Roger Gale, Alan Duncan and Richard Shepherd, and Lords Beaverbrook and Pearson of Rannoch. From the ranks of journalism came Charles Moore, the Editor of the *Daily Telegraph*, followed by columnists Simon Heffer of the *Daily Mail* and Bruce Anderson of the *Spectator*. From the law came Sir John Nutting QC, Bruce Steather and Richard Sykes, while from Lambeth Palace came the Archbishop of Canterbury's Chief of Staff, Bishop Richard Llewellin. Eminent though these visitors were in their own walks of life, none of them had one-tenth as much impact within the prison as the old friend who came to see me twice: Sir Frank Williams, boss of the Williams Formula One motor racing team.

In his headier moments Frank Williams has been heard to say, 'There would be no Williams F1 if it hadn't been for Jonathan Aitken.' This is a huge exaggeration although a very kind one. All that happened was that back in 1976 when the Williams motor racing team was a small and struggling outfit in the world of Formula One, I encouraged various Saudi friends to provide some early sponsorship. In particular, the son of the King of Saudi Arabia, HRH Prince Mohammed bin Fahd, expressed his passion for motor racing by making his company Al Bilad the lead Williams sponsor. As a director of Al Bilad, I had some of the responsibility for getting the (usually late) cheques signed and delivered. In the course of these sponsorship activities I had a lot of fun on the grand prix circuits of the world and developed a great respect and admiration for Frank Williams.

Frank, who has had his own far greater blows of suffering in life, was the quintessence of loyalty and kindness to a friend in trouble. Although we had been out of touch for some years, he came charging to my rescue at the worst of times in the best of ways. One of them was visiting me in prison.

The population of Standford Hill was not overwhelmed by the procession of MPs and former ministers who descended on the jail to see me, but when a 'real man' in the shape of Frank Williams turned up as my visitor, both the cons and the screws were truly impressed. For Sir Frank is to motor racing what Sir Alex Ferguson is to football – one of the all-time greats among team managers. I had no previous understanding of the hero worship his name, let alone his presence, could generate until he turned up in the visiting hall. In that not altogether friendly arena, applause rang out, autograph hunters stampeded and two of our most respected prison officers came over to pay homage to my guest.

One of those officers was Mr Joe Johnston, who supervised my wing cleaning duties. He turned out to be an enthusiastic, indeed obsessional, F1 fan and so was his son. Impressed by the Johnston family's devotion to the sport of motor racing, Frank Williams decided to do them a favour. When he got back to the Williams F1 headquarters at Grove, near Wantage, he sent a parcel of goodies to the prison. I believe these included a Jenson Button helmet, a set of bright-yellow driver's suits and a couple of tickets for the next grand prix. Frank often makes such generous gestures. Unfortunately the powers that be at HMP Standford Hill (i.e. the Governor and the POA) could not cope with them. As the parcel was sent to me with a note inside saying, 'FW says give these to that nice prison officer', the mail censors at the prison thought they had got a case of contraband, perhaps even bribery, on their hands, and an inquiry started. Poor Mr Johnston, the straightest of the straight arrows, was in a state of torment. He longed to acquire legitimate ownership of the gifts sent to him by Frank Williams and offered to pay the full commercial price for them. This solution was acceptable to the

Governor but not apparently to all members of the POA where jealousies from other motor-racing enthusiasts came into play. The eventual solution was that the F1 goodies were offered as prizes in a regional Christmas raffle attended by prison officers from all over Kent and Essex. Mr Johnston bought a record number of raffle tickets but alas was unsuccessful in the draw. My heart bled for him.

My heart nearly had to bleed for my gentlest visitor, Father Philip Chester, Vicar of St Matthew's, Westminster. In a comic misunderstanding he was 'apprehended' at the prison gates (the verb comes somewhere below detained and arrested in prison officer vocabulary), on suspicion of smuggling an illegal package out of the prison. Under Standford Hill rules, all inmates were allowed chaplaincy visits from their home parish priests. Father Philip came to see me once a month, a pastoral record way beyond the call of duty. As his church was located two minutes' walk from my house in Lord North Street, I asked him if he would take a couple of large envelopes back there for me on his homeward journey. He kindly agreed to do so. Neither of us had the slightest idea that we might be breaking prison rules, for an inmate is allowed to send out all the letters he likes in envelopes large or small through the post without interference or censorship. There seemed nothing wrong in sending letters out in the same large envelopes by hand delivery – indeed at the end of the day there was not. The intervening excitements were in retrospect amusing.

Having finished his chaplaincy visit to me with a prayer, Father Philip picked up my envelopes and began walking towards the prison gates. Some vigilant person noticed he was carrying out two 'suspicious objects' which he had not carried in, so the authorities swooped on the innocent vicar. He was apprehended and questioned. However, as there was no disputing that I had given him the so-called suspicious objects, he was allowed to go on his way, leaving the envelopes behind with the gate officers.

That afternoon I was summoned to see Governor 4, Mr Elliott. He ordered me to open the envelopes in his presence. To his surprise, all that poured out of them were about 600 letters from well-wishers, most of them ending up 'I am praying for you'. Each one was ticked to confirm that I had answered them in my own handwriting. I explained to Governor Elliott that I had sent out these letters by hand delivery in order to comply with the prison rules, not to break them. Two days earlier a woman prison officer had inspected my cell and had warned me that the piles of correspondence stacked up under my bed could be a fire risk and were in any case violating the 'volumetric control rule'. This was almost exactly the same warning that I had been given in HMP Belmarsh three months earlier.[1] Because of the incomprehensible no-stamps rule which prevailed in HMP Standford Hill, I could not post the large envelopes back to my home address. Hence my request to Father Philip to act as courier. I pointed out that as there was no ban on sending these envelopes home by mail, it seemed illogical for there to be a ban on sending them by vicar.

Governor Elliott looked perplexed. He agreed that this was not a case of smuggling out illegal materials. He accepted that the volume of mail I was receiving was a problem for me and for the prison. With a frown he mentioned that the job of handling and censoring my incoming mail was costing a lot of extra staff overtime. He even conceded that the no-stamps rule (unique to Standford Hill among British prisons) 'probably needed to be reviewed'. Sensing an opportunity, I asked whether he could give the rule a temporary review on the spot and allow me enough stamps to post these envelopes home right away. Governor Elliott was underwhelmed by my revolutionary suggestion, explaining that any such review would have to be carefully considered by a committee. However, he did come up with a judgment of Solomon; as a special concession I would be allowed to send the envelopes out by freight service or by courier. That way there would be no breach of the no-stamps rule.

Later in the evening, over my usual cup of soup with my cell neighbour Mickey Aguda, we both had a good laugh about the inflexibility of prison bureaucracy. Then I said to him, 'But I'm still left with an ongoing problem of how to send out too many letters with too few stamps. Can you think of any way to get round this crazy no-stamps rule?' 'I'll put on my thinking cap,' replied Mickey. Mickey Aguda's prison job was cleaning the visitors hall area including the visitors' toilets. Using the inside knowledge he derived from these duties, he thought up an ingenious scheme to beat the no-stamps rule. It turned out to be foolproof.

Every female friend or relative who came to visit me in prison was sent a message asking if she could bring several books of stamps in her purse or pocket. When she was sitting at my table in the visiting hall, I would explain the prison's no-stamps rule and the difficulties it was giving me. Then I would say, 'Please go to the ladies at some time during this visit. When you get there, lock yourself into the toilet where you will see a metal waste bin. Inside the waste bin is an inner plastic container which is easily lifted out on its two handles. When you have lifted it out, put your books of stamps at the bottom of the metal bin. Then replace the plastic container and your mission is accomplished.'

At least a dozen titled ladies, MPs' wives, lawyers' wives, ambassadresses, peeresses and Aitken female relatives accomplished this mission, codenamed Operation Dirty Drop. Their deposit of the stamp books was the first half of the operation. Secret agent Aguda looked after the second half which was collecting the stamps when he cleaned the ladies toilet the following morning. By that time, the entire visitors area had undergone its daily search for contraband, meaning drugs, by prison officers with sniffer dogs. But these canine detectives were not trained to bark at the scent of postage stamps, nor did their handlers ever think of looking into the lower regions of the waste bins for illegal items. As a result, the Aguda plan kept me amply supplied with all the stamps I needed for the rest of my sentence.

My favourite female visitors, with or without stamps, were my three daughters. Victoria came only twice because she had to go to Washington to start her degree course at Georgetown University. Petrina and Alexandra paid me several visits. Usually they came with my sister Maria or my mother, but on one memorable occasion Ally came on her own, travelling down from London on 'The Toms' Bus'.

'Tom' is the word criminals use to describe a girlfriend. It comes from tomfoolery = jewellery, something the ladies of the robber classes are often given. In the interests of keeping prisoners' families together, the welfare officers at the three jails on the Isle of

Sheppey organized a special fortnightly bus service running from the East End to Standford Hill, Elmley and Swaledale.

'How was the journey down on the bus?' I asked Ally as we kissed in the visiting hall. 'A-mazing,' replied my 19-year-old daughter. 'All the other girls were sooo nice to me. And they gave me incredible advice on how to handle men. My ears were practically popping out!' At least one Aitken was getting some education out of Standford Hill. Ally and I were on our own together in the visiting hall for two and a quarter hours. We had a marvellous father–daughter conversation. At the end of it I thanked her for giving up most of an entire day to come down and see me. 'Don't thank me, Daddy,' she replied. 'I've loved every minute of it. Do you realize that I've never had over two hours of one-on-one conversation with you before! All those red boxes, ministerial phone calls, lawyers and everyone else got in the way of long conversations – until now.' It was a heart-rending reminder that I might have got my family priorities badly wrong in my days of power.

My son William gave top priority to visiting his incarcerated father. With the help of his sympathetic Eton housemaster Charles Milne, he was given leave to come to Standford Hill regularly, usually accompanied by a senior boy who could drive. These visiting schoolboys were fascinated by prison life and they interrogated me about it with a curiosity and concentration rather greater than that which they applied to their studies at HMP Eton. I shall always remember the afternoon when William's best friend, 17-year-old Ben Goldsmith, was questioning me about the crimes the various villains sitting around us in the visiting hall had committed. At a moment when the general buzz of conversation in the visiting hall went uncannily quiet, Ben's piercing voice rang out on an imperious note of command that reminded me of his late father Jimmy, 'Jonathan, will you point out one or two more murderers for me!' Several lifers in the immediate vicinity turned sharply away from the Aitken party of young visitors and one shaved head actually ducked under the table!

My most wonderful but also my most tearful visitor was my mother. Because of the shortage of drivers in the family, she was the most frequent chauffeuse for the children, who regaled me with

1. Jonathan Aitken's daughters Alexandra, Victoria and Petrina enter the Old Bailey on June 8th 1999.

2. *(above)* Paddy, the co-founder of the HMP Standford Hill Prayer and Fellowship Group with his wife and baby daughter (also JA's God-daughter) with JA in February 2000 at 8 Lord North Street.

3. *(below)* Jonathan Aitken and Mickey Aguda outside their adjoining cells.

4. Jonathan Aitken on the 3rd floor landing of A Wing
at HMP Standford Hill.

5. *(top)* HMP Belmarsh, Britain's highest security prison, where Jonathan Aitken started his 18 month sentence.

6. *(left)* Jonathan Aitken walking out of HMP Elmley carrying his possessions in a bin-liner on the morning of his release January 7th 2000.

7. *(right)* Jonathan Aitken and his bride, Elizabeth Harris, cut the cake on their wedding day June 25th 2003.

8. Four old Standford Hillians reunite at the wedding reception June 25th 2003.

From left: The Revd. Clinton Davis (prison chaplain), Phil Allen-Taylor, Jonathan Aitken, Mickey Aguda.

9. Jonathan Aitken and fellow Wycliffe Hall students in formal academic dress outside the Oxford University Examination Schools after taking Part I of the BTh exam.

Jonathan Aitken's mother, the Hon. Lady Aitken.
Portrait by Simon Elwes RA, 1928.

stories of her near-misses on the M2 motorway during the 70-mile journey from London. 'It's far more dangerous for us to be driven here by Pempe [my mother's family nickname, an abbreviation of Penelope] than it is for you to be locked up with a whole lot of violent criminals,' cracked Ally.

Cracking up was my mother's problem when she visited me in prison. Although she was a strong lady who had experienced more than her fair share of adversity in her 88 years, the sight of her 'little boy' in prison uniform was more than she could bear. Although there was always plenty of fun and laughter during a two-hour visit from my mother, every so often she could not prevent her upper lip from trembling, and then she would break down in tears. Inevitably I found such moments extremely difficult but I understood my mother's pain and never discouraged her from coming.

One visit I encouraged my mother to make was on the occasion of the prison Harvest Festival service. The home team permitted to attend this event was a mixture of prisoners who regularly attended chapel, prisoners who worked on the farm and prisoners who knew how to work the system. The first attraction for all three categories was that they were allowed to invite guests who were not part of the regular quotas permitted under the Visiting Order rules. The second attraction was that the guests could be entertained in far easier conditions than the strict surveillance of the visiting hall. The Harvest Festival took place in a huge barn filled with bales of straw, stacks of hay and stalls of produce. Visitors could move around freely. They could also walk around a farmyard area where sheep, cows, horses and other animals were tethered. For the well behaved, this event provided an opportunity to see family and friends in a relaxed setting. For the less well behaved, there were opportunities for romps in the hay with girlfriends or assignations behind the barn with old partners in crime. For such purposes, some of the prison's sharpest operators had been signing on as regular chapelgoers or transferring to jobs on the farm in order to get a ticket for the Harvest Festival. The chances of 'getting nicked' at the event were negligible, or so I was informed. It was therefore a surprise that the only person who nearly got nicked was the Hon Lady Aitken MBE JP.

My mother arrived in one of her mischievous moods. As she inspected the farm produce she announced at the top of her voice, 'Those tomatoes are from Tesco's. I can see a Tesco's label stuck to one of them.' A blushing farm manager explained that because the Standford Hill tomatoes were not yet ripe he'd gone out shopping to augment the display. 'Caught red-handed eh?' teased my mother. Several prisoners fell about laughing.

Laughter surrounded my mother for the rest of the afternoon. She sat down on a bale of straw surrounded by an admiring circle of inmates, telling them her stories and listening to theirs. She opined that the chaplain's Harvest Festival sermon had been 'rather boring' and declared that 'anyone can tell that Jonathan's no good with his hands, so whoever put him in charge of a concrete mixer must have been mad'. Some bright spark offered her a glass of 'special water' which turned out to be smuggled vodka. 'I'd like another glass of that, please,' said my mother, winking at the purveyor of it and telling him, 'You are far too handsome a young man to waste your life locked up in here.' The young man in question was more than happy to be flirted with by an 88-year-old grandmother, so he fetched her a second glass of special water.

Emboldened by her refreshment, my mother produced a small camera from her handbag and started clicking away. At first, no one in authority noticed her as she snapped Mickey, Paddy, the vodka supplier and other interesting faces. However, a lady who was a member of the chaplaincy team did observe my mother's photographic activities and drew them to the attention of a prison officer. He came over and began saying something to the effect that bringing a camera into a jail was an offence under the Prisons Act 1952.

'Think of the 'eadline in tomorrow's *Sun*,' said one old lag. ''er Ladyship gets nicked. Grassed up by Christians.' 'Very unchristian,' agreed my mother. More laughter. The chapel lady took umbrage. The prison officer told the Lady Aitken fan club that this was no laughing matter. My mother seemed to disagree, 'Oh I'm quite ready to be put in handcuffs,' she said, cheerfully extending her wrists. Just as the situation seemed to be getting decidedly tricky, a saviour appeared in the form of the Rt Hon Michael Alison MP who had driven my mother down from London. During his years as

Margaret Thatcher's parliamentary private secretary he had acquired some skills in handling headstrong women. He was a master of the emollient word. Somehow Michael managed to soothe everyone's feelings. He explained away the misunderstanding by referring to my mother's great age and her ignorance of the 1952 Prisons Act. With good grace the prison officer closed the incident by asking for the camera to be put back in the handbag. My mother seemed rather disappointed. 'Well, darling, I nearly managed to join you in being locked up here,' she said as she kissed me good-bye. After this particular maternal visit I was relieved to see her car driving out of the prison gates, and I was equally relieved that the story never appeared in the tabloids.

For a few merciful weeks, press interest in my prison journey seemed to wane. However, it revived as soon as I passed my FLED date and became entitled to town visits. A prisoner's Facility Licence Eligibility Date (FLED) occurs when two-thirds of a sentence has been served. Thereafter an inmate has 'enhanced status', entitling him to some minor privileges inside the prison, and the major concession of monthly exeats outside it.

These exeats, known as town visits, are designed to help a prisoner prepare for his release by reconnecting him with his family and friends in a normal setting. The town visit licence that grants the temporary exeat has several conditions. It lasts for six hours, it is restricted to the area within a 55-mile radius of the prison and it prohibits the consumption of alcohol or drugs. These restrictions seem minimal compared to the huge joy of having a day out from jail. Most prisoners look forward to their town visits with eager anticipation and plan them meticulously. I was no exception.

If an inmate happens to live within a 55-mile radius of his prison, then a town visit becomes a home visit. But since most prisoners live further afield, their only option is to visit a nearby town where they reunite with their families in a hotel, rented room, borrowed caravan or whatever. When I came to organize my town visits, I realized that they would be ruined if they turned into a media circus, so I planned them in great secrecy and with military precision. The secrecy was easy (or so I thought) because I told no one my plans. The military precision was supplied by Colonel Edward

Sharp, late of the Royal Engineers and with a long record of clandestine missions with the SAS and other parts of the secret world. Having been on a mission or two in the Middle East with Ted Sharp, I knew I could trust him completely. Moreover he had a secure base camp – his own home – in Sittingbourne, a mere ten miles from Standford Hill. In guarded phone calls, with careful use of codewords, we set up a plan for a media-free town visit.

The essence of the plan was that on the Sunday morning of my exeat (date unknown to anyone other than me, Ted Sharp and the Governor) I would leave the prison at 9 a.m. to be met at the gate by Ted and one of his old military pals. Both of them would have cars, one of which would be a decoy or paparazzi-obstructing car. Between them, these cars would get me to base camp Sharp where we would later be joined for a festive lunch by a gathering of Aitken friends and relations.

Meanwhile, back in what used to be called Fleet Street, at least three newspapers were preparing their battle plans to get the first exclusive pictures of Aitken's day out from jail. We knew this because my closest companions in the prison, including the faithful Mickey Aguda, were offered many hundreds of pounds for the vital details of my town visit. Playing the disinformation game, though not for money, I authorized the leaking of the wrong details. So far so good.

My plan started to go wrong when the licence papers on my town visit were passed by the Governor's office to the A wing office the Saturday night before I was due to begin my exeat at nine o'clock on the Sunday morning. One or two officers working on A wing had long been suspected of passing Aitken information to journalists. Now these suspicions were, to my mind, confirmed, because when I emerged from Standford Hill at the start of my town visit, four paparazzi were waiting for me on the ground, and a fifth one was snapping away from the branches of a nearby tree.

Despite this unwelcome ambush, Colonel Sharp's irregulars were more than a match for the tabloid troops. I was bundled into Ted's Mercedes and, with the escort car behind me driven by his friend whom he referred to as 'the Major', we shot off towards Sittingbourne. The paparazzi drivers were slow off the mark from the prison, but they had thought their battle plan out carefully and had one advance driver stationed half a mile down the road from the prison. He now took up the chase. The Keystone Cops had nothing on the race that followed. The only weakness in the Sharp pair of hotrod wheelmen was that they were retired military gents in their seventies with some vestiges of respect for road safety. The paparazzi were at least 20 years younger and prepared to drive at least 20 miles per hour faster. So after several miles of grand prix racing along the B320 between Sheppey and Sittingbourne (why hadn't I thought of asking Frank Williams to send a couple of his F1 trained drivers to help with my town visit?) the bad guys caught up with the good guys.

Just as I thought the battle for privacy was lost, old military cunning triumphed over raw paparazzi speed. We approached a big round-about and encircled it not once, but thrice. Soon we were in a confusing crush of two Sharp vehicles and two photographers' vehicles going round and round in circles. It felt rather like the dodgems. Then Colonel Ted came up with a dodge of his own. After exchanging hand signals with the escort car driven by the Major he swerved into a fast left turn off the roundabout. Immediately behind us the Major slammed on his brakes and slewed sideways, neatly blocking the exit from the roundabout. In the wing mirror I could see the photographers getting out of their vehicles to have words with the Major. As our car roared away the Colonel was jubilant: 'Damned good show,' he exclaimed. 'Those blighters are well and truly buggered.'

We reached our destination without further alarms, excursions, or sight of pursuers. Colonel Ted and his wife Clare laid on a sumptuous Sunday lunch at which we were joined by my mother, sister, two daughters and a group of friends which included Malcolm Pearson, Alan Duncan, Bruce Anderson, Richard Shepherd, actress Tsai Chin from Hollywood and Ambassador Dick McCormack from Washington, DC. It was a wonderful day out for me in perfect conditions of normality, hospitality, friendship, happiness and – or so we thought at the time – privacy.

Unfortunately the paparazzi had the last laugh. For the most resourceful of the newspapers involved in the battle for exclusive pictures had not been in the Keystone Cops car chase nor outside

the prison; instead they had obtained Colonel Sharp's address –
almost certainly from my town visit licence papers – and had done
a deal with his neighbours. Under this arrangement, photographers
took over the upstairs bedrooms of the house next door. From this
vantage point they shot all the pictures an editor could possibly
want of me, the guests, and our eating and drinking. It was an unexpected breach of the Colonel's defences, but we discovered it too
late for the party to be spoiled, so a good time was had by all on my
first town visit.

Later town visits were quieter. I went back to the Sharps on a subsequent media-free Sunday. I had a day out in my old haunts at
Sandwich Bay where my former neighbour Julian Seymour hosted
a lunch for me with guests who included Norman Lamont, Algy and
Blondel Cluff and E.W. Swanton, the doyen of English cricket writers who came in fresh from a round of golf at Royal St George's. Jim
Swanton had been a Japanese prisoner of war, and my ordeals were
trivial compared to what he had endured. Nevertheless we had a
deep conversation about getting through captivity with the help of
God. I shall always cherish my memories of our discussion because
I never saw Jim again. He died at the age of 92 a few weeks later.

My most peaceful town visit was when Jim Pringle drove me to
Canterbury Cathedral on Sunday 19 December where we attended a
beautiful Eucharist service. At the giving of the sign of peace, several
members of the congregation, led by the Archbishop's director of
communications Jim Rosenthal, came over to shake hands with
me. I was overwhelmed by these gestures of kindness, which continued after the service as the Dean and Canons, some of whom I
had known for years, were exceptionally warm in their welcomes.
Then, after lingering rather too long over a good lunch *à deux* with
Jim in the nearby Tuo et Mio restaurant (a favourite Aitken family
watering hole), we had to drive back to Standford Hill at breakneck
speed to make the 3 p.m. curfew deadline for town visits. As I got
out of the car with seconds to spare, I thanked Jim and said, 'Only
18 more days of my sentence left to serve. Coming into the home
straight I feel at peace.'

[1] See Chapter 4, p. 64–5

CHAPTER 10

Last Lap

I felt increasingly peaceful during the final months of my sentence. Several factors contributed to this change of mood. One was the arrival of a new governor of HMP Standford Hill, who took decisions which made life more straightforward for me and for many other prisoners. Another was the extra visits and minor privileges that came my way as a result of becoming an 'enhanced' prisoner once I had passed my FLED[1] date. A third source of peace was a victory I won over my creditors in the High Court. The greatest blessing of all was the progress of our prison prayer group and the impact it had on my own life.

The arrival of Governor John Robinson was like the proverbial breath of fresh air. Like a brisk new headmaster taking the reins of a school that had fallen into bad habits, he made his presence felt by smartening the place up and introducing sensible changes. We prisoners thought the Governor was good news because he was decisive, accessible and always ready to talk to any inmate. Among the officers he got mixed reviews, but it was clear that some of them were pleased to feel a firm hand on the tiller.

I was one of the earliest beneficiaries of the Robinson regime because my reapplication to be allowed to do education had been sitting on his predecessor's desk for weeks. 'Of course you're entitled to do education,' said the new Governor. 'Start on Monday.' Strange though it sounds, a part of me was sad to give up the job of wing cleaner. It was not that I had fallen in love with my duties involving the Harpic, the rubber gloves and the plunger, but I did enjoy that special status in the prison community which a wing cleaner can sometimes occupy. I had become a confidant, a counsellor and a calming influence on the wing in a number of tense situations. Two instances, which were appreciated by both officers and inmates, are worth mentioning.

The worst outbreak of tension followed the sudden death of an inmate in circumstances rumoured to be highly suspicious. I knew and liked the young man who died. He was an Afro-Caribbean American called Bob, serving four years for a series of frauds. The judge who sentenced him had ordered the freezing of his bank accounts and other assets. However, all this had to be confirmed by a subsequent confiscation order hearing. Bob was a volatile character who loved to boast and to gossip. He was the wing laundryman, a job which provides even more opportunity for conversation with fellow inmates than the job of wing cleaner. Because Bob and I were two of a rare category of prisoner – those who do not leave the wing to go to work – we spent a fair amount of time drinking coffee together.

Over those mugs of coffee Bob told me about his master plan for avoiding the confiscation of his assets. The essence of it was to get the legal formalities of confiscation postponed beyond the six-month time limit after which the trial judge's freezing order automatically expired. This could be achieved, said Bob, if the confiscation order hearing were adjourned for some legitimate reason such as the absence of the defendant due to serious illness.

As the date of the confiscation order hearing approached, Bob became increasingly volatile as he revealed the details of his plan. He was going to make himself seriously ill. This was easy, he explained, because he had suffered for many years from sickle cell anaemia, which required him to take daily doses of medication. If he overdosed himself with this medication he would fall into a coma, making it impossible for him to attend the confiscation order hearing, yet the coma itself was not dangerous. Bob assured me that any doctor or hospital could easily revive someone from a sickle cell anaemia coma. He knew this because he himself had been revived from such comas several times.

On the eve of the confiscation hearing, Bob was energetically implementing his plan. He was uninterested in my own and others' warnings that going into a coma might be dangerous. Not only did Bob have his medication overdose measured to the last milligram, he was aiming to make his coma deeper by spending the hours before taking the overdose immersed in water, a practice which he said would cause his condition to deteriorate. There was no stopping him from putting into effect what he began calling his 'fail-safe' master plan.

On the morning when he should have been going to court for his confiscation order hearing, Bob missed the 7.45 a.m. roll-call. Officers went into his cell and found him unconscious. Realizing that they were dealing with a medical emergency, they pulled him out on to the landing, summoned an ambulance and took him to hospital. A few hours later he was dead.

Sudden deaths in prison can create a whirlwind of rumours. Bob's certainly did. One rumour was that he had been beaten up in his cell in the night after getting lairy (cheeky) with an unpopular officer. Another was that the officers who pulled him out of his cell treated him so brutally that he suffered brain damage. A third rumour suggested that Bob was a CIA agent who had been murdered with the connivance of the Home Office because he 'knew too much'.

As Bob had been an energetic and popular character, these stories spread like wildfire. His death, in the prime of youth and apparent good health, seemed inexplicable to many prisoners whose angry grief made them willing to believe the wildest of explanations. Those of us who knew the real story became worried as the emotional temperature in the prison rose to feverish levels. When we heard of reprisals being threatened against Bob's alleged 'murderers' among the officers, it seemed time to act, so I got together three other inmates who knew the score. One was Mickey Aguda, and the other two were Afro-Caribbean friends of Bob's in whom he had also confided. Should we tell the authorities what we knew? Should we tell the other prisoners? All four of us thought we should, but someone was worried that this might lead to accusations of grassing.

'You can't grass up someone who's brown bread,' said Mickey Aguda. He was obviously right, so we spread the word around the wing and we also told the officers everything we knew. The tension slowly subsided, although the genuine sorrow over Bob's tragic death continued. A memorial service was held in the chapel for him. This calmed the atmosphere still further.

Two days later, Bob's widow Catherine came to Standford Hill accompanied by a friend who appeared to be a lawyer. A Senior Officer escorted them to Bob's cell and gave them a tour of the prison. Many inmates came up and expressed their condolences. However, in the course of their visit, Catherine and her companion made it clear that they were thinking of suing the Prison Service for negligence. Later in the afternoon, the four of us who were Bob's friends had tea with Catherine in a private room. In sad truthfulness we gently told her what we knew about her husband's master plan for avoiding the confiscation order. After that, the talk of litigation, at least against the Prison Service, faded from the agenda. The tea and sympathy ended with us regaling Catherine with our good memories and stories about her late husband which she clearly appreciated. After we said our sad farewells and waved to Catherine as the car pulled out of the prison gates, the officer in charge of the visit, Principal Officer Jeffries, paid us a generous compliment. 'I'd like to thank the four of you very much indeed,' he said in a voice thick with emotion. 'You helped a lot, you really did.'

Another tense situation on the wing which we helped to defuse was occasioned by a stupid new rule. One morning a notice was sent round to all prisoners who had passed their FLED date. It decreed that in order to qualify for the enhanced inmate's privilege of being able to use our visiting orders (V/Os) both on weekends and weekdays, we must all move into cells on B wing by 1 November. This meant a massive upheaval. It required about 60 prisoners to pack up their cells and move to a different wing. What was the purpose of it? Why should the issuing of V/Os have anything to do with the location of a prisoner's cell? What was the point in changing a V/O system which was working perfectly well? To these sensible questions the officers gave no sensible answers. 'It's an administrative matter, so you have to do it,' was the best we got.

Amidst much grumbling, about half the enhanced prisoners made the move. Then a nasty incident occurred. One of the A-wing movers got beaten up when he arrived on B wing – allegedly for no other reason than for being a newcomer. Fear began spreading on A wing, as did vocal resistance which threatened to turn into physical resistance. Many people knew that I was far from enamoured of the prospect of being made to move, so they came to ask my advice. 'Let's try to see the new Governor,' I suggested. 'He seems pretty reasonable. Let's get up a petition and ask if he will hear our case.'

Governor John Robinson was a fast operator when faced with these nascent stirrings of prison democracy. Within a few hours of receiving our petition signed by the reluctant movers, he sent word that he would like to meet the organizers on the wing at 3 p.m. The organizers came down to me and Mickey Aguda, as no other signatories wanted to front up. So Mickey and I waited on the Governor, who arrived on the wing and asked the officers on duty to find a room where he could talk to us. With ill-concealed surliness a door was unlocked and the three of us entered one of the dirtiest rooms I have ever seen. 'This is awful,' said Mr Robinson. 'I do apologize to you. It will be cleaned up later today.'

A governor who opens a meeting by apologizing to his inmates for shortcomings in his own prison is a rare bird in the higher management of the Prison Service, so it was no surprise that he gave us a good hearing. Mickey did most of the talking. In his role as the voice of the people, he gave a cogent summary of the reasons why most enhanced inmates did not want to be compulsorily moved over to B wing. I tried to be the voice of logic, pointing out that there was no rhyme or reason in the position that prisoners needed to move to a new wing in order to qualify for their entitlement to have extra visits.

'I entirely agree with you,' said the Governor. 'You can all stay where you are and have the same V/O allocation as you are entitled to wherever your cell is in the prison.' End of problem and end of tension, although there were some noticeably grumpy faces among the officers who had been in charge of the move to B wing.

*   *   *

Mickey's presentation to the Governor was well argued and did him a power of good. He had applied to be transferred to a resettlement prison, HMP Latchmere House in Richmond, which operated a day release scheme that would allow him to work in the community for the last six months of his sentence. Places at Latchmere were hard to come by, but the Governor recommended Mickey for one of them, and his application was granted in mid-November. When he left Standford Hill, I knew I would miss Mickey enormously during the last seven weeks of my sentence, but I also felt sure that our friendship would endure outside the prison walls. So it has done, as later chapters will tell.

Although Mickey was irreplaceable as a 'best mate', I had made several good friends by this stage of my Standford Hill journey, so I did not lack interesting company. One colourful character I came to know well was called Les. He had such a fearsome reputation from his murderous gangland past that he was often referred to as 'The Guvnor', 'The Boss', 'Mr Big', or 'The Big Face'.

The population of Standford Hill was a strange mixture of short-sentence men doing six or nine months for petty crimes like booze smuggling; white-collar criminals serving longer terms for offences like fraud or forgery; drug dealers doing sevens, tens or even more; and lifers coming towards the end of their tariffs. Les was a lifer who had completed almost all of his 20-year tariff. When I met him he was within three months of being released, and he talked enthusiastically about getting home to his family. As with all lifers, however, this timetable was conditional on good behaviour. A single foolish incident involving drugs or violence can keep a lifer inside for another three years. My rapport with Les came about because I narrowly prevented him from hitting a prison officer and losing his release on licence.

The prison officer concerned was widely regarded as an officious oddball. Known among the cons as 'the White Dog', he enjoyed 'nicking' prisoners for trivial breaches of the rules, such as coming back a few minutes late from their jobs on the farm, that were normally ignored by, or earned perfunctory warnings from, other officers. I myself had a bizarre brush with the White Dog, on the occasion when he burst into my cell at 2 a.m., shouting, 'Don't move. You're both nicked.' Apparently he had been listening at the keyhole of my cell door and thought he heard two men's voices.

Suspecting that I was engaged in a homosexual tryst, he flashed his torch aggressively round my cell and under my bed for at least a couple of minutes. This is a long time for a search, considering the physical impossibility of concealing two bodies in a space the size of a shoebox. Even so, this ultra-suspicious officer seemed reluctant to accept my explanation that I was alone listening to my tape recorder. The tape I had been playing was a sermon on forgiveness by the Reverend Dick Lucas of St Helen's, Bishopsgate, so it seemed appropriate to practise what had been preached, and I ignored the excessive zeal of the nocturnal search.

However, Les the Big Face was not so well schooled in the practice of forgiveness on the occasion when he lost his temper after an incident involving this same officer, the White Dog aka Mr X. The incident occurred inside a Portakabin in the prison grounds known to the cons as 'the piss room'. It was where our Mandatory Drug Tests (MDTs) always took place. I was tested for drugs six times while at Standford Hill, so I became well used to the MDT procedure. The prisoner being tested stands in a room with two officers, removes his trousers and underpants, then provides a urine sample which is carefully labelled and put into a refrigerator. The whole process has to be observed by the officers to make sure that no ingenious tricks for distorting MDTs are played.

On the morning of the incident involving Les, I was one ahead of him on the list of MDTs. My test followed the usual pattern but with one slightly peculiar addition. Just before I gave my urine sample, the officer conducting the test, Mr X, brought his eyes down to the level of my genitals. From a distance of about three feet, he stared at them for some ten seconds. As this had never happened at any previous MDT, I did think it rather odd but put it down to Mr X's notorious officiousness. It was strange and mildly humiliating but I was in no mood to make a fuss about it.

When Les had his MDT a few moments later, his private parts were given the same close inspection by Mr X. Fortunately Les managed to control his temper for the few more seconds it took him to give the urine sample, but by the time he stormed out of the Portakabin he was apoplectic with rage. As I was the nearest inmate in sight, he ran over to me shouting, 'Did that effing bastard X perve at your Niagaras [Niagara Falls = balls]?' 'Yes he did. I think he's a bit of a nutcase,' I replied. 'Nutcase? He's a —— and I'm going to —— him.'

I don't think I have ever seen a human being fly into such an uncontrollable fury as the one that possessed Les for the next couple of minutes. His face went bright red, he screamed at the top of his voice, he stamped with both feet on the ground, then he started punching the wall of an adjacent building with such savagery that his bare knuckles split open. As blood poured from them I could see the white of the bone underneath his ripped flesh. Impervious to the pain he was inflicting on himself, Les kept on pounding the brick wall with his fists, screaming obscenities and kicking out with his legs as if he were attacking some invisible kung-fu opponent. He was berserk, totally out of control.

At first, Les was incoherent as well as incandescent in the passion of his tantrum, but suddenly he chilled into a more deadly mood of menace. His face changed colour from red to white, there was a grinding sound from his mouth as his upper and lower molars clenched together. Then with a vicious snarl he said, 'I'm going to serve up effing bastard X. He's worse than any nonce. I'm going to smash his face in. I'm going to kick him in his Niagaras until he screams for mercy. I'm going to ...' Before he could get to the end of his repertoire of potential acts of revenge he started to run towards the Portakabin. From the expression on his face I knew he was crazy enough to do something violent to Mr X. I was alarmed.

After a second or two of internal panic I started to run after Les. He was a colossus of a man, but his elephantine bulk made him a slow mover. Because I had kept fit by fairly regular jogging around the prison football field, I was able to catch up with him. I grabbed him by the arm and shouted, 'Les, don't be an idiot. They'll never let you out of here if you hit a screw. You'll never get released!' Les heard me, even though he was shaking off my feeble grip on his arm. He broke his stride and slowed down. Turning on his heel towards me he said through gasps of panting, 'You're effing right, aren't you?' 'Yes I am. You'll never see that granddaughter of yours if you go in there and start serving up that bastard X.'

146

Mentioning the granddaughter, whose photo Les had proudly showed me a day or two earlier, did the trick. Les dropped his hands to his side. Puffing and blowing out his cheeks, he repeated, 'You're effing right. I lost it. I nearly effed up. It's me worst fault me temper.' 'Well at least you know it,' I said. 'I didn't. That's me problem. I can't control it when I get like that. But you knew it and you stopped me. I owe you, Jonno. I owe you big-time.' 'We all have our problems when we get angry,' I said.

*   *   *

Although my anger problems were not physical, I had been suffering from a lot of them myself earlier in the summer. Tossing and turning on my bed at night, I had been boiling with a different kind of fury directed at the people I misguidedly called 'my tormentors'. By this I meant my principal creditors at the *Guardian* and Granada and my Trustee in Bankruptcy, Mr Colin Haig, a partner in the accountancy firm Baker Tilly.

In fact Colin Haig was a fair-minded and experienced insolvency practitioner. However, as he later conceded in private conversation, he had never handled a high-profile bankruptcy like mine. Nor had he ever presided over such a creditors committee. During the summer of 1999 the more militant members of that committee pushed Baker Tilly into territory where no insolvency practitioner had ever been before. The result was that Mr Haig came a terrible cropper in the courts and in the press. This was the unprecedented case of *Haig v Aitken*.

The battlefield of *Haig v Aitken* lay in some 5,000 pages of private correspondence I had exchanged over the past 20 years with personal friends and acquaintances. It covered a huge range of people and subjects: family correspondence; ancient love letters; notes scribbled in Cabinet; letters to members of the Royal Family; confidential medical records; letters to priests and spiritual mentors; correspondence with intimate friends; correspondence with political figures in Westminster and across the world – in short my entire personal archive.

The existence of this archive was known to my Trustee in Bankruptcy because his assistant Ms Louise Brittain of Baker Tilly had seen it on a visit to my office a few days before my sentencing. She had asked to look at these personal files to see whether they contained any financial information relevant to my affairs in bankruptcy. I agreed. After further consultations with her superiors at Baker Tilly, Louise Brittain had come back to me with a request to take away the entire archive for inspection. I balked at this on first hearing, but Ms Brittain pointed out that my Trustee could easily get a court order allowing him to remove all my papers as part of his duty to look into my financial records with due diligence. 'But there isn't a single file relating to my financial affairs,' I objected. 'These are all personal letters.'

With the wisdom of hindsight I think I should have taken a stand against my Trustee at this point and forced him to go to the courts to seek an order from a judge to inspect my personal letters. They were of no relevance to my bankruptcy and in the light of subsequent judicial decisions I think the High Court would have protected my privacy. But at the beginning of June 1999, I was emotionally, physically and legally exhausted. Less than a week before going to the Old Bailey to be sentenced, the last thing I needed was more court appearances and more newspaper headlines. The most important consideration was that I had nothing to hide from my Trustee in Bankruptcy. Although the letters in my archive of private correspondence were personally sensitive, they were not in the least financially sensitive, so in a spirit of cooperation with my Trustee, possibly mixed with a spirit of appeasement, I allowed him to take possession of all my files of private correspondence. Three days before I was due to be sentenced, Ms Louise Brittain turned up at my office with a van and removed ten large boxes of letters. Before they were handed over, I asked for an assurance that the privacy of the letters would be protected, particularly from journalists associated with my creditors. I also asked for all my files to be returned to me by Baker Tilly as soon as Mr Colin Haig had completed his due diligence. Louise Brittain gave me those assurances. I am sure she gave them in good faith, for nobody with her experience of insolvency practice could possibly have anticipated the unprecedented legal moves which were subsequently taken over this archive.

While I was getting on with serving my sentence, various lawyers acting for the Trustee in Bankruptcy and certain members of his creditors committee were getting on with reading my private letters. Nothing of any financial significance was found in them. One member of the committee took a much more favourable view of me and my character than he had previously expected as a result of reading through the archive. This was Mr Peter Thackeray, a senior inspector from the Inland Revenue. Two years later when we met to sign off the necessary tax releases just before the annulment of my bankruptcy, Mr Thackeray told me, 'There was nothing in those files of interest to the Revenue. But I did take away from them an impression of you as a man which was very different from the man I had read about in the newspapers.'

Unfortunately my private letters had a high value to the newspapers. Mr Haig and his legal team soon realized they had their hands on a treasure trove of correspondence which would fetch a good price if it could be deemed to be an 'asset' and auctioned for the benefit of my creditors. Never before in the history of insolvency had a bankrupt's private correspondence been considered an 'asset' in this way. It was a risky strategy but Mr Haig embarked on it.

His first move was to get my ten boxes of letters valued by an auctioneering house, Messrs Gorringes of Tunbridge Wells. Their expert valuer reported to Baker Tilly, 'We believe that these sensitive files are of value and that the market lies in the publishing arena. On the basis of the limited research we have been able to undertake we have reason to believe that if the boxes were to be offered to newspapers and publishers a six figure sum would be easily obtainable.'

The ostensible reason why such a high price (by the standards of the 1990s) might be paid was that among my correspondents over the years were many famous names. Handwritten letters from figures such as Margaret Thatcher, Richard Nixon, George Bush, Sr, John Major, Michael Portillo, Norman Lamont, Ken Clarke, Alan Clark, Princess Margaret, Prince and Princess Michael of Kent and Sir Robin Butler would no doubt be grist to any features editor's mill. But the real inducement for the bidding war which the

Trustee's valuers obviously expected to be unleashed between newspapers, so that 'a six figure sum would be easily obtainable', was the intimate nature of so many of the letters. Sitting in my prison cell, I found it all too easy to imagine what a tabloid newspaper could do with the emotional wrestlings of my heart and soul which had been recorded on paper in those files at various moments of drama over the past 20 years. I thought of the family upheavals no one outside our family knew about; the secret affairs that had remained secret; the embarrassing comments about well-known people; the plots and feuds in the passion play of politics; the unexpurgated gossip; and my more recent spiritual outpourings to personal or priestly confidants in confessional mode. At best, my papers in the wrong hands might make Alan Clark's diaries look boring. At worst, they could be turned by the tabloids into a journalistic orgy of salacious sensationalism which would be harmful to me and hurtful to others.

Lying awake at night at Standford Hill, with my mind wandering across the minefield of potentially explosive revelations that lay in my private archive, I became tearful, fearful and furious. I expressed my anger orally to Mr Colin Haig, when he visited me in prison to explain his proposed course of action. I expressed it in writing for the court pleadings, claiming in an affidavit that the sale of my letters would amount to 'a gross violation of human rights, civil rights, privacy, confidentiality, trust and secrecy – not only against me but against the individuals who have corresponded with me'.

A handful of these individual correspondents were protected by the intervention of the Treasury Solicitor, who managed to cull from the archive certain letters written by politicians and civil servants who had served with me in government, but this tiny concession by my creditors barely dented the journalistic and financial value of the archive. What was still at stake was the big issue of principle relating to the law of privacy and the law of insolvency: did a Trustee in Bankruptcy have the right to seize and sell the private letters of a bankrupt for the pecuniary benefit of his creditors?

For the reasons set out above, I thought this issue was important and worth fighting for, but, for all the brave words in the pleadings I sent to the court, I was deeply despondent about my ability to fight the case and my chances of winning it, for I had no money to pay lawyers to represent me. Under some obscure section of the prison rules, I was not allowed day release leave to attend the hearing to defend myself in person. Even if I had been granted this leave, I think I would have been a poor advocate in my own cause, for I was too emotional in my feelings and too ignorant of the statutes and the precedents on which the case would be argued. All things considered, I was helpless and my legal position looked hopeless. The only thing I could do was watch and pray – with considerable support from my prison prayer group.

There was one unexpected development just before *Haig v Aitken* came to court. A young barrister who was unknown to me, Mr Tom Lowe, heard about the case from one of my former legal advisers Ms Rachelle Preston. Mr Lowe felt such a sense of outrage about the issues of principle at stake that he volunteered to defend me *pro bono*, or free of charge. A lawyer offering to fight a case in the High Court without being paid for it was one miracle. A second was having the trial presided over by a judge with no sympathy whatever for the case my creditors tried to argue. Mr Justice Rattee's judgment in *Haig v Aitken* made newspaper headlines and legal history. It was witnessed in Courtroom 40 of the Queen's Bench division by a large crush of the other side's lawyers, my creditors, journalists plus court staff. I was defended by the lonely figure of my *pro bono* counsel Mr Tom Lowe and supported by just two friends, Richard Shepherd MP and Jim Pringle. From their written and oral accounts, plus the press reports, it is possible to give an accurate account of what happened on this fateful day in court.

Mr Justice Rattee showed his colours early in the proceedings by displaying considerable scepticism towards the arguments put forward by Mr Marshall, the barrister acting for my Trustee in Bankruptcy and my creditors. 'You wish to sell his private correspondence to newspapers?' asked the judge in tones of incredulity. Mr Marshall argued that there was no confidentiality over my papers because I was planning to write a book about my life based on these records. I don't know where he got that idea from, but the judge wasn't having it anyway. 'I find that a rather extraordinary proposition,' he said. 'Are you saying that everything in these papers is open to public scrutiny?' Mr Marshall said it was. Mr Lowe said it was not, adding that he thought his learned friend was 'putting lipstick on a very repugnant animal'. 'Yes,' said Mr Justice Rattee in a voice which Jim Pringle described as 'somewhere between a whoop and an amen'.

Matters got even worse for the Trustee and his counsel. The judge took a dim view of the fact that my papers had been handed over ostensibly so that they could be checked for financial information but had then been valued for sale without the permission of the court. 'That won't do,' said Mr Justice Rattee. He then got both counsel to agree that the court had 'unfettered discretion' to allow or to forbid the sale of papers. After that came the judgment which *The Times* rightly described as 'scathing'. 'The concept of such a gross invasion of privacy is morally repugnant,' said Mr Justice Rattee. Throwing out the plaintiff's application to sell my letters he declared, 'Is this really what Parliament envisaged by passing the Insolvency Act, that a bankrupt's correspondence should be available for publication all over the world by being put up for sale at the behest of the Trustee in Bankruptcy? Everyone including Mr Aitken has the right to the respect of privacy over their correspondence.'

After those pearls of judicial wisdom it was game, set and match to me, the defendant, while the unfortunate plaintiff, Mr Colin Haig of Baker Tilly, had to endure many critical newspaper headlines highlighting the judge's words about the 'repugnant' nature of the action brought against me. So seriously did Baker Tilly take these criticisms that its Chairman, Mr Clive Parritt, felt obliged to defend his partner Colin Haig in a letter to *The Times*. 'The activities of my partner, Colin Haig, as trustee in bankruptcy for Mr Jonathan Aitken, may require clarification in the light of Mr Justice Rattee's refusal to allow Baker Tilly to sell Mr Aitken's personal correspondence', read the opening sentence of this attempt to close the accountant's door after the judicial horse had bolted. The 'clarification' that followed in the next 40 lines of print was as clear as mud. Its main point seemed to be that Mr Haig had conducted himself entirely properly, correctly, helpfully, wisely and in line with standard practice. The letter concluded, 'Mr Haig is a highly respected insolvency practitioner with 20 years of experience. In seeking to maximize the recovery for the bankrupt's creditors he proceeded in accordance with standard professional procedure.'

Readers of both *The Times'* report in its news pages of *Haig v Aitken* and this letter about it in the correspondence columns must have wondered whether the two items could possibly be about the same case. I felt that the Chairman of Baker Tilly could never have heard of the old adage, 'if you're in a hole, stop digging'. This impression was reinforced when Mr Haig's defeat on the major issue of the case was followed by a second day in court when he was defeated again on the secondary issue of my books. Although less important than the issue of principle about confidentiality of correspondence, this was still a matter of considerable literary and journalistic significance. My creditors had applied to the court to sell my collection of about eight hundred books located on the shelves of my study and drawing room at 8 Lord North Street. I claimed that the Insolvency Act did not allow them to do this because one of its clauses specifically excluded 'the tools of his trade' from a bankrupt's estate. My argument was that when I came out of prison I would be earning my living as a professional writer and biographer. This had been my trade in the past. As an example of its application to the law I could show that one part of my library consisted of some two hundred books about the Presidency of Richard Nixon. I had needed this collection as my tools to write Nixon's biography. I would need the same tools again for my next project which was writing the biography of Charles W. Colson, Nixon's White House aide. The rest of my library would also be used for research work on newspaper articles and future books. I was therefore entitled to prevent the Trustee from selling these books for the benefit of the creditors by relying on the 'tools of the trade' safeguard clause in the Insolvency Act.

Although Mr Haig's valuer had assessed my entire library as being worth 'less than £10,000', nevertheless another session in court was set aside to argue the Trustee's case that I was not a professional writer, that I had no prospects for earning my living as an author, and that the 'tools of the trade' clause could not apply to me.

'Mr Aitken's books are mine to sell,' said Mr Haig, rejecting witness statements from Sir Martin Gilbert, Kenneth Rose, Simon Heffer, Charles Colson, Professor Alister McGrath and other distinguished figures in support of my claim that I was a genuine professional author who needed his reference library.

For the second time, Mr Justice Rattee became decidedly ratty with the arguments put forward to the court by counsel for Mr Haig. 'Why are we spending all this time and money about books which have only been valued at less than £10,000?' he demanded. After this and other observations from the bench that were less than helpful to the plaintiff's case, an adjournment was requested and a deal was struck. Of the eight hundred or so books in my library, I could keep seven hundred and fifty under the 'tools of the trade' clause. The remaining fifty, all of which were in fine leather bindings, could be sold at auction by Baker Tilly on the grounds that I could buy cheaper editions as replacements. Although I had no say in this out-of-court settlement, when I heard about it I felt that my *pro bono* counsel Tom Lowe had once again done me proud. My library had been almost entirely saved. It was a sweet success, soured only by my feeling that this part of the legal proceedings had been brought to cause pain for the bankrupt rather than to save money for the creditors. However, the bottom line was that I had won two big victories on important issues in the High Court.

*   *   *

Back at Standford Hill, I was not the only one rejoicing at the result of *Haig v Aitken*. There had been so much advance media coverage of the case that half the prison seemed to know that my books and letters were up for grabs. In the days before the court proceedings started, inmates who were virtual strangers kept coming up to me and saying things like, 'bleeding liberty they're taking over them letters of yours', 'just not proper to sell off anybody's private correspondence', 'what bastards they must be to try pullin' that one'. When news of the victory was reported, the same prisoners came up to congratulate me. 'First time in me life I ever heard of a judge saying something sensible,' was one comment that made me laugh, but the comments that pleased me most came from the regular members of our prayer group.

Ever since Paddy, the Irish burglar, had set about recruiting add-itional members to our original two-man prayer partnership, the PFG (Prayer Fellowship Group) had gone from strength to strength. Inevitably we had our setbacks and dropouts. Yet Thursday evening after Thursday evening, a hard core of about a dozen regulars, and sometimes double that number, met together in a room set aside for us in the chapel to share in the fellowship and to pray. Always we shared our problems and prayer needs. The most amazing results were seen in lives that began to change and prayers that were clearly answered.

'Show the fruits of your repentance,' was the command of John the Baptist in Matthew 3.8. It is a good biblical test of whether or not someone's repentance is genuine, particularly inside a prison where, when parole reports are being written, many an inmate is prepared to say with his lips, 'I'm sorry. I'm going to change.' Changing lives with true sincerity of heart is a much more serious business. Yet it clearly happened with not one, but several, of our PFG regulars. At first I could hardly believe what was happening. I doubted the reality of some of the reported changes in attitude and behaviour. Yet as the weeks rolled by and I knew that V really had stopped swearing, W had thrown away his porn maga-zines, X had got back in touch with his estranged wife and forgiven her infidelities, Y had written apologetic letters to his victims and Z had broken his drug habit and stayed clean, the clear evi-dence of these changes showed that something extraordinary was happening.

In addition to the visible changes in some PFG members' lives, we witnessed some spectacular one-off answers to prayers. One that stunned us involved our Chaplain's father-in-law. The Reverend Clinton Davis, who came to our PFG meetings as often as he could manage, told us one evening that his most urgent prayer need was for his father-in-law, an active and energetic man in his seventies. Climbing over a gate on a country walk, Clinton explained, his father-in-law had fallen on his shoulder, dislocating it badly. Various doctors and osteopaths had tried to get the injured and apparently frozen shoulder working again but with no success. With a note of despair in his voice, Clinton Davis said that he and his family were beginning to fear that the injury was permanent. If so, it would mean permanent pain and disability for his father-in-law, who could no longer drive a car or move his arm without acute discomfort. For some reason, the prayers of the PFG members for Clinton's father-in-law seemed to be exceptionally fervent. I remember how one prisoner, appropriately named Christian, was carried away to such heights of eloquence that the best word to describe his prayer would have been the Welsh term *hwyl*, except that Christian was from Nigeria. But he was only one of ten prayerful voices on fire that evening. Between us all we certainly called to the Lord with passion for Clinton's father-in-law to be healed.

I next saw Clinton Davis at the 8.30 service of Morning Prayer in the prison chapel the following day. Five or six of those present were regular attendees at the PFG. Calling us together, the Chaplain said that at about 7.30 the previous evening his father-in-law had been in his bathroom when his shoulder had suddenly clicked back into place. It was still sore but the pain had gone. For the first time in weeks, he could move his arm normally; the dislocation was healed. 'Praise the Lord!' said Clinton. An extraordinary element in this story was the time of the healing: the shoulder had clicked back into place at almost exactly the same time, 7.30 p.m., as the prayer group was coming to the end of its meeting with those fervent prayers for Clinton's father-in-law. Was it a coincidence? Or was it a God-incidence? The members of the PFG had no doubt.

I brought many of my own problems to the PFG for shared prayer, including my agonies over the prospect of having my private letters sold to the newspapers. It was a cause which everyone seemed to become involved in. On three or four successive Thursdays we had particularly passionate group intercessions for the case to have the right result. One of our PFG members was a former solicitor who knew the psalms well. As part of our Bible study he read out some very appropriate verses from Psalm 37 which ran, 'Do not fret ... Trust in the Lord ... Commit your way to the Lord ... He will make your righteousness shine like the dawn, the justice of your cause like the noonday sun.' When the books and papers case ended in victory we read the psalm again in the PFG, giving joyful thanks for its promises coming true.

Far and away the most joyful of the experiences arising from prayer group was the baptism of Paddy's baby daughter. Paddy was not just the founder and recruiting sergeant for the PFG, he soon became its most committed member. His lapsed Catholicism turned into a burning and living faith. He gave his life to Christ, he repented of his sins, he became a changed man in his character and behaviour. These changes were genuine and wonderful to behold. To this day, I think of Paddy as one of the great spiritual influences on my life because I could so clearly see the transforming power of God's love at work in him. There were many fundamental changes in Paddy, but almost as an aside to them he said at a meeting of the PFG, 'I've been thinking a lot about my new baby who's been born since I was sentenced. She's ten weeks old and now I'm a real Christian I want to have her baptized here in the prison chapel. So I'm making an application to the Governor to be allowed to have the service here.'

I will remember the baptism of Paddy's daughter for as long as I live. It was a beautiful service full of humorous touches, deep emotion and profound spiritual symbolism. I was involved in it on many levels, not least because Paddy had done me the great honour of inviting me to be the godfather (of the Christian kind!) to his baby daughter Kathleen Veronica. Paddy's relatives turned up dressed to the nines in great style and colour. The baby was the best dressed of all, in a magnificent white christening gown with frills, folds, ruffles and bows worthy of a royal princess. However, on closer inspection this splendid garment was not a baby's christening dress – it was an adult lady's bridal gown.

If in retrospect I had been asked to guess which particular lorry this bridal gown might have fallen off, I would have said it was a lorry on the way to the outsize woman's shop, for it was made for an extremely large and buxom bride, quite possibly for a Wagnerian soprano. When lowered into this amply proportioned creation, the baby resembled a tiny little boat on the crest of huge billowing white waves. It was a combination with predictable consequences – she capsized, not once, but several times. As Standford Hill's

Catholic Chaplain, Father Kevin McElhinney, began the service with the opening prayer, the baby slipped towards the left-hand side of the dress and vanished into one of its large sleeves. She was rescued by her father and by various members of the congregation (all members of the PFG) who lovingly pulled her out with many kind words of encouragement like, 'God bless you my little darling', as they kissed her and quietened her down. But before Father Kevin could make much progress with the liturgy of Baptism – whoops! – the baby was submerged again, this time in the centre-folds of the dress. Once more she was brought to the surface to be comforted by prayers and kisses from the prisoners surrounding her before – whoops! – she disappeared again beneath yet more billowing waves of white silk.

By this time we had quite an audience participation service going as the cycles of the baby's appearances, disappearances, emergence and submergence repeated themselves amidst more and more pulls, kisses, prayers and 'God bless you my little darlings'. Standing up at the altar alongside the parents and godparents, at first I was amused by the *mouvementé* spectacle around my tiny goddaughter. But soon a deeper and more spiritual thought entered my head. 'What are we all doing here in this chapel on this Sunday afternoon?' I asked myself. 'We are here to bring an innocent new-born baby into the family of Christ. Her innocence makes a sharp contrast with the past villainy and criminality of just about every-one else present. Yet whose hands are helping this baby with such gentle touches of love and prayers? These are hands which in the recent past have had fingers on triggers, fists in bar brawls and out-stretched palms to receive payment for drug deals. Yet now these same hands are bringing this tiny child into a symbolic relationship with God with angelic words and actions. Something has happened to change these hands and the characters of those they belong to. The reason for the change is the transforming power of Christ's love.'

These musings of mine were silent at the time, but they re-inforced my conviction that I too was travelling on a journey of change. To pray is to change. The practical and human results from our prayer group taught me this far better than any priest or book of religious instruction. Looking back on my prison sentence, I know that my prayer partnership with Paddy and its enlargement into the PFG was the biggest single influence on my spiritual journey. How strange that I had to go to prison to learn that God changes the lives of those who pray to him in penitence and faith.

The tabloids reporting these events in the chapel of HMP Standford Hill did not repent or change. Under the headline 'GOD-FATHER AITKEN', the *Sunday Mirror* published a burlesque account of how 'Paddy the Tinker' had interrupted the usual Sunday services, breached the prison rules and brought in relatives who embarrassed everyone by turning up for the christening. It was such a travesty of the facts and of Kathleen Veronica's beautiful baptism service that the Catholic Chaplain lodged a complaint with the Press Council. It was an annoying end to a moving event but I was moving on myself. The end of my sentence was drawing near, and before that I was entitled to take five days of home leave over Christmas.

[1] Facility Licence Eligibility Date. See Chapter 9, p. 135

CHAPTER 11

Christmas and New Year Surprises

Every prisoner is entitled to five days of home leave in the month before his release to help him reintegrate with his friends, family and community. As my release date had been set for 7 January 2000 I could take my home leave any time in the month of December. Naturally I chose the period over Christmas. It turned out to be a visit full of surprises.

My excitement at the prospect of coming home for a few days was unfortunately shared by the media. Because no one knew the exact time or date when my home leave would start, the paparazzi began a stake-out at the prison gates from 21 December onwards. This surveillance created first tensions, and then outright hostilities, between the photographers and the prison officers. As mutual dislike deepened, the prison officers began thinking of ways to outmanoeuvre their enemies at the gates. Eventually a solution was reached which delighted me. 'The Governor feels we've got a duty to protect your privacy and the privacy of all the other inmates going out on home leave over Christmas,' said the SO in charge of A wing, 'so we've got a plan to fool the media if you're prepared to play ball with us and keep it secret.'

Unaccustomed as I was to this new solicitude for my privacy, I immediately agreed to cooperate, and was taken off to see Principal Officer Peck, the head of security. Mr Peck seemed to be enjoying his role as my cloak-and-dagger protector. My licence for home leave was scheduled to begin on the morning of 24 December.

'Normally that would mean from 8 a.m. on 24 December,' explained Mr Peck, 'but so long as it's on 24 December it's within the law, so how would you like it if your home leave was brought forward to five minutes past midnight on that morning?' 'I'd like that very much indeed,' I replied. 'Well then, don't tell a living soul. This is how we'll do it,' explained the Principal Officer as he outlined his top-secret plan. He would himself arrive on A wing at midnight. Not even the wing officers (some of whom were suspected of being sources to the tabloids) would know he was coming. I would get into his car and crouch down in the back seat with a rug over me. Mr Peck would drive me out through the prison gates and run the gauntlet of round-the-clock paparazzi. 'Those camera boys won't be taking no notice of my car,' said Mr Peck. 'All they'll see is one PO at the wheel going home at the end of a midnight shift.'

Having got past the paparazzi, the Peck plan required a pick-up point somewhere near the prison where we could rendezvous with a friend or relative who would drive me home. Together we pored over a map and pinpointed a filling station at a crossroads on the Isle of Sheppey. 'That'll do foine,' said Mr Peck who had an old-fashioned rustic accent that reminded me of Walter Gabriel in *The Archers*. 'Do you come from east Suffolk by any chance Mr Peck?' I asked him. 'Now you're a smart one you are. How do you know that?' he responded.

'I thought I recognized a Suffolk accent.' 'Well you're roight boy,' said the Principal Officer relapsing into broad Suffolk. 'My hoom used to be at Hollesley Bay and gort my furrst job in the Prison Service at that there Borstal.' 'Yea borr, strike a loight,' I said, showing off my fluency in broad Suffolk, 'oi grew up in them there parts too. My hoom was at Playford, 'longsides Wudbridge, and my furrst job were in that there borstal at Hollesley Bay too.'

'Strike a loight!' exclaimed Mr Peck, who was evidently enjoying this stage dialogue with a fellow native, 'and what were yew been doin' at Hollesley Bay Borstal, I'd loike to know.' Dropping the accent, I explained that back in 1961 at the age of 19 I'd had a summer job as an assistant to a Borstal housemaster, Peter McNeil, who later went on to be Governor of Wakefield and other prisons. 'Well I'll be darned,' said Mr Peck. 'I knew Mr McNeil. He were a gudd'un he were.'

From that conversation onwards Mr Peck and I were friends. It was fun plotting my nocturnal exit with him. His plan worked perfectly. We drove past the bored paparazzi at 12.10 on the morning of Christmas Eve, with none of them taking the slightest interest in a car driven by a single uniformed officer. At the Sheppey filling station we were met dead on time by Alan Woods, my former driver, who had chauffeured me in better circumstances for the past 12 years. As I took my leave of the marvellous Mr Peck, he said cheerfully, 'Oi shall enjoy telling them there photographers in the mornin' that yew be already gorn.'

I was gone with the wind, arriving back in London as Big Ben was striking half past one. As my car drove round Parliament Square, Alan Woods's mobile phone rang. It was William, anxious to speak to me: 'Er, um, Daddy there's been a slight technical hitch,' he began. 'I'm not actually waiting for you at Lord North Street with the others. You see I went out to a bar to celebrate your return home and got into a sort of discussion with a girl, and her boyfriend sort of biffed me in the eye, I'm absolutely fine but I've got a tiny little cut above my eye and so I rang Dr Wheeler. Actually I'm at his surgery now and he's very kindly just stitching me up.'

I drove straight to the surgery of Dr Roger Wheeler at 85 Sloane Street. The injury to William's pride was worse than the damage to his eyebrow. A couple of stitches and some paternal advice about not chatting up someone else's girlfriend put him back in good shape. We drove back together to Lord North Street and ate a delicious breakfast with the girls, washed down by large glasses of champagne, to an accompaniment of large gales of laughter. The first breakfast of my home leave was much happier and tastier than 'the last breakfast' of my sentencing day seven months earlier.

The rest of Christmas Eve was full of good and joyful news. I had a long conversation with Malcolm Pearson who had been discreetly raising funds for the Aitken Children's Trust (ACT). Thanks to his efforts, ACT, whose purpose was to educate, support and house my children, now had £600,000 in the bank. This was a wonderful result. The generosity of my friends touched and overwhelmed me. However aggressive my creditors became, they could not now prevent my children from finishing their education and having a roof over their heads even if it was not to be the roof of the home they had grown up in. Thanks to Malcolm's wonderful fund-raising, I now had financial peace of mind for the first time since going into prison. No friend could have supported me more loyally or more practically throughout my troubles. It was good to be able to sit in Malcolm's drawing room and thank him face-to-face for his heroic endeavours.

More good news came to me from Bruce Streather. He knew that about 50 leather-bound books of mine (the only casualties of the *Haig v Aitken* case in the High Court) were about to be auctioned by my creditors. Some of them had already been saved thanks to individual purchases made by generous friends such as Antonia Fraser, Jim Pringle and my school contemporary, Winston Churchill. However, that still left a residue of books which were special to me because of the inscriptions from their authors, among them Michael Foot, Roy Jenkins, Robert Blake, Richard Nixon and my great-uncle Lord Beaverbrook. Bruce, who knew how sad I would be to lose these volumes, said he would try to organize a rescue operation. His chosen rescuer-in-chief was Ken Costa, a deputy chairman of the UBS bank and a leading figure at Holy Trinity, Brompton. Although I had never met him, in an amazing act of kindness and generosity Ken Costa stepped in and bought all the books I wanted to save: they were back on my shelves by Christmas. I could not have had a finer present. and there was, the added delight of starting a friendship with Ken Costa, whom I have come to admire greatly for his chairmanship of Alpha International.

The Alpha course, a ten-week series of introductory talks on the Christian faith, had played a crucial role in my spiritual journey before going to prison.[1] Its booklets had been an important teaching resource for me and other members of the PFG at Standford Hill, so it seemed natural to celebrate the first communion of Christmas at the midnight service in Holy Trinity, Brompton, the mother church of Alpha. Accompanied there by my children, by Michael and Sylvia Mary Alison, and seeing many old friends in the congregation, I felt at home and at peace as we celebrated the joyful coming of the Word made flesh.

I should have felt equally at home and at peace in our local parish church of St Matthew's, Westminster on Christmas morning, but as I walked there with my mother we were ambushed by the paparazzi. 'Don't you guys ever take a day off even at Christmas?' I asked plaintively. In fact I felt rather sorry for one of the photographers whom I recognized from a TV news bulletin the day before in which Principal Officer Peck had read out a statement about my home leave to a bedraggled group of journalists outside the gates of Standford Hill, in the pouring rain. What a life to be an Aitken watcher and to have to miss your own family Christmas standing outside jails and churches. At first, the media presence in and around St Matthew's made me edgy, but I later relaxed and co-operated in posing for photographs with the Vicar, Philip Chester. It was the first time for about three years that I had not felt hounded by the cameras. To be in a cooperative rather than an adversarial relationship with the paparazzi was in itself a new beginning.

We ate a gargantuan family Christmas lunch in my sister's hospitable home in Kennington Road, and after that I had two good days of chilling out, sleeping late, and enjoying life at home with the children. Yet all the time I was conscious of the clock ticking away towards the 3 p.m. deadline on 28 December when my licence expired and I would again be prisoner.

I was driven back to Standford Hill by my friend Tony Richardson. When we approached the prison I saw a larger than usual media circus congregated at the main gate, but two hundred yards before it I also saw a single officer unlocking a back gate into the prison grounds. 'Can I come in this way?' I asked him. 'I'm just back from my home leave and I'd like to dodge the cameras if I can.' 'Of course you can,' said the officer warmly. 'Hope you had a nice Christmas. Just check yourself in with the SO at the visits office.'

So I checked in with the SO who told me to sit down and wait until all the other home-leavers came up from the main gate to be searched and processed. When they arrived on a bus, the officer in charge seemed very relieved to find me already in the office. 'Thank goodness you're here,' he said. 'We thought you might have been kidnapped.' 'Kidnapped?' I said in astonishment. 'I'm afraid there's a security scare about you,' he replied. 'Governor 2 is waiting for you upstairs. You needn't wait for the usual search here. I'll take you up to see him right away.' I was led to a room occupied by the Deputy Governor, an SO and two other officers. 'I'm sorry to have to tell you that we've uncovered a plot against you,' began the Deputy Governor. He had a thick cold, and was croaking so badly that I could hardly hear what he was saying. Other officers soon joined in, reading from notes in the brown files on the table in front of them. I was astounded by what they told me. My prison journey had been full of unexpected twists and turns but this was the biggest surprise of all.

The essence of what later newspaper headlines called the 'Aitken drugs plot' was that three Standford Hill inmates had been arrested and moved to a high-security prison on suspicion of plotting to drug me. It was said that they had been overheard talking to representatives of a tabloid newspaper on the prison phones. Exactly who had said what to whom was unclear, but the plot itself was all too clear. For an agreed price of £40,000, these three musketeers were allegedly going to kidnap me and force me to take an immobilizing drug called Rohypnol. Their plan was to then strip me naked and put me in bed with another prisoner. Photographs would then be taken and the tabloid would have a world exclusive 'Aitken is gay' story in return for its investment.

'Sounds pretty far-fetched to me,' I said, 'but thanks for the warning. I'll watch out. I've got some good friends who will watch my back for me too.' The Deputy Governor was taking the matter far more seriously. 'Oh no, we can't possibly keep you here,' he said. 'We haven't got the staff to protect you round the clock. We're going to move you to Elmley. You'll be in a cell in the high-security hospital there for the rest of your sentence.'

I was upset but knew it was useless to protest. HMP Elmley was a brownstone B-cat prison half a mile from Standford Hill. Being held under high-security conditions there, even in the hospital, would be a miserable start to the new millennium and a depressing end to my sentence. My friends in Standford Hill had been planning to give me a good send-off with farewell fruit-and-trifle parties. These festivities now would not take place, nor would I be able to join in the anticipated celebrations for bringing in the year 2000.

I was genuinely disappointed. 'Oh well,' I said. 'I shall miss you all. I suppose I'd better go back to my cell, pack up and say a few good-byes. What time am I being shipped out?' The Deputy Governor shook his head. 'I'm afraid we can't let you back on your wing,' he said. 'There may be more prisoners involved in this plot. It's too dangerous. These two officers will pack up the contents of your cell and any property that's being held for you in the property depart-ment. In the meantime you must stay here. When they come back with your belongings they will drive you over to Elmley.'

Once again it was useless to protest. In the privacy of my own thoughts I wondered whether this stranger-than-fiction plot could be more of a fantasy than a reality. I also wondered whether the high command of Standford Hill could be overreacting to it. But I could see from the sombre expressions on the faces of the uni-formed officers around the table that they were seriously worried. Two hours later I was driving through the gates of my third prison in seven months to begin my second spell of incarceration in high-security conditions.

*   *   *

HMP Elmley was not as tough as Belmarsh, but many of the same conditions and atmospherics prevailed there. Once again I was back in 'the cage', or communal reception cell, although this time I was all alone in it since my admission was taking place on a day when the nation's courts were closed. Once again I was put through the mill in a property department which confiscated most of my belongings because of the stricter security rules of a B-cat prison. Particular attention was paid to any item in my possession which by the wildest stretch of the imagination could be a potential suicide weapon – e.g. a tie or a large handkerchief. The explanation, I later discovered, for this special solicitude was that I was heading for the prison hospital. 'The screws thought you was a fraggle,' one of the property orderlies told me some days later. The word fraggle, which comes from the children's TV series *Fraggle Rock*, is prison slang for an inmate who is mentally ill.

The high incidence of mental illness is a big problem in Britain's prisons, and during the last ten days of my sentence I saw some of the worst aspects of it at first hand in the Elmley hospital. Most of my neighbours on the hospital wing (about 15 prisoners in all) were indeed 'fraggles'. The first one I met in the corridor had the rolling-eyed look of the Ancient Mariner about him as he stopped me to say, 'I know you! I know who you are! You're General Custer! I know what you did to those Cree Indians.' Being greeted each day by this deranged man with military salutes and 'Good morning General Custer sirs!' soon palled, but his behaviour was nothing compared to the screams that rang out in the night from my immediate neighbours in the padded cells across the corridor. A male nurse told me that many of the worst cases were suffering from the after-effects of drug abuse. 'They blow their own minds and then it can take weeks of medication to get them back into some sort of equilibrium,' he told me. 'Waking up in the middle of the night screaming from a nightmare they've been having is quite a normal sound on this wing I'm afraid.'

Also 'quite normal' in the Elmley hospital were paranoiacs, schizophrenics and self-harmers. On my second morning I was joined in the communal showers by an obviously disturbed prisoner whose body was criss-crossed by angry red scars. 'I can see you lookin' at me mars,' he grunted. 'Can't really miss them, can I?' I replied. 'No yer can't,' he said in an affable tone, 'but don't worry. I don't do violent. I done 'em on meself. But I'm all right when I take me pills.' I got to know more about the mars man. He told me he was a schizophrenic who had been in and out of prisons and mental institutions for years. His main trouble seemed to be a tendency to imagine he was cured, then to throw away his pills, and then to lurch into burglary, looting or any other crime that entered his head. That was his story. If it was true he shouldn't have been in a prison at all.

For all the good medical care it offered, the Elmley prison hospital was atmospherically far more of a prison than a hospital. My accommodation was a cell almost identical to the one I had in Belmarsh, with iron bars on the window, a heavy iron door, a loo without a seat and an observation panel in the door for round-the-clock surveillance.

News of the Aitken drugs plot soon reached the outside world in colourful stories and lurid headlines. However, news that I had been transferred to a high-security jail for reasons for which I was blameless did not seem to have reached the prison officers of Elmley. Within 48 hours of arriving there, I was subjected to a very aggressive cell search by the drug squad. After taking all my possessions apart – right down to the unscrewing of pens and the emptying of shampoo bottles – no drugs were found. However, one highly suspicious object was confiscated on the grounds that it constituted a danger to prison and indeed national security. This was my address book.

I pleaded with the officers to be allowed to keep it in my possession. 'But I've had my address book with me all through my sentence in Standford Hill and in A-cat Belmarsh,' I said. 'I really need it right now as I am writing about 30 letters a day.' 'Sorry, it's too much of a security risk. It contains the telephone numbers of the Royal Family,' said the officer in charge of the search. 'That's the Buckingham Palace switchboard number,' I replied. 'It's in the phone book.' The officer stood his ground, 'And it contains Margaret Thatcher's home address, Sir Edward Heath's home address and similar details about many other famous people,' he replied. 'It would be a serious breach of national security if it were stolen from your cell.' 'But how can it be stolen from my cell?' I objected. 'I'm shut in here for most of the day and the door's always kept locked when I'm out of the cell.' 'We decide on the security risks here, not you,' was the officer's parting shot as he swept out carrying my precious address book under his arm.

I appealed to the SO in charge of the hospital wing, and an elaborate compromise was reached. The address book would be kept in a safe in some undisclosed high-security location within the prison. However, if I needed to check anyone's address for the purposes of my correspondence I could write down their name and give it to an officer, who would give it to the SO. He would get another officer in the high-security location to unlock the safe and copy out the address required from my address book. That second officer would get a third officer to bring the information back to me on the hospital wing. As I was writing about 30 letters every day in an attempt to clear the backlog of my Christmas correspondence from friends and well-wishers, this elaborate procedure had to be put into action to obtain well over a hundred addresses. I certainly did my bit to create jobs for the boys in HMP Elmley.

Prisoners on the hospital wing did not go to Association or to Exercise. As a result, we were kept in our cells for over 22 hours a day. The only breaks were for meals or for an opportunity to brew up tea or coffee. Although this austere regime brought a few pangs of loneliness, on the whole I made the most of my solitude. I wrote a large number of letters, several of them to my fellow prisoners in Belmarsh and Standford Hill thanking them for their companionship during my sentence. I read voraciously, particularly enjoying Andrew Roberts' biography of the first Marquess of Salisbury, Robert A. Caro's second volume on Lyndon B. Johnson, and Metropolitan Anthony's *The Essence of Prayer*. I also plugged away at my New Testament Greek, testing myself morning and evening on a vocabulary list which consisted of over seven hundred words. I could usually score over 90 per cent on any section in this list, which was not bad considering that seven months earlier I had not known a single word of the language.

The arrival of the new millennium nearly passed me by. I was actually asleep, having taken no notice of the oral message passed to me and other occupants of the hospital wing: 'Kick yer door down at midnight.' Every other inmate, it seemed, did obey this call to arms. For as Big Ben sounded the first stroke of 12, Elmley exploded with the noise of six hundred pairs of prisoners' boots slamming into the iron doors of their cells. The iron doors won the contest, but not before several minutes of extreme noise had tested my eardrums to the full.

On New Year's Day, a team of investigators from Standford Hill came over to Elmley to ask me questions about the Aitken drugs plot. I was willing to help, but as I didn't know the first thing about it I was no use. The next day, Governor John Robinson came on his own to tell me the names of the three men who had been arrested on suspicion of being the plotters. I was amazed. 'My gut instinct tells me you've got the wrong suspects,' I told him. 'I thought X, Y and Z were pretty straight shooters. They wouldn't get mixed up in a sordid deal with a tabloid for taking photos of me in the nude. In their language they wouldn't think it proper.'

My gut instinct penetrated closer to the truth than the labours of the Standford Hill investigating team. The evidence from overheard conversations about the plot was strong against the tabloid but weak against the unidentifiable prisoners on the other end of the line. X, Y and Z were eventually sent back to D-cat prisons without any charges against them. Nobody dared charge the journalists who had offered the money to their unknown accomplices. So in the end it was just another sequence in the media's *Carry On* film that had been playing ever since I arrived on the Isle of Sheppey.

One other visitor who came over from Standford Hill to see me in Elmley was the Chaplain, Clinton Davis. After a long conversation we said our farewells with emotion on both sides. As I hugged him, my last words were, 'Thank you Clinton. You have done more than you can ever know to help me into a right relationship with the Lord.'

Prison chaplains do not get enough thanks. They carry an impossibly heavy load of administrative duties (why should a chaplain be in charge of booking overseas telephone calls?) and welfare work which the prison officers should do themselves. Yet despite these pressures, the two chaplains I got to know, David Powe at Belmarsh and Clinton Davis at Standford Hill, were remarkable pastors with great gifts of spiritual leadership. I don't think I missed a day of Clinton's Morning Prayer services in chapel and I heard almost all his Sunday sermons. A graduate of Wycliffe Hall, Oxford whose preaching showed a deep knowledge of scripture, Clinton Davis was a great inspiration to me and many other prisoners.

There was one more inspirational surprise on the final night of my prison sentence. Just after 11 p.m. on 6 January 2000, I was packing up the last of my belongings into a black bin-liner. My release time was less than nine hours away and my mood was a mixture of contentment and excitement. Suddenly I heard the sound of someone knocking on the door of my cell. I was startled, for at this hour of night prisoners are banged up and there is little or no movement on the hospital wing. 'Who's there?' I asked, going over to the door whose observation panel had been slid open from the other side.

'My name's Mr Smith,' said a soft voice. I saw a pair of brown eyes peering intensely at me through the aperture. Because the corridor behind them was dimly lit, I could barely see the face of my visitor. 'Who are you?' I asked. 'I'm a prison officer. I was just wondering if I could pray with you.' There was something in the gentleness of these words, as well as the surprise they gave me, which made me start to choke up. 'I'd love that,' I said. 'Please come in.' 'I can't come in,' he replied. 'I'm on night duty on C wing and I don't have a master key to the cells on this unit. I shouldn't really be here at all.'

We were whispering to each other through the observation panel. Our faces were about six inches apart, separated by the thickness of the iron door. 'Thank you so much for coming,' I murmured, conscious that Mr Smith must have taken some sort of a risk by his visit. 'Oh no, don't thank me. I really felt God's call to come over and pray with you,' he said. 'I know you're being released tomorrow, and as your brother in Christ I wanted to send you on your way with a prayer. Could we just say one here and now?' So we prayed together beginning with the Lord's prayer. The spectacle of Prison Officer Smith and Prisoner CB9298 Aitken whispering these holy words together through the grill of a cell door was all but impossible in the prison culture, but with God all things are possible, so for the next seven or eight minutes we shared some wonderful extempore prayers. Eventually Mr Smith said, 'I'd better be getting back to C wing, but before I go, is there any one special prayer need you have that I can pray for – not just tonight but in the months and the years ahead of you?'

As he said these words in the flickering light of the corridor behind him, Mr Smith seemed like an angel. He had come out of the darkness with an offer to pray for me in the future. So I searched for the right request and found it. 'My greatest prayer need is something I pray for every morning,' I replied. 'It's a short prayer I wrote myself while I was in Standford Hill. It is particularly right for tomorrow morning. Could I read it to you?' 'Yes, please read it,' said Mr Smith. So I went back to my bed, picked up my prayer notebook and turned the pages until I found a prayer which I called 'Coffee with God' because I usually said it first thing in the morning while drinking coffee. Returning to the door, I read these words to Mr Smith through the observation panel:

> Heavenly Father, I thank you for this new day; for the sunlight streaming through the bars of my cell; for the taste of this warm coffee; and for your presence as you hear my prayers.
>
> Lord as each day dawns I thank you for bringing me a step closer to freedom. Not just my physical freedom; far more importantly I thank you for the freedom of a new relationship with you.
>
> Lord you have liberated me from the darkness of my past. Help me to stay faithful to you in the future – on this day and every day for the rest of my life. Through Jesus Christ our Lord. Amen.

'Amen,' whispered Mr Smith, 'and it's a good prayer for me as well as for you, asking the Lord to keep us faithful to him. I'll be praying it for both of us. God bless you!'

And with that, Mr Smith melted away into the dingy twilight of the corridor and was gone. A few moments later my head was on the pillow and I slept peacefully until 6.30 on the morning of my release.

[1] See *Pride and Perjury* (Continuum), pp. 271–3.

CHAPTER 12

Released and Depressed

The early-morning preliminaries to my release began with the deranged inmate on the hospital wing saluting me smartly and saying, 'Good morning General Custer sir! They tell me you're going on leave. Watch out for those Red Indians. You could easily get an arrow in your back.' In the light of the later events, perhaps he was not so mad after all.

The first 'Indian' I met (from Southall rather than from the Wild West) was a bureaucratic one. He was in charge of an office within the prison which dealt with all the forms an inmate has to sign before being released. There were forms reminding me to see my probation officer within the next 12 hours; forms returning my property; forms explaining the terms of my 'tag' or Home Detention Curfew; and finally a form which gave me a release grant of £41.50. I pocketed the cash gratefully and was escorted to the main gate by a friendly woman prison officer.

'I hear you're writing a book,' she said. 'Don't be too hard on the prison staff, will you? Most of us are pretty much OK.' 'I know you are,' I said, thinking of Mr Smith the night before and then of the vast majority of the officers in Belmarsh, Standford Hill and Elmley who had treated me with fairness and often with kindness. 'I'm not an unqualified admirer of your higher management up in head-quarters,' I said, 'but I do admire those of you who work on the front line of the Prison Service. I think most of you do an extremely difficult job pretty well under enormous pressures. That's what I'll be saying and writing.' It was a promise I have done my best to keep.

The doors of Elmley prison are two huge steel behemoths with a small postern gate cut into them to allow individual exits and entrances on foot. I stood alongside this lesser portal as the gate officer looked at his watch. 'Two minutes to eight,' he said. 'We do things punctual here. There's quite a crowd of photographers out there waiting for you, by the way.' 'How many?' I asked. 'Maybe 50 or 60. Anyway we've got them all behind a long barrier about 40 yards back from the gate, so they can't mob you. What I advise you do is to walk half a dozen paces forward to let them get their pictures. Pause for five or ten seconds, then turn right on your heel and 20 paces ahead of you you'll find your car and driver. Chin up now – and out you go.' 'Thanks,' I said, feeling that this officer had missed his vocation as film director. He unlocked the postern gate, swung it open and I stepped out into the chill January sunshine. I was free.

There is a much reprinted photograph of my exit from prison which shows me emerging from the gates, clasping a black bin-liner in my right hand, dressed in a pair of faded blue jeans and a black tracksuit top. In the background are the dark bars of HMP Elmley, and in the foreground my face has an expression that is half-startled, half-quizzical. The startled part came from the sight and sound of several dozen flashbulbs going off in my direction. The quizzical look sprang from the question that was going through my head in those first moments of freedom, 'What on earth am I going to do next?'

My immediate next move was to get into a Renault car which Frank Williams had kindly loaned me, and to be driven to London by Alan Woods. It soon became apparent that we were being pursued by at least four cars and three motorcyclists. 'Can we shake them off?' I asked Alan. Although the Renault Laguna was a fast car with good acceleration, we were no match for the motorcyclists. I was anxious not to be followed by a cavalcade of paparazzi to my first port of call which was a rendezvous with Malcolm Pearson and other friends who were helping me put together a settlement proposal for my creditors, so I picked Alan's brains for 'the knowledge' he had acquired as a London taxi driver. Could he think of any little sidestreets or backstreets where we could stymie our unwanted entourage and escape?

'How about that little alley on the edge of Victoria Station which you sometimes used when you were in a hurry to catch a train to Ramsgate?' he suggested. 'Brilliant,' I replied. 'Those boys will have a hard job catching up with me down there if I can make a quick getaway.' Alan's plan worked perfectly. The alleyway he had recommended was a path for pedestrians linking the Wilton Road perimeter wall of Victoria Station with platform 16. As the car braked to a sudden halt in Wilton Road, I leapt out and sprinted down the alley, across the station platforms and down into the tube. Emulating the story I had heard in Belmarsh about Slim, Smasher and Pee-Wee and their getaway from their jewellery robbery using the underground, I leapt on to the first incoming train, changed at Charing Cross, then headed slowly to Malcolm Pearson's house un-followed and unobserved. Meanwhile, back at Victoria Station Alan Woods was enjoying the spectacle of the three media motorcyclists pulling off their helmets, cursing me and arguing amongst themselves about what to do next. 'AITKEN GIVES HATED PACK THE SLIP', said *The Times'* headline the next day.

After a good meeting with Malcolm I was able to slip into Lord North Street unnoticed by the crowd of journalists congregated outside our front door. This was achieved by using a back entrance via North Court, a block of flats in Great Peter Street which contained my mother's ground-floor granny flat. It shared a garden with us which we had used as an escape route in many previous paparazzi sieges. So I had a happy reunion lunch with my mother, after which I settled down to await my next two visitors – a probation officer and a team of electronics experts who were going to fit me up with a tag.

My probation officer, who had visited me in Standford Hill about three weeks before my sentence ended, was Mr Bah Opong of the London Probation Service. He was a considerate official who was doing me a favour by coming to Lord North Street. Normally all released prisoners have to visit their probation officers within 12 hours of leaving jail. These meetings almost always take place in the local office of the Probation Service, which puts great emphasis on protecting the privacy of its visitors. A visit from me on my first day of freedom, however, was bound to attract the paparazzi who would have thrown my privacy and everyone else's to the winds. When Mr Bah Opong realized that I could not prevent a large number of cameramen from following me to his office just off the Marylebone Road, he decided to come and see me. I was grateful for his kindness.

Mr Opong explained that I had to be interviewed by him once a week for the next four weeks and once a fortnight for the eight weeks after that. The purpose of these interviews was to deter me from reoffending by reviewing my attitudes, lifestyle, relationships and personal circumstances. This is a formula which may well be appropriate for many newly released prisoners who need the help and guidance of the Probation Service. In my case it was difficult to envisage the circumstances in which I was likely to commit my crime again. Another libel action against the *Guardian*? Another night in the Paris Ritz? When I tried to speak light-heartedly about the improbability of such repeat performances, Mr Bah Opong's face remained a mask of solemnity. He was a 'do it by the book' man, so we did it by the book at that first afternoon interview in Lord North Street and in the same way over and over again for every one of my succeeding interviews. To a large extent it was an empty ritual of predictable questions and predictable answers. Yet I saw his point of principle which is that the post-release monitoring of prisoners is a valuable exercise. Making exceptions from these procedures would be difficult. So I cooperated fully with Mr Opong on all aspects of my statutory three months on probation.

Having done my best to reassure my probation officer that I was not thinking of reoffending, I waited for my taggers to arrive. Meanwhile I was deriving some amusement from watching the TV news bulletins which were being transmitted live from Lord North Street. 'The suspense is mounting here because Mr Aitken is five minutes away from being in serious breach of his licence,' said one excitable commentator, obviously unaware that I had arrived five hours earlier by a side entrance. 'If he is not back in his home behind this front door by the curfew deadline time of 7 p.m. he could be taken back to prison tonight.'

A few minutes before seven, a technical team of electronics specialists arrived with their tagging equipment. They were from Premier Monitoring Services, contractors to the Home Office for the Home Detention Curfew (HDC) scheme. HDC was a little-known part of the criminal justice system in early 2000. It had been in existence for less than a year, and only a few hundred prisoners had ever been given early release under it, so the tagging of Aitken had news and novelty value. The leader of the technical team for Premier Monitoring Services was Andy Homer, and his No. 2 had the appropriate name of Mr Alan Tagg. They had been warned by the Home Office that their visit to my home could be the focus of media interest. Even so they were startled by the size of the crowd of reporters and the intensity of their questioning. 'This is the biggest publicity the electronic monitoring of offenders has ever had,' said Andy Homer cheerfully.

The first job a team of tagging experts has to do when they arrive at the home of a 'curfewee' (the legal term for the tagged offender) is to create an electronic envelope which equates to the boundaries of the property. No. 8 Lord North Street gave the technicians no small problem because it is a rambling five thousand square-foot eighteenth-century house with ten bedrooms, a cavernous basement, a courtyard and a ballroom-sized drawing room extending like a separate peninsula into the garden. 'Not quite your usual south London semi,' observed one member of the tagging team as they rose to the challenge of creating the most diffuse and difficult electronic envelope in their experience of monitoring released prisoners.

Just when the technicians had achieved electronic mastery over the complex shape of our house, my mother came across the shared garden from her flat and engaged in conversation with Andy Homer. Applying all her charm she said to him, 'How brilliant of you to be able to make your envelope fit Jonathan's house. But you will make it fit my flat too, won't you? You see we're both part of one big family home, and Jonathan will be coming over to me all the time for his meals. So could you please make your envelope just a tiny bit bigger, so Jonathan can have his suppers with his old mother?'

Although this request sounded more like Lady Bracknell than Lady Aitken, Andy Homer generously agreed to do his best to accommodate it. He needed to get the consent of the authorities at HMP Standford Hill for such an extension, so a fax was despatched to Governor John Robinson who gave his consent immediately. As a result of this efficient cooperation, my HDC envelope was enlarged by another 2,500 square feet to include my mother's granny flat and the garden that gave access to it. I was delighted. I calculated that as a tagged prisoner I could now move around in a space almost a thousand times larger than the dimensions of a prison cell. This felt like real freedom, even if I was a curfewee.

The electronic tag is a small device about the size of a wristwatch. It is fitted around the curfewee's ankle where it must stay 24 hours a day for the two-month tagging period. It was so unobtrusive when concealed under my sock, and so lightweight, that wearing a tag never physically inconvenienced me.

The feeling of carrying a moral burden did, however, stay with me throughout my 60 days on HDC. The presence of the tag was a constant reminder that I was still a prisoner under surveillance. In fact there is no surveillance between the daylight hours of 7 a.m. and 7 p.m. The tag only operates as a form of house arrest for the next 12 hours. During those night hours the curfewee must stay within the electronic envelope around his home. If he steps as much as a few inches outside his front door during the curfew period, the tag sends an alarm signal to the regional monitoring headquarters of the HDC scheme. Almost immediately, one of the HDC monitors will call on the 'hotline' – a specially installed telephone which shrieks with the decibel power of a fire alarm. If the curfewee picks up the receiver, identifies himself with a series of codewords, and can give a reasonable explanation as to why the alarm signalled a breach of the curfew, no further action is taken. But any serious breach of the HDC conditions such as going down to the pub during curfew hours can result in rearrest and re-imprisonment. It is hardly surprising that over 95 per cent of all tagged prisoners comply fully with the terms of their HDC licence.

I had little difficulty in coping with the rules of my tag. As a middle-aged man still feeling bruised from the experience of imprisonment, I had no desire to be out on the town, pubbing, clubbing or partygoing. I much preferred the home comforts of reading or watching television and I hugely appreciated the home cooking of my mother. Although she was now in her ninetieth year, she showed amazing energy in organizing supper parties for me. These took place three or four nights a week throughout my tagging period and were a wonderful way of reconnecting me with my circle of old friends and new supporters.

I did breach my tagging conditions once, but fortunately only by about 90 seconds, so it involved no penalty. The cause of this breach was my over-enjoyment of the one and only big party I attended in the early weeks after coming out of prison. It was the wedding of my former secretary Fiona Mellersh to Robert Syms MP. After an afternoon marriage service in the Crypt Chapel of the House of Commons (it felt strange to be back in the Palace of Westminster for the first time since May 1997) the assembled guests moved to the Carlton Club in St James's Street for a sumptuous seated dinner which began at 5 p.m. With champagne and other good wines flowing freely, I did not keep as close an eye on the clock as I should have done. I was particularly enjoying sitting next to Gillian Shephard MP with whom I shared many reminiscences about our times together in John Major's Cabinet.

As this wedding feast was reaching the dessert course, the MC came to the microphone and declared, 'As it's coming up to seven o'clock, ladies and gentlemen, we'll take a comfort break now and than have the speeches.' The words 'coming up to seven o'clock' made me break away in acute discomfort. The exact time was five minutes to seven and I felt like Cinderella discovering she was still at Prince Charming's ball on the edge of midnight. Without saying goodbye to the bride, groom or Gillian Shephard, I sprinted out into St James's Street and luckily found a taxi immediately. As we hurtled round Parliament Square almost on two wheels, the chimes of Big Ben began to strike. Dashing through the front door of Lord North Street at one minute past seven, I heard the HDC hotline emitting its high-pitched scream. Grabbing the receiver I panted out the confirmation that I was present, correct and within the electronic envelope. It was a close shave.

My social life while on the tag consisted almost entirely of suppers around my mother's dining room table. On the rare occasions when

I went out, I felt slightly awkward and uncomfortable. Paparazzi continued to pursue me, although as single spies rather than in battalions. I therefore turned down most invitations, but one that I did accept had some strange consequences.

My old friend Winston Churchill, who had been in the House of Commons with me for 23 years, invited me to lunch at his home in Belgrave Square in late January. Joining us for pre-lunch drinks were his wife Luce and a young woman barrister called Karen Phillips. Her name meant nothing to me. We chatted pleasantly and that was that. In the following days I had several phone calls from Karen Phillips. There was nothing of substance to them. She seemed to be keen to ask how I was getting on and to wish me well. To reciprocate her kindness I asked her to come to one of my mother's supper parties. Karen arrived with a pot plant for my mother and talked animatedly all evening to me and the other guests. She went home on her own.

The day after that supper my mother, ever the matchmaker, said to me, 'Darling, I think you need some fun in your life. Why don't you see more of Karen? She has rung up to invite both of us to lunch, but I'm sure she'd rather see you on your own. I think she finds you rather attractive and I'm sure you feel the same about her. Why don't you have a date with her?' Soon after these maternal manoeuvres, Karen Phillips called me again. Some sixth sense made me decide not to follow my mother's suggestions, so at the risk of sounding priggish I explained to Karen that I did not feel like going out with anyone at this time. Karen, on the other end of the line, said she entirely understood. So our platonic telephone calls fizzled out. That should have been the end of our non-story, but amazingly it became headline news in the gossip columns soon after the death of George Carman QC.

Although George Carman had been counsel for Granada and the *Guardian* in my 1997 libel action, he had known me before the case and treated me fairly during it. I liked him. We had a memorable conversation some months after our duel in the witness box, when he let slip several fascinating tit-bits of information about his clients. He was particularly disenchanted with their post-trial triumphalism. Far from being harsh or judgemental about me, Carman was reported as saying in August 1997, 'Jonathan Aitken was not a liar. He told a lie, like many of us do, and had to live with the consequences.' The reason why George Carman came back into my post-release story was that soon after his death it became publicly known that Karen Phillips had been his mistress during the last years of his life. She was living with him at the time of my libel case against the *Guardian*. She claimed to have played a dramatic role in the turning point of that courtroom drama by suggesting to Carman that he should start his legal team searching for the air tickets of my ex-wife's visit to Paris. If true, that claim made Karen Phillips a pivotal figure in my ruin because it was the discovery of the air tickets in mid-trial that had snatched victory from the jaws of defeat for the *Guardian*.

After George Carman's death, which was marked by fulsome obituaries and personal tributes including a warm one from me, there was a row between his son Dominic Carman and Karen Phillips who each published somewhat conflicting accounts of the great man's controversial lifestyle. In the wake of the journalistic excitements caused by these revelations, the gossip columns got wind of the story that Karen Phillips had been seeing me in the months before Carman's death, and various insinuations were made about our encounter. These were unfair because not even the smallest sparks of romance had ever been kindled between us. Karen Phillips later said that she had made her phone calls and visits to me entirely as acts of kindness. So far as I know, that is true. However, it was curious that she never mentioned her relationship with George Carman to me, nor indeed to Winston Churchill who had introduced us on the day he gave me lunch at his home in Belgrave Square. So what did all this mean? At the end of the day, nothing much. The only effect the episode had on me was to induce a great wariness, in the months ahead, of single ladies bearing pot plants or invitations to lunch.

Like many a newly released prisoner I found the period of adjustment to freedom a difficult experience. Even after my tag was removed I felt uncertain about almost all personal relationships outside my immediate family. I worried whether people were being artificially kind to me out of false politeness when they made contact. Then if people I was hoping to see did not communicate I became unreasonably disappointed. These mood swings were irrational. All they really indicated was that I was a long way from settling down. Gradually it became clear that a lot of the people and places in my old world were subtly changing their attitudes towards me. At this time I often thought of these lines from Browning's poem 'The Lost Leader':

> Life's night begins: let him never come back to us!
> There would be no doubt, hesitation and pain
> Forced praise on our part – the glimmer of twilight
> Never glad confident morning again!

The biggest single obstacle to 'glad confident morning again' was my bankruptcy. In the early weeks of the year 2000 I seemed to be getting an aggressive letter from my Trustee almost every other day. A typical missive from him would open,

Dear Mr Aitken

I am now in a position to issue legal proceedings in the matter of your Parliamentary Pension Fund and your Occupational Aitken Hume Pension Fund ...

Simultaneously I would receive letters from my ex-wife's lawyers threatening both me and my Trustee with proceedings over her rights to chattels in Lord North Street and to her rights over the property itself.

Although I felt caught in the crossfire between these warring parties, I also felt that a lot of time and money was being wasted by them on expensive legal bills. There was a far better way of finding an honourable solution to my bankruptcy than complicated litigation. It was a well-known route out of insolvency known as an IVA – an Individual Voluntary Arrangement – which is an agreed settlement between a bankrupt and his creditors with advantages to both sides.

In late January 2000 I put forward an IVA cash offer of £1.5 million which was all I could possibly raise or borrow after a sale of Lord

North Street. Fifty per cent of those sale proceeds would go to my ex-wife Lolicia from whom I was divorced in 1998. In discussions with my Trustee in Bankruptcy Mr Colin Haig, he seemed to think that my offer had a good chance of being accepted. One of its greatest advantages was that it would avoid all future litigation over my assets and debts. However, the hawks on the creditors committee had already signalled that they wished to fight in court to seize my parliamentary pension, my small occupational pension, and to oppose Lolicia's right to 50 per cent of our matrimonial home. For my part, I still had the right to get the £2.4 million of legal bills claimed by the *Guardian* and Granada subjected to taxation – i.e. umpiring by a costs judge. So if we did not settle the matter by an IVA agreement, the alternative was to spend at least a couple more years in litigation over the libel case costs, over whether or not my two pensions could be seized and over the division of the sale proceeds of 8 Lord North Street. If these court cases were to go ahead I was advised that I would succeed in sub-stantially reducing the legal costs, and defeating the challenge to my pensions, and that Lolicia would succeed in being awarded 50 per cent of her former marital home. Yet even if I won all these cases, they would in one sense be pyrrhic victories, for they would tie me up in court paperwork and court hearings for long periods just at the time when I desperately wanted to be free to start a new life. As I put it in the final paragraph of my IVA proposal to my creditors,

It is now coming up to the five year anniversary of the issuing of the writ in the *Aitken v Guardian* libel action. I confess to being weary of the saga and wearier still at the prospect of it dragging on for two more years ... I sincerely hope that the Trustees of the Scott Trust [owners of the *Guardian*] and the Board of Granada plc will feel as I do that all of us have better things to do with our lives than to prolong our legal and court-room contests into the New Millennium and that the settlement deal offered is the best and most commercial way forward in the interests of the creditors.

Unfortunately the creditors did not see it this way – or at least not for another two years, when they eventually did come round to an IVA solution. I thought there were two main reasons why my proposal was rejected. One was to do with pride, the other with suspicion.

The pride of the Trustee in Bankruptcy had been badly wounded by the drubbing he had received in the judgment of Mr Justice Rattee in the books and papers case of *Haig v Aitken*. The media criticism had stung my creditors and was beginning to sting them again over their attempts to confiscate my parliamentary pension. As the *Daily Mail* said in a leading article,

> For once it is difficult to avoid a certain sympathy with Aitken's plight. Never before has a former MP faced the loss of a pension in such a way. Moreover civil servants don't lose their entitlements when they are declared bankrupt ... It may be that Aitken's principal creditors the *Guardian* newspaper and Granada Television are legally entitled to their pound of flesh. But in human terms the hounding of Jonathan Aitken to the very limit smacks of petty vindictiveness.

In the sheltered world of insolvency practitioners and lawyers, public criticism of their activities in national newspapers is an unwelcome novelty. I knew that such press comments severely upset Mr Haig and his advisers, so I guessed that wounded professional pride was a factor in making them stick to their legal guns and fight on.

Suspicion was another key element in prolonging the fight over my bankruptcy. My principal creditors were implacable in their misguided belief that somewhere in the world I had stashed away a huge fortune which journalists had labelled 'Aitken's arms-dealing millions'. In my book *Pride and Perjury*, I wrote at the start of the 'Arms Deals' chapter,

> So to set the record straight: I have never in my life made a penny from an arms deal, either by way of commission or in any other way. The extraordinary labels that have been slapped on me by some sections of the media such as 'merchant of death',

'missile salesman', 'arms dealer', 'notorious arms dealer', and even 'illegal arms dealer', are quite simply false.

This is, and always has been, the truth. But it was not believed by my creditors, whose suspicions about my huge hidden fortune from arms deals were much inflamed by a front-page story in the *Guardian* on 31 May 2000 headlined 'AITKEN'S SECRET SWISS BANK ACCOUNT REVEALED'. Although the source (an Arab who had admitted fraud and embezzlement) was dubious, the details were precise since the bank was named as Credit Suisse with an account number 332771021 and an amount in it of £2.7 million. Had this been true, at least it would have solved all my bankruptcy problems, but it would also have got me into more trouble because I had already made a declaration of all my assets which did not, alas, include an extra £2.7 million.

Although the story of my secret Swiss bank account made many headlines, its only immediate effect was to postpone all hopes of an IVA settlement since Mr Colin Haig had to investigate the story, as did the Inland Revenue. I cooperated fully, writing letters of authority to Credit Suisse to open up account number 332771021 for inspection. I also asked Credit Suisse to confirm that I had never had any bank account with them under any other number or code-name. At the end of his investigation, Mr Haig was satisfied that what I had told him was true. When my bankruptcy was finally settled by IVA and annulled in court, he issued a press statement making it clear that I had not concealed any assets from my creditors.

Although my bankruptcy eventually came to an end in an atmosphere of mutual confidence and cooperation, in the summer of the year 2000 relations between me and my Trustee in Bankruptcy were characterized by mutual suspicion and hostility. He thought I was hiding assets. I thought he was leaking unhelpful material from my financial records and correspondence to certain journalists who put their own pejorative slant on them. This made me fed up. I knew I had no assets other than the ones declared, but the drip of suggestions to the contrary unnerved me as false rumour after false rumour kept on appearing in print. I became despairing about getting back to the peaceful life I longed for. I was down and depressed.

There were other factors in my depression besides my difficult relationship with my Trustee in Bankruptcy. Being prevented from getting started on my biography of Charles Colson was a huge source of frustration. This project was dealt a devastating blow when officials of the Immigration and Naturalization Service of the US Embassy in London rejected my application for a visa. The grounds for the rejection were that I had committed a criminal offence involving 'moral turpitude'. This development plunged me into a black mood of despair. No visa meant no book contract and no prospects of travel to a country I loved. It also meant that I could not visit my daughter Victoria who was in her final year at Georgetown University. It felt as though I was being punished twice over, with imprisonment in Britain being followed by exile from America. The visa refusal worsened my money problems. If I could not write books for my US publishers, could I earn a living as an author? The answer was far from clear.

To add to my gloom, my plan to study theology at Wycliffe Hall, Oxford, looked as though it might be crumbling. Before going to prison I had been offered a definite place at Wycliffe. This had been confirmed in correspondence with the college and by a conversation with Wycliffe's Principal, Professor the Reverend Dr Alister McGrath, when he kindly visited me in Standford Hill. However, by the spring of 2000 the Wycliffe trumpet was giving an uncertain sound. I discovered that some of the tutors had been unsettled by the negative newspaper stories that kept appearing about my bankruptcy. To make matters worse, Wycliffe had admitted an ex-prisoner as a student at the beginning of the previous academic year and the experiment had failed. That failure had been veiled in obscurity, but any comparable weaknesses by me would be guaranteed maximum publicity, so the college was nervous about admitting a second ex-prisoner who might damage its reputation. It was also worried about being under permanent siege by paparazzi. I had an uneasy interview with Alister McGrath in which he wondered aloud if it might be wiser of me to postpone my entry to the college for one year. I came back from this meeting in Oxford saying to some of my closest friends, 'I'm not at all sure that Wycliffe wants to admit me as a student.'

Amid my deepening anxieties about these Wycliffe worries, US visa disappointments and bankruptcy problems I went to a Sunday evening service at Holy Trinity, Brompton. Nicky Gumbel preached a powerful sermon about trusting in God. Towards the end of the service he invited all those who wanted to be prayed for to come forward. In spite of all of my good experiences of communal prayer on the Alpha course and in prison, I had still not entirely lost the instincts of a traditional member of the 'church-reticent' wing of Anglicanism. The idea of coming forward to the front of a packed church in this way turned me off. But my need was greater than my reluctance. So with leaden footsteps I did go forward for the first time in my life to be prayed for.

When I reached the front of the church, Nicky Gumbel asked me what my prayer need was. In ten or fifteen seconds I summarized my problems, saying that I felt 'under attack'. Nicky thumbed through his Bible, and in a quiet, peaceful voice he read me the first few verses of Psalm 37. As soon as I heard the familiar words, 'Trust in the Lord ... Commit your way to the Lord ... trust in him and he will make your righteousness shine like the dawn, the justice of your cause like the noonday sun', I remembered how the same prayer had been said for me on the eve of the High Court hearing of *Haig v Aitken* by members of our Standford Hill prayer and fellowship group.

Almost immediately I realized that I had been sinning with my own failure to trust God. Of course he would sort out the unfair stories about my 'secret Swiss bank account'. Of course he would decide whether or not I should go to Wycliffe. Of course I would get the right answer from him on whether or not I should write the Colson biography and on the related visa problem. Instead of fuming, fretting and getting depressed about these apparent reverses in my life, I should surrender them to God's will. I was being tested and had so far failed the test. I would only pass if I learned the lesson from these pressures and yielded my will to God's will on all of them. This moment of truth in Holy Trinity, Brompton brought peace to my troubled soul. I went home that night and said prayers of surrender instead of prayers of request. Nothing happened quickly with the problems, but at least I was content in my heart to be leaving the solutions in God's hands.

The solutions duly arrived. My Trustee in Bankruptcy appeared to lose interest in 'Aitken's secret Swiss bank account', presumably because he and his team of investigators found it did not exist. I was invited to come to the US Embassy where a sympathetic Vice Consul in charge of the visa department interviewed me about the remorse I felt for my crime of moral turpitude. Ten days later I was granted a 'waiver', which gave me a two-year multiple-entry visa for unlimited visits to the United States: the Colson biography could go forward. As for Wycliffe, my close friend and prayer partner Michael Alison went to see the key tutors there and reassured them about the sincerity of my commitment to the Lord and the falsity of the newspaper stories suggesting that I was dishonestly with-holding funds from my creditors. I did nothing except continue to pray. Soon the third answer to prayer arrived in the form of definite confirmation that I could start at Wycliffe, as originally planned, at the beginning of the new academic year. So after nearly nine months of being down and depressed I became joyful and thankful as I set off for Oxford University in September 2000 for a new life as a mature student.

CHAPTER 13

Wycliffe and Oxford

Going back to Oxford to read theology at Wycliffe Hall gave me two of the happiest years of my life, but I did not settle in easily. Becoming an undergraduate again at the age of 58 to face an academically demanding regime of lectures, tutorials, weekly essays and examinations was one challenge. Another was accepting and getting accepted into the spiritual atmosphere of a theological college on the evangelical side of the Church of England, whose primary purpose was to prepare the majority of its students for ordination. A third hurdle was adjusting to yet another upheaval out of my familiar world and into a completely new culture and environment.

Arriving at Wycliffe on 27 September 2000, I unpacked my trunk with a mixture of eagerness and anxiety, rather like a new boy on my first day of school. The eagerness came from my spiritual hunger to get to know God better by studying his word and teachings. The anxiety came from a mass of self-doubts: Would Wycliffe be the right place for me? Would I get along with my fellow students? Would I be intellectually and theologically capable of meeting the required standards? Was this new chapter of my life in accordance with God's will?

Getting along with my fellow students became easy after our first evening together, when we all had to take part in a process of public self-introduction equivalent to baptism by fire. In accordance with tradition, the entire college of about 120 students and 20 staff assembled to hear each newcomer give a two-minute summary of his or her background, history and reasons for coming to study at Wycliffe. This was a bonding event, for although every individual found it difficult to do their own solo turn, it was universally agreed that listening to the totality of the presentations was an experience which united and knitted us together. What awed me was the rich variety of backgrounds from which the new entrants in our year had come. I had left a prison cell to go to Wycliffe, which was not exactly a sacrifice, but my fellow Wycliffeians had given up impressive occupations and careers to respond to God's call. Our first-year students included: a surgeon, a doctor of chemistry, a doctor of physics, a solicitor, an artist, an RAF officer, a head teacher, a miner, a movie actor, a Gallup poll executive, a psychologist, a ballet dancer, an architect, a business tycoon, a TV presenter, a missionary, and a former Home Office civil servant whose career had included spells as an anti-terrorism expert and as a private secretary to two Home Secretaries. Bringing up the rear of this galaxy was yours truly, an ex-prisoner and ex-Cabinet minister with enough additional X's against my name to make me unqualified and unsuitable for just about everything except membership of the body of Christ.

My self-introduction to the body of Wycliffe reflected these hesitations. I told the story of my encounter with the psychiatrist of HMP Belmarsh which got a good laugh, although several of the self-deprecating presentations were far more interesting and amusing than mine. As we broke up for drinks in the Junior Common Room at the end of this session, one ordinand commented, 'Well it sure proves that God has a sense of humour. He is the only one who could possibly have got us lot together.'

'Us lot' gelled well and quickly. The shared purpose of seeking a life of service to the Lord was the common thread that bound us together, but there were three additional forces that deepened our sense of unity. The first was the excellence of Wycliffe's spiritual and academic leadership. The second was the prayer life of the college. The third was our work in the outside world, particularly our participation in college-organized evangelistic missions and events.

I realized at my first Sunday morning service in the chapel that Wycliffe's leadership was exceptional. The Principal, Alister McGrath, preached on Isaiah 6.1–8. This is the passage that describes the call of the young Isaiah. His encounter with God, one of the most magnificent experiences of theophany in the entire Bible, is followed by Isaiah's abject penitence and sense of unworthiness before the divine presence as he says, 'Woe is me! I am ruined. For I am a man of unclean lips and my eyes have seen the King, the Lord Almighty.'

The words 'I am a man of unclean lips' had more than a little resonance with the only convicted perjurer in the congregation. However, just about every Wycliffeian seemed to be spellbound by Alister McGrath's exposition of these verses, especially their climax which is Isaiah's unconditional response to God's call, 'Here am I, send me!'

I remember being overwhelmed by three powerful reactions to this visionary sermon. The first was a dawning realization that the only reason why I was sitting in that chapel at all was that God had called me to be there. The second was that I was totally unworthy of his call. 'Join the club,' said one dry Wycliffe cleric after the service when I told him of my reaction. The third was that I had absolutely no idea of how, when, with what vision or in what way I should respond to the call. All I knew was that I was willing to make the commitment even if it meant being sent anywhere God wanted. For the time being, that appeared to mean spending two years as a resident theology student of Oxford University.

There were several coincidences that encouraged me just before and after my arrival at Wycliffe. One big one (perhaps a miracle rather than a coincidence) was that an amazingly generous benefactor paid all my fees and accommodation costs up front in the form of a £15,000 donation to Wycliffe. This gift came out of the blue from Robert Edmiston, a Midlands industrialist and Christian philanthropist. Our paths had crossed on one memorable evening of shared prayer two years earlier, yet I hardly knew him. His magnificent support stunned me not only by its generosity but by my belief that it was such an extraordinary gift that it must surely have been guided by God.

The second coincidence was my failure to negotiate a settlement to my bankruptcy. If my creditors had agreed to an IVA in January 2000, I think I would have felt it my financial duty to start trying to earn money immediately in order to support my family. The two-year delay before those same creditors came round to much the same IVA were the two years I spent in full-time theological study, prohibited by the rules of my bankruptcy from earning more than my own subsistence costs.

The third coincidence was finding that I had an enthusiasm, perhaps even an aptitude for studying theology. Its range as a subject covers philosophy, history, linguistics, literature, ancient codes of law, intellectual reasoning and an exploration of spiritual faith. I was soon captivated by the heights and depths of these disciplines. So I worked hard at my course, partly because I was inspired by my tutors and partly because I was stimulated by my immediate peer group of fellow students.

I will never forget my first Wycliffe tutorial, because I shared it with three of the cleverest students the Oxford Faculty of Theology has produced in recent years. Two of them were young women scientists in their mid-twenties, starting their training for ordination. One was Jill Duff, a doctor of chemistry who had given up a promising career with Esso. The other was Rosie Dymond, a cognitive neuroscientist with a doctorate in physics. Both were doing the BA course in Theology. Two years later they were both awarded firsts which complemented their earlier first-class degrees in science.

The third member of our quartet was Joanna McGrath, by profession an NHS consultant clinical psychologist and by marriage the wife of Wycliffe's Principal, Alister McGrath. As a mature student taking a year out from NHS duties, Joanna was doing the Diploma of Theology course. She too was awarded a Distinction, the equivalent of a first, by the University examiners. In such company I naturally felt the tail-end Charlie of our tutorial group.

As members of the new student intake of the academic year 2000, at the end of what Oxford calls 'first week', we handed our initial essays on the subject, 'Was Jesus inevitably a political figure?' in to our tutor Dr David Wenham. When we gathered in his study for our first tutorial, I soon gathered from the discussion and analysis of our essays that the intellectual challenges of Wycliffe were going to be far more formidable than I had envisaged. At that time I did not know the academic histories of Jill, Rosie and Joanna. I simply assumed that their standards of scholarship were the ones required to read theology at Oxford in 2000. It seemed a far cry from the lackadaisical spirit of 'winging it' which was just about all that my tolerant tutors seemed to require when I read law at Christ Church, Oxford, in the early 1960s. But times and colleges had changed. As a young law student I had expected success: as a mature theology student I feared failure. To overcome that fear I worked at least four times more diligently than I had done in my first incarnation as an undergraduate, spending long hours in the library, dutifully attending university lectures, sweating away at my Greek and Hebrew, and targeting all these endeavours on the four subjects which I would have to master to get through Part 1 of the university examinations in March 2001. These subjects were: the synoptic gospels with special emphasis on Matthew; the Pauline epistles with compulsory Greek translation questions on I Corinthians; the pre-exilic Old Testament prophets with compulsory questions on Isaiah chapters 1–12; and the fourth book of the Psalms, which required a smattering of Hebrew.

*   *   *

As the examinations approached, I had to grapple simultaneously with a huge off-stage distraction. In early 2001 my Trustee in Bankruptcy won a battle to enforce the sale of 8 Lord North Street even though the sale proceeds would have to go into an escrow account to await further litigation battles between my creditors and my ex-wife's lawyers.

Although in one sense I was a bystander to these legal and physical upheavals since as a bankrupt I had no rights to the house, nevertheless the emotional pressures they created took a heavy toll on me. I once read in some magazine that the three greatest stresses on a family are bereavement, divorce, and losing the family home. The last two were like omnipresent black clouds hanging over me in early 2001 as my ex-wife's lawyers fought for her rights to her former matrimonial home and chattels; as my children reluctantly prepared to move out of Lord North Street; and as the Trustee's lawyers fought for every stick, stone and item of property with the same ferocity as they had displayed in the books and papers litigation.

I was powerless and helpless on the sidelines of these dramas. The only success I achieved was in saving my mother's granny flat from the wreckage. My mother, once she had won that battle, fought like a tigress to save the family pictures and items of furniture which she had loaned to us in Lord North Street. After much huffing and puffing, the creditors did not challenge her claims in court for they were far too well documented. The same could be said for most of Lolicia's claims to pictures and chattels, but the saga was complicated by mismatches between the descriptions on the inventory compiled by the Trustee and his valuers and the descriptions from the original auction houses where Lolicia had bought the disputed chattels. The argument over these different descriptions caused many frictions. I recall one about a painting which Gorringes, the Trustee's valuers, called '17th Century Hens and Ducks', but which Christie's had described as '18th century still life of game'. The Trustee's lawyers said the first belonged to the creditors; Lolicia's lawyers pointed to the legal agreement which made the second her property. The trouble was they were the same picture. These arguments were not about priceless heirlooms: as Alan Clark had disparagingly written in his diaries, the Aitken collection of objets d'art consisted of 'pure art dealer's junk'. Hardly any items were worth more than £5,000. So as usual in such prolonged disputes, it was the lawyers on both sides who collected most of the loot.

There were heroes and heroines in the disorderly retreat from 8 Lord North Street. One was my mother, by now in her ninety-first year, who acted as commander-in-chief of the packing-up and moving-out operations. On 2 December 2000, during the last weeks of our ownership of the house, she organized a memorable ninetieth birthday party for herself, attended by over three hundred guests from her remarkable range of friends in the worlds of politics and theatre and from the local pub where she was a Saturday regular. By the time of these festivities, 8 Lord North Street was largely denuded of furniture and pictures. One that survived, because it was her property, was a famous portrait of my mother, aged 20, by Simon Elwes with whom she had eloped in 1930. Standing beneath this hauntingly beautiful painting, my mother responded to the toast to the birthday girl with a scintillating speech which began, 'I feel just as good as I did at 18. In those days the map of the world was painted British Empire red all over and a joint was something we had for lunch on Sundays.' After more in this vein her audience cheered her to the rafters. It felt like the end of an era as well as the end of a house.

The battles over the ending of the house were far from finished, as throughout the early weeks of 2001 the commander–in-chief fought more rearguard actions over individual disputed knick-knacks, right down to spoons, chinaware and tiny figurines in porcelain. Her foot soldiers in these battles included Mickey Aguda, who had been released on licence in the autumn of 2000 and had become my mother's driver, shopper and close confidant. 'Meet my bullion-robber friend,' she would say when introducing him to her sisterhood of titled ladies. Another heroine was Ashley Merry, a former army officer who turned herself into an executive PA to the Aitken family. She carried out invaluable secretarial duties for me in return for a modest remuneration provided by my friend David Hart who had said when he visited me in HMP Standford Hill, 'I reckon what you'll need most in your post-release life is some secretarial help, so take whatever you need and I'll pay the bills for it for a year.' In a similar spirit Frank Williams' loan of a car became a gift. With friends like these, no wonder I survived!

The final and perhaps greatest heroine of the retreat from Lord North Street was my sister Maria. Her home in nearby Kennington Road became the new family base camp. William lived there for the next two years. I weekended in her one-bedroom basement flat, while Petrina and Ally, who were respectively involved in fashion modelling and studying at art college, and Victoria, when she came over for London visits from Georgetown University, were regulars around Maria's kitchen table for lunches and suppers. Maria's hospitality, supported by my mother's love and care in the secondary Aitken base camp she created in her small flat, did much to soften the blow of losing a family home, but it was still a painful one.

In the final days of the move out of Lord North Street I found the desolation there almost unbearable, so I hunkered down in my Oxford bunker, burning the midnight oil in preparation for the Part 1 examinations. On the day when this challenge dawned, I found it strange having to put on the regulation subfusc dress (mortarboard, white bow-tie, grey suit and gown) and go down to the same building in the High Street, known as 'Schools', where I had sat for my law finals 40 years earlier. I was better prepared for this academic ordeal in 2001 than I had been in 1961, and when the results were published I was overjoyed to discover that I had scored high 2:1 marks on two of my papers and alphas or first-class marks on the other two. If I could keep up this level of performance in my second-year papers and theses, I would be headed for a First or Distinction. This fired me up with tremendous enthusiasm for the next phase of my theology course.

Although Wycliffe's academic standards were high, the real purpose of the college was spiritual, with prayer at the heart of our student life. In addition to the daily services in chapel, we were divided up into fellowship groups and cell groups. The former included senior members of the teaching staff, the latter were gatherings of students. In addition, there were often ad hoc prayer meetings or individual prayer partnerships which met regularly. One way and another, my time at Wycliffe was suffused with prayer. Including the chapel services, I reckon that around 18 hours of my average week were spent in some form of personal, collegiate or group prayer. This was nothing exceptional by Wycliffe standards. The college was a truly prayerful place and it showed.

My fellowship group was headed by Alister McGrath and Canon Michael Green. I could not have had two finer spiritual mentors. Both were brilliant scholars. Alister guided me down the paths trodden by great Christian saints and writers such as Augustine of Hippo, Thomas à Kempis, Julian of Norwich, Martin Luther, John Calvin, Thomas Merton, Dietrich Bonhoeffer and John Stott. Michael was more pastoral in his fellowship, caring for me like an elder brother and gradually persuading me to take up the challenge of lay evangelism – of which more later.

Student friendships and prayer partnerships were the lifeblood of Wycliffe. There is nothing like sharing in prayer for building and strengthening human relationships. I already knew this from my experiences in prison. At Wycliffe my understanding of how God changes the lives of those who pray to him continued to deepen. I can illustrate this by highlighting one or two individual stories that inspired me.

Paul Zaphiriou became my closest friend at Wycliffe. I had met him as a fellow coffee-pourer on an Alpha course. He was then a successful businessman in his early fifties, wondering whether or not to accept a job offer that would make him the Chief Executive of a major international company. Coming from a Greek background he was neither an Anglican nor had he much knowledge of the Church of England. His lifestyle in early 1998 was clearly troubling him, for he came across as restless, unfulfilled and hyperenergetic and he mentioned that he was about to get divorced. I took an immediate liking to Paul, not least because of the warmth and openness of his somewhat frenetic drive which I imagined would soon lead him to higher and higher positions in the world of Mammon. The idea that he might one day be wearing a clerical collar in the service of God never entered my head. Having temporarily lost touch with Paul Zaphiriou in the whirlwind of my prison dramas, I was amazed to see his name on the list of new Wycliffe students as an approved candidate for the ordained ministry.

In the intervening two years Paul had been through some spiritual whirlwinds of his own. The Alpha course brought him to Christ. In subsequent months he was baptized, confirmed, and became a key figure in the lay leadership of Holy Trinity, Brompton. Then he felt God's call to ordination and was approved by the Church of England's selection board three days *after* the Wycliffe term began. So the first communal prayers in which I participated at the college on the evening of the self-introductions meeting were for our not-yet-arrived student Paul Zaphiriou to get through his selection process and to be able to take the place allocated to him.

Paul and I travelled far together as friends and prayer partners. So many of our prayers were answered that it seems invidious to start mentioning the best of them. Yet one theme that did run through our supplications was the painful loneliness we both occasionally felt as divorced middle-aged men in a college largely made up of happily married fellow students. I do not think we directly asked the celestial dating agency to find us marriage partners, but God must have got our drift, for within two years he blessed both of us with wonderful wives in Bonnie and Elizabeth. He also blessed Paul with an appointment as Assistant Vicar of St George the Martyr in Holborn, London, a church whose congregation has quintupled in size since he arrived there.

Perhaps the most original and at times wayward student in my year at Wycliffe was Patrick Malone, a young Irish film actor of great style and charm but with a semi-detached approach to some of the usual theological college disciplines such as getting up early enough to attend morning chapel, being punctual at lectures and handing in essays on time or indeed at all. Yet these weaknesses were supplanted by immense strengths. For Patrick was a superb communicator of the gospel message. His thespian skills converted into evangelistic skills, his gregariousness into prayerfulness. I prayed a lot with him, often to help resolve his constant crises with essays, girlfriends, revision for exams, and finances. But a God who created order out of chaos had no difficulty turning Patrick's chaotic existence into a centred and focused life of Christian service in which exams were miraculously passed and all ordination commitments fulfilled. Today Patrick Malone is the Assistant Vicar of the Christ Church Fulham, where he has a wonderful ministry.

Outside the student body I found other remarkable prayer partners for whose guidance on my spiritual journey I shall always be grateful. One was Canon John Collins, the former Vicar of Holy Trinity, Brompton, who was living in retirement in North Oxford. John's pastoral care and spiritual teaching (at its deepest to me on the Cross) was a source of growth and inspiration. The same could be said of a new friend I made at Wycliffe, James Jones, the Bishop of Liverpool.

Bishop James Jones, although chairman of Wycliffe's board of governors, was in the college as a humble student. He had taken a period of study leave away from his diocesan duties in order to read and write about the theology of the environment. This later resulted in an excellent book *Jesus and the Earth*, but in the spring of 2001 James was usually earthed in libraries by day, while by night he could often be found in deep conversation with his fellow Wycliffe students, myself among them. At a time of some turbulence in both our lives we shared many prayers, confidences and good glasses of wine in the Norham Gardens basement flat which Wycliffe had allocated to me as my student lodgings. My new friend's sources of turbulence were at a loftier level than my mundane troubles with bailiffs, bankruptcy men and removal vans, for Bishop James Jones was at this time a strong contender to become the new Archbishop of Canterbury in succession to George Carey.

I hope I was some small help to James as a prayer partner in those difficult days when he was at the centre of media speculation, political pressure and ecclesiastical in-fighting. He was an enormous help to me as a spiritual mentor, not least with guidance at the time when I thought I might have met the new love of my life – of whom I say more in the next chapter. Anyway we became and have stayed good friends. James's prayers and advice have been a great blessing during my post-prison journey.

The final prayer partner who deserves a special mention in my pantheon of Oxford heroes was Sir Andrew Green. He had recently retired from a distinguished diplomatic career to the Oxfordshire village of Deddington. Our paths had previously crossed in Whitehall and in British embassies abroad, and we were reintroduced by a mutual friend. Andrew was grappling with the after-effects of a cancer operation and adjusting to retirement. His stoical courage in the face of the first and his determination to do something of national importance in the second made my little local difficulties of grappling with the aftermath of prison and adjusting to theology seem very small beer. We soon discovered that we were both travelling together along similar roads of spiritual searching, so we began praying together.

Andrew Green's urge to do something of 'national importance' was related to his last job in Whitehall. He had been a special adviser to Prime Minister John Major on various Home Office and national security issues. The most politically sensitive of these was immigration. During his stint inside No. 10, Andrew had concluded that the official statistics relating to asylum seekers, work permits, overstayers, legal and illegal residents – in short the whole numerical base of immigration and citizenship policy – was a complete mess. Nobody knew the whole picture. Nobody understood its implications for the future of British society. The collection and presentation of immigration figures were seriously flawed. Andrew Green knew this and was deeply troubled by it.

When Andrew first told me what he had discovered while at No. 10, I believed him but was worried that he had bitten off far more than he could chew in his desire to raise immigration statistics to the level of a serious national debate. For his part, Andrew did not lack courage but he was worried by the prospect of being pilloried as a racist, a right-wing nutter or a political propagandist. We both discussed the Christian dimension to this problem. The search for truth and statistical accuracy could not be attacked as unchristian – or could it? Even to start talking about immigration figures in the neutral language of statistics seemed like entering a minefield. So before Andrew set off on his quest, much prayer was needed.

It would be wrong to give the impression that the Green–Aitken prayer partnership was all about immigration. It was not. As with all such relationships, most of our prayer life was personal. Yet so high were these immigration concerns on Andrew's personal agenda that we did give them priority in prayer and in conversation. Out of this dialogue – or rather trialogue, with God the unseen participant – there emerged what I believe to be the encouragement and the wisdom for Andrew to go ahead and launch Migrationwatch – an independent, non-political think tank to monitor Britain's elusive immigration statistics.

Nearly five years on from those first prayers and discussions of Andrew Green's worries about immigration (worries which he shared with older Christian sages in Oxford like John Collins and Michael Green), it is possible to see what has been achieved by Migrationwatch and its founder, whose personal story reminds me of the words of Edmund Burke: 'One man with conviction makes a majority'. For Migrationwatch has changed the administrative practices of the civil service and the policies of the major political parties on asylum seekers, work permit criteria and numerical totals. It has introduced integrity and accuracy into the previously misleading government statistics on immigration. The level of understanding of the subject in all serious newspapers and broadcasting organizations has been improved. Britain may or may not have the right answers to immigration questions, but we certainly now have a far more informed debate on them. All this has been achieved by one man, against whom no one can say that he is racist, biased, unhinged or unchristian. I think prayer had something to do with this. It certainly seemed to protect and strengthen Andrew Green both in his Christian convictions and in his conviction that his work with Migrationwatch was ethically, morally and spiritually right.

*   *   *

My new friendships with companions like Paul Zaphiriou, Patrick Malone, John Collins, Bishop James Jones and Andrew Green were one reason I found my two years as a retread Oxford undergraduate so enriching. Another was the sheer *joie de vivre* rekindled by re-entering the university environment, for in addition to the work I had plenty of play. Another set of new friends, most of them some 40 years younger than me, got me laughing, talking, drinking and arguing over coffee long into the Oxford nights. The sort of project I hugely enjoyed was my involvement in the production of a new play, written by a Trinity undergraduate James Mumford and directed by Patrick Malone, called *Play the Man*. An historical drama based on Cranmer and the Oxford martyrs, *Play the Man* had its first read-through with its cast of student actors in my Wycliffe basement flat in October 2001. It was performed for a week-long run on an open-air stage in Broad Street in the summer term of 2002. I was coffee-boy and assistant publicity officer for the production, which attracted large student audiences and excellent reviews. For me, *Play the Man* was simply great fun, reviving my interest in the theatre which had lain dormant for far too long.

I also had great fun in my social life at Oxford. Several dons invited me to dine as their guests at various college high tables.

Michael Beloff, President of Trinity; Jeremy Catto, the senior tutor at Oriel; and John Drury, the Dean of Christ Church, were exceptionally hospitable. Many more invitations came from fellow undergraduates in their late teens and early twenties. I enjoyed the cut and thrust of discussions over their student suppers of spaghetti and red wine. However, I could not help noticing one big difference between the content of undergraduate conversations in 1961 and 2001. In the 1960s almost all such suppers sooner or later took on a political flavour. The burning issues that excited Oxonians then included the Vietnam War, nuclear disarmament, civil rights in the American South, apartheid in South Africa, equal rights for women, and communism versus socialism versus capitalism. Almost everyone was politically engaged in such issues. By contrast, in the 2000s almost no one seemed to be burning with political zeal. Detachment from great causes was the prevailing attitude. Undergraduate conversation was far more materialistic than idealistic. The hottest topics in the Oxford of 2001 seemed to be Clifford Chance's next cocktail party, Goldman Sachs' latest level of starting salaries and the forthcoming recruitment dinners being organized by City of London merchant banks and stockbrokers. '*O tempora! O mores!*' I said to myself. Perhaps I was just failing to keep up with the times.

I was also kept busy with speaking invitations from student dining clubs and societies. On one occasion, I addressed the Oxford University Law Society on the subject of 'Trials I have known'. The room was full of young students, but with a light sprinkling of older faces. A white-haired figure sitting six or seven rows from the back looked vaguely familiar but I could not place him. Probably a senior don whom I had met when dining at some high table, I thought. At the end of the meeting, after I had finished my talk on the various *causes celèbres* I had been involved in over the years, including the *Aitken v Guardian* libel case, the white-haired gentleman came over to me. 'Oliver Popplewell,' he said, extending his hand. My failure to recognize him was excusable, for the last time I had seen, him five years earlier, he was wearing a judicial wig and red robes and presiding as Mr Justice Popplewell over the case of *Aitken v Guardian*. We talked warmly for several minutes. Our encounter amused the student President of the Law Society, Rupert

Abbott, who did his best to persuade Sir Oliver (who had retired from the bench and become a mature Oxford undergraduate reading philosophy, politics and economics) to join us for dinner. 'Terribly sorry but I've got an essay crisis,' said the retired High Court judge. I understood his pressures for they were similar to mine at Wycliffe as a mature student.

Wycliffe introduced me to a new activity which needed much preparation but brought great fulfilment. This was the work I was led into by Michael Green on evangelistic missions. For all his erudite scholarship and lifetime of service to the Lord, Michael was an original free spirit when it came to the teaching of evangelism. A former adviser to various Archbishops of Canterbury, Michael in his seventies had become the Wycliffe senior tutor leading all the college's missions in Britain and abroad. He had no difficulty persuading me to join his team. Soon I was travelling with him all over the UK, to Europe and to America on mission trips. This work gave me the first taste of what was to become a major activity in my life – evangelism through outreach speaking.

In the jargon of modern evangelical Christianity, an outreach speaker is someone (usually a layperson) who reaches out to audiences of the unchurched, the uncommitted and the unbelieving with talks which resonate to the secular world yet have a strong spiritual message. Under Michael Green's tuition, I soon found that I could be a fairly effective communicator in this field. My earliest outreach efforts were to prisoners. The first jail which welcomed me as a speaker was HMP Spring Hill, a D-cat prison for short-sentence inmates located about 20 miles from Oxford. I began my talk there with a line I have used ever since when speaking in penal institutions across the world: 'I have been where you now are.'

There is a mystical wavelength which connects prisoners serving their sentences with ex-prisoners who come back into jails to try and help them. Once I discovered how to tune into this wavelength I made good use of it, but I soon learned that giving a talk to the inmates is only one part of prison ministry. Listening, praying, counselling and guiding a searching soul into a right relationship with the Lord is the most sensitive work in this kind of evangelism. Wycliffe began to train me for it. At Spring Hill our team went down so well with the inmates that the prison Chaplain, the Reverend Michael Chantry, invited us back for three successive outreach events in response to popular demand from his flock.

In no time I was travelling to prisons around the UK and in America where my friendship with Charles Colson led to my appointment as a director of Prison Fellowship International. I well recall the occasion when Colson first asked me to share a day of prison ministry preaching with him. We had travelled to Parchman State Penitentiary, Mississippi, one of the toughest jails in the United States. The temperature was 105 degrees and I was dripping with sweat, induced not just by the heat but by the searing experience of having just prayed with the men awaiting execution on Death Row. After emerging from that section of the prison, it was my job to give the opening address to a large and rather restless crowd of inmates corralled in an exercise compound. When I came to the microphone I was suddenly petrified that I would fail to connect with my audience. I was worried that my Eton and Oxford accent might not go down too well in darkest Mississippi. But the legendary 1960s civil rights leader, John Perkins, introduced me so warmly that my fears subsided and I opened up as usual with, 'Brothers, I have been where you now are.' Almost immediately the crowd of prisoners stopped their restless movements and listened to the Gospel message in pin-drop silence. Because of my discomfort in the hot sun, I know I did not speak well, but on the Pauline principle that when we are weak, God makes us strong, I also know that, for reasons entirely due to Him, the address that afternoon in Parchman prison touched the hearts of many inmates.

Giving all the glory to God was the key principle of the Wycliffe missions led by Michael Green. He specialized in going into a geographical community, for example Plymouth, Folkestone, Guernsey or eastern Pennsylvania, and planning a week-long mission with churches and civic organizations many months in advance. Michael took 20 of us Wycliffe students to Guernsey in Holy Week 2002. My assignments included a day in the prison, a breakfast address to 250 financial services industry bosses, a tea for 400 women, a dinner for the Members of the States (Guernsey's Parliament), and delivering a series of reflections on the Cross throughout the three-hour Good Friday service in a local church. It was testing work but wonderfully satisfying if you believe that the whole purpose of a mission is to please God and that you, the speaker, are his unworthy and unimportant servant. Such an approach is the complete antithesis of political speaking, yet I have found infinitely more fulfilment in outreach missions than ever came my way on the hustings.

The oxymoronic label 'a celebrity Christian' was sometimes stuck on me during my outreach activities. I hated it and did my best to avoid it. One route to such avoidance was to travel outside the UK, so I did quite a lot of travelling in voluntary work for Christian Solidarity Worldwide (CSW), the admirable charity headed by Baroness Cox which fights for those who are being persecuted for their faith. New Year's Day 2002 found me flying in to Beijing as part of a small CSW team headed by the charity's Chief Executive Mervyn Thomas. We were met by Wang Zhiyong, a superb English-speaker and former corporate lawyer to blue-chip US corporations such as Bechtel and Coca-Cola. Wang Zhiyong had, however, turned away from all his legal and financial success to become Pastor Paul Zhiyong, the leader of an underground Christian church in central Beijing.

Pastor Paul was our guide and interpreter for the next few days, as our CSW team witnessed at first hand the astonishing growth of Chinese Christianity. The People's Republic of China now has between 70 million and 100 million believers with a claimed rate of 100,000 new conversions every week. Whatever the statistics, there can be no doubt of the fervour of many Chinese congregations, despite their frequent harassment and persecution by the authorities in various cities and provinces. I shall never forget being taken by Pastor Paul to a clandestine meeting of Christian students close to Beijing University. After James Bond-like manoeuvres with decoys and car changes in order to slip away from possible secret police pursuers, we eventually arrived at a tenement block of low-grade housing accommodation. After climbing eight or nine flights of dirty stairs, we entered a small room which was full to bursting with 40 or 50 teenage students all reading their Bibles and listening to an exegesis on the parable of the Good Samaritan from an elderly professor, Lu Chen. Our CSW delegation was given the warmest of welcomes, with hymn singing and prayers. We learned that the students in the room ranged from strong believers to serious doubters, but all seemed eager to learn more about the gospel. The abiding impression I took away from this and many other similar encounters was that huge numbers of young Chinese people are on fire over the teachings of Jesus Christ. No amount of harassment or even persecution is likely to prevent this fire from spreading far further and faster than most people in the Western world have begun to envisage.

At the end of our visit to China I said my goodbyes at Beijing airport to Pastor Paul Zhiyong. He had become a real friend and brother to me during our intense week of conversations and prayer. As we bade farewell in the departure lounge, he said how much he envied me going back to Oxford University to study theology under modern professors and lecturers. 'I have had to learn my theology here from old books and very old men,' said Paul with a note of sadness in his voice.

'Could you come and study theology in Oxford if we could make the arrangements?' I asked him. 'Oh I don't think that would ever be possible,' was Paul's regretful reply. 'But with God all things are possible,' wrote his namesake St Paul in the New Testament. Against inconceivable odds, Pastor Paul Zhiyong of Beijing became a resident student in Oxford within four months of our airport leave-taking. He spent a full term at Wycliffe, where Alister McGrath found a place for him at short notice. CSW raised the funds for his air ticket and tuition fees. Paul himself was miraculously given a visa by the Chinese authorities. He was an outstanding Oxford student, a life-enhancing addition to our college, an inspirational preacher of the gospel and a brilliant outreach speaker. He has now returned to Beijing where despite all the difficulties he has a successful and growing ministry as pastor of an increasingly above-ground church. When I look back on my years at Wycliffe I some-times think that my greatest achievement there was making it possible for Pastor Paul Zhiyong to join the college as a fellow student.

At the end of January 2002 my bankruptcy was annulled in the High Court. This legal process, which in the law of insolvency meant that it was cancelled as though I had never been bankrupt in the first place, was made possible because my creditors decided to accept an IVA remarkably similar to the one they had rejected in January 2000. No new assets were provided by me or found by my Trustee between the first and second of these IVAs. All the earlier newspaper headlines about my 'secret Swiss bank accounts', 'deceptions', 'lies', 'evasions' and 'hidden assets', turned out to be irrelevant nonsense. My Trustee in Bankruptcy was good enough to acknowledge this by making it clear in a press release issued at the time of the annulment that I had never withheld or concealed any assets from my creditors.

What brought about the IVA was, first, that the sale of my biggest asset, 8 Lord North Street, achieved a significantly higher price, £2.4 million, than anyone had expected, so there were more funds to distribute, and Lolicia made life easier for everyone by generously giving her share of the house sale proceeds to our children via the Aitken Children's Trust.

Secondly my creditors were understandably keen to save themselves over £250,000 of tax that they would have had to pay to the Department of Trade and Industry if my bankruptcy had ended in a discharge. A bankruptcy which ends in an annulment and an IVA requires the creditors to pay no tax.

Thirdly, the retirement of some of the most militant members of the creditors committee at the end of 2001 had made a settlement in 2002 much easier. There was no longer any enthusiasm for prolonged litigation over my parliamentary pension or against Lolicia.

So that was the way my bankruptcy ended: not with a bang but with a whimper – and even a few friendly handshakes.

It felt strange to be free of the shackles of bankruptcy, for I had got used to a life largely unencumbered by possessions, and to an income that was remarkably low by my previous standards and lifestyle. Adjusting to straitened circumstances had been made easier by living in an Anglican theological college where most of my fellow students were even more impecunious than a bankrupt. In this environment, I learned some good tips about how to make ends meet. One weekend, at a low moment in my bankruptcy, when I was living hand-to-mouth on a slender income from freelance journalism, a vital cheque was delayed in the post, so I had only just over £20 in my pocket. Unfortunately this shortfall came at a time when I urgently needed to buy extra food because my son William (whose appetite had not diminished since 'the last breakfast') was coming to visit me from school. I asked a fellow Wycliffe student if he could help me out with a temporary loan. He could, but he had a better idea. Did I know that every Friday night at ten o'clock the local Somerfield supermarket sold off, at half-price or less, all perishable food that had reached its sell-by date? This was news to me, but I hurried to Somerfield and seized the opportunity. As I walked home with my shopping bag full of bargain-price sausages, eggs, bacon, hamburgers and lamb chops, I thought for a moment of all those breakfasts in Claridge's, lunches at Harry's Bar and dinners in Annabel's on which I used so casually to spend three-figure sums. Then I burst out laughing. After that, until my bank balance improved, I spent many an evening laughing all the way to the sell-by-date sales.

By the middle of 2002 my spirits were lifting for a variety of reasons, some of them spiritual, some of them academic, some of them romantic.

Spiritually my two years at Wycliffe had been a period of growing and strengthening in faith. There is a splendid verse of scripture which opens,

> To your faith add goodness, to your goodness knowledge, to your knowledge self-discipline ...   (2 Peter 1:5)

I am not so sure about the goodness bit, but Wycliffe had certainly educated and disciplined me to a level of theological and biblical knowledge far higher than anything I had ever dreamed of attaining. Some of this knowledge derived from the theses I was having to write for Part 2 of my exams. These 7,500-word compositions had titles like 'A comparative assessment of Luther's theology of the Cross and Ignatius of Loyola's theology of the Cross', 'The Christology of Luke's Gospel', 'A comparative study of the contributions made to English spirituality by Julian of Norwich and Evelyn Underhill' and 'A theological assessment of the characters in the

Book of Job'. Such topics may seem like dull fare to many, but to me they were the theological equivalent of caviar and smoked salmon, so I devoured them eagerly. More importantly they were a diet which found favour with the university examiners, for when the class list was published I was awarded the only Distinction in my year. This was a cause of great rejoicing, although a wise student of this subject should remember that one definition of a theologian is 'someone who knows how little they know'.

On top of the many internal blessings of Wycliffe there was one more external blessing, which was causing me the greatest rejoicing of all. She was a lady called Elizabeth with whom I had fallen in love.

CHAPTER 14

Enter Elizabeth

'Boring movie rekindles exciting passion' would be a fair headline to describe the opening scene of the romantic reunion which resulted in my marriage to Elizabeth Harris.

The boring movie, which ran for precisely one performance, was *Subterrain*, an esoteric short film in a genre its producer described as 'art house with social conscience'. Its plot (?) featured suicidal depression, glue sniffing, malnutrition, loneliness and a tramp's death on a haunted London Underground station after it had shut down on Christmas Eve. *Subterrain* would not be my choice for a cheerful evening of cinema-going, but I turned up for its opening (and closing) night in the summer of 2001 out of family loyalty. For my nephew, actor Jack Davenport, was starring in the film – shot long before he began starring in rather more popular movies such as *Pirates of the Caribbean* – and his wife Michelle Gomez was its producer.

Although family loyalty kept me in my seat for the mercifully brief duration of *Subterrain*, as soon as its titles faded I headed for the bar in need of a drink. In the queue with many others who evidently felt the same need, I observed to my sister Maria, Jack Davenport's mother, that the only people who could possibly have come to see the film must surely be closely related to the members of the cast. This was a prophetic utterance, for ten seconds later I saw a beautiful, immaculately coiffured and elegantly dressed woman queuing at the opposite side of the bar. She was the mother of the other leading actor in *Subterrain*. Her name was Elizabeth Harris.

Elizabeth and I did not need to be introduced. Some 25 years earlier, when we were both young and single, we had been much in love. Our passionate two-year affair in the mid-1970s might easily have developed into marriage, but we had gone our separate ways and seen each other only at occasional social events during the ensuing quarter of a century.

I congratulated Elizabeth on her son Jamie's portrayal of the suicidally depressed glue-sniffer in *Subterrain*. After that we chatted about old times with much sparkle. I thought of asking her whether she was free for dinner but then thought better of it. Elizabeth kept her thoughts to herself. I now know that she too thought our conversation at the bar was creating a few sparks, but equally she felt no sudden urge to start seeing her old flame again. So once more we went our separate ways, returning to lonely suppers in our respective homes.

And there it might all have ended had it not been for the intervention of my sister Maria, an experienced director both on and off stage. She had noticed the electricity in my encounter with Elizabeth and thought that a revival of our relationship might merit a long run. She enlisted the help of my 90-year-old mother who like many a family matriarch enjoys matchmaking. The supporting cast soon expanded. To this day I am not entirely sure who was writing the script, directing the action, and playing their cameo roles knowingly or unknowingly as the plot thickened. There were exits and entrances by Michael and Sandra Howard, actress Tsai Chin, playwright Ronald Harwood, Michael Portillo, Lady Annabel Goldsmith, the Bishop of Liverpool and last but not least Elizabeth's first husband Richard Harris. With such players, the path of true love inevitably turned into quite a saga.

The first move came from Maria who was full of sisterly concern, never mentioned to me, that I had become a lonely wallflower in theological Oxford. Loneliness cure No. 1 was produced in the shapely form of Tsai Chin, star of *The World of Suzie Wong* and many other musicals and movies. Tsai, an old family friend, had flown into London from Hollywood. Elizabeth gave a dinner party in her honour to which she invited Maria and her husband, Patrick McGrath. Maria asked if she could bring me along too, so I took an evening off from theology and enjoyed the party. Sitting between Tsai and Elizabeth at dinner, I had plenty of jokes with these two lively ladies both of whom seemed just as beautiful as they were when I had dated them back in the 1970s. However, the glittering soirée ended with me playing the part of Cinderella rather than Prince Charming. For on the stroke of midnight I made my excuses and left, explaining that I had to get back to Oxford in order to do a reading at the 8 a.m. service in Wycliffe chapel.

After I had departed, Maria made a charitable appeal on my behalf, announcing to the assembled company that what her poor brother needed was more life, more dinner parties and, above all, a girlfriend. 'Surely he's got lots of girlfriends at Oxford,' said Elizabeth, who was unversed in the lifestyle of Anglican theological colleges. 'Well he's surrounded by religious women, but they're all far too *worthy*,' said Maria, enunciating the sentence as though she was back on stage in a Noel Coward comedy.

A week or two later, Elizabeth answered this sisterly *cri de coeur* for me to be introduced to unworthy people. She invited me to another of her dinner parties. On this occasion, the guest list featured Michael and Sandra Howard and the playwright Ronald Harwood. Again I enjoyed myself. I was particularly pleased to see Michael. At the time he was Shadow Chancellor of the Exchequer, but press rumours suggested that his days on the Tory front bench under the new Leader of the Opposition, Iain Duncan Smith, were numbered. I recall telling Michael that he should hang in there, as the party would really need him sooner or later. This was not a fashionable view in the autumn of 2001.

Soon after this dinner, Elizabeth received a thankyou letter for it from someone who had not been present – my mother. The message of her maternal epistle was that it had been wonderful to know that Jonathan 'had been back on his best form' at two successive dinner parties in London. Could St Elizabeth please continue to rescue me from the miry pit of theological Oxford? And by the way if Elizabeth ever needed an escort to accompany her to the theatre, the Lady Aitken dating agency had just the right man (her son) for the job.

By now Elizabeth must have been feeling that I was a complete basket case. In the reports of my nearest and dearest I was being portrayed as so lonely and depressed that I would have made a suitable member of the cast of *Subterrain II*. This was a complete misunderstanding by my mother and sister, for I was loving Wycliffe and felt happy there. However, I was also happy to come up to London in response to Elizabeth's next invitation which was for an evening at the theatre. I enjoyed it greatly, and we followed it with three or four more such evenings over the next month or two.

By this time I was starting to feel Cupid's darts shooting into my heart. I think Elizabeth was experiencing similar emotions. However, by the standards of modern dating we were having a Victorian courtship. Instead of a passionate reunion of ex-lovers it was our practice to part on Elizabeth's doorstep after exchanging chaste goodnight kisses.

This restraint was so unlike my previous pattern of romantic behaviour that I felt a need to explain it to Elizabeth. One evening, over a candlelit dinner at La Poule au Pot restaurant in Chelsea, I said to her, 'Do you understand that God now comes first in my life?'

Elizabeth debunked this over-pious pomposity by retorting that she had never asked to come first in anyone's life ahead of God. This exchange had the effect of setting us off on a series of deep conversations about faith. I was humbled to learn that Elizabeth's private commitment to the Lord in prayer was every bit as strong as my own. This discovery was important because it opened up the way for me to become deeply committed to her. I do not think such a commitment would have been possible if we had not shared a living faith.

As our relationship strengthened, we thought it was time to tell our children about it. The news was well received, although with varying degrees of seriousness. Top prize for the lightest touch went to Elizabeth's youngest son Jamie, who told his girlfriend, 'Guess what? Mum's new boyfriend is an ex-con.' The bossiest reaction came from my daughter Victoria who e-mailed me from New York: 'I think you should hurry up and marry Elizabeth. She is very good for you. Don't waste time talking about it to other people or you will lose her.'

One key person who had to be talked to about it was Richard Harris. He had married Elizabeth in 1957, when she was 18 and he a penniless drama student. Their tempestuous relationship, much tested by the temptations of Hollywood when he soared to mega-stardom, broke down in acrimonious divorce by 1968. Yet the bond of raising their three sons Damian, Jared and Jamie gradually brought Richard and Elizabeth together again in a relationship which matured into deep friendship and total trust.

In the spring of 2002, Elizabeth told Richard about her new romantic involvement with me. He reacted positively, indeed enthusiastically. Most of this enthusiasm seemed to be based on his unusual view that anyone who had done time in HMP Belmarsh must be a good bloke. After checking me out with a number of Old Belmarshians with whom Richard seemed to be surprisingly well acquainted he discovered that I had done my bird there without making complaints, asking for favours or grassing anyone up. That made me an even better bloke.

Impressed by these credentials, Richard began taking rather a proprietorial interest in his ex-wife's romance. He sent her several notes (complete with illustrations) and wrote me one delightful letter offering his suggestions on how we should proceed. These billets-doux of encouragement were delightfully eccentric but alas unprintable. But it was good to know that we had the Richard Harris seal of approval.

Soon after Richard joined the supporters club of the Elizabeth–Jonathan relationship, the press got wind of the story. Unbeknownst to us, we were secretly stalked by a reporter equipped with a miniature camera. The stalk produced nothing more exciting than a shot of us holding hands, but it was enough. 'SMITTEN AITKEN STEPS OUT WITH HIS NEW GIRLFRIEND' was the headline over a full page article in the *Daily Mail*. That set the rest of the media off in hot pursuit of follow-up stories on the theme of 'Aitken finds love again'. The received wisdom of the var-ious gossip columnists who wrote these pieces seemed to be that a poor defenceless theology student had been lured away from his monastic existence in Oxford by 'a scarlet woman'. The most exotic of these articles was a two-page spread in the *Daily Mail* headlined 'THE RETURN OF THE TEMPTRESS'. The subheadline began, 'her exes include Richard Harris and Rex Harrison. Now Elizabeth Harris has persuaded Jonathan Aitken to give up celibacy'. Many colourful photographs of Elizabeth illustrated the article, as well as one of me captioned 'Husband No. 4?'

This media overkill produced welcome and unwelcome consequences. On the good side, several of our friends rejoiced at the news and started to invite us out together as a couple. The first big party we went to together was given by Annabel Goldsmith. We had a memorable evening in her hospitable home on Richmond Common. Many of her guests came over to say how delighted they had been to read that Elizabeth and I had found happiness together. The obvious warmth of these conversations touched us and reinforced our feelings that our relationship was on the right track.

On the bad side, I started to receive a surprising number of letters telling me that our relationship was on the wrong track. These came mainly from members of the evangelical Christian community who had been so supportive of me during the darkest hours of my dramas. Then their letters had been full of love and forgiveness: now the tone had changed to one of judgement and condemnation. Expressing anxiety, and sometimes outrage, about the newspaper reports of my romance with Elizabeth, the message of these communications was, 'Stop it'. Citing passages of scripture, the general thrust of these epistles was that getting involved with a three-times divorced woman was unacceptable if not sinful behaviour from someone who professed to be a follower of Jesus Christ. 'You are a total hypocrite' was how one critic ended his letter.

I occasionally wondered what Jesus would have said about the attitudes reflected in these missives. Certainly they were a long way from his teaching in the Sermon on the Mount, 'Judge not that ye be not judged.' Yet for all the answers that could be made to these letters, they nevertheless unsettled me quite badly. Indeed there were days when I felt I was being pulled apart by two different kinds of passion. One was my passion for Elizabeth for whom I felt a great and growing love. The other was my suffering over worries triggered by the hostile letters. I became fretful that my love for Elizabeth was somehow dragging me back into the very areas of sin and hypocrisy that I was so anxious to avoid in my new life as a committed believer.

I shared these worries with Elizabeth. She immediately said that she did not want to take me away from the faith which she knew was at the centre of my life. If she was becoming a problem to my fellow Christians, then she would prefer to back out of the relationship.

Elizabeth and I had begun praying together early in 2002. Initially the idea of praying out loud with another person had been as alien to her as it had been to me back in 1997 when a Baptist friend, Mervyn Thomas, first suggested I should try it at the height of my troubles. Elizabeth's faith was very private. Remembering my own reticence in religious matters, I well understood her hesitation over the concept of sharing oral prayer with me. But at least she was willing to try it as an experiment. Soon the experiment became a regular part of our daily routine, and gradually developed into the cornerstone of our relationship. Its importance is best summarized by the dedication of my recent book about prayer: 'To Elizabeth, my nearest, dearest and closest prayer partner.'[1]

Fortunately, not all Christians felt the same way as those who sent me harsh letters. At Wycliffe, which is Britain's leading evangelical college, my tutor Canon Michael Green and my student prayer partners offered nothing but criticism-free love when I described my growing feelings for Elizabeth to them.

Another wise counsellor at this time was Bishop James Jones. While we were both in residence at Wycliffe, James and I spent many a good student evening together over coffee and conversation. His sympathetic advice to me on the future of my relationship with Elizabeth was, 'Commit it to God in prayer.' This I did in many different settings.

Although I did not say it directly to Elizabeth in the summer of 2002, I was becoming increasingly certain that I wanted to ask her to marry me. That July and August, I had to spend several weeks on my own in the USA, trying to complete my biography of Charles Colson. As I toiled away in the sweltering heat of a Washington summer, phone calls to Elizabeth seemed no substitute for her presence. The more I missed her, the more I agreed with a profound saying by Stendhal, 'Absence extinguishes small passions and increases great ones, just as the wind blows out a candle and blows up a big fire.'

As the winds and fires of love increased in their intensity, Elizabeth and I decided to take a summer holiday together. Encouraged by Richard Harris's considerable interest in how her relationship with me was progressing, Elizabeth called her ex-husband. 'Richard I want to ask you a favour,' she began. 'No need to ask. I know what you want,' replied Richard. Without pausing for breath he continued, 'You want to have a holiday with Jonathan staying in my house in the Bahamas. Favour granted. The house is all yours! Stay there and enjoy yourselves for as long as you like.'

Intuitive telepathy and generous hospitality were attractive characteristics of Richard Harris. We immediately accepted his invitation and booked our airline reservations. I was so delighted by the prospect of holidaying on the legendary Paradise Island where Richard lived that I began to wonder whether a moonlight walk on one of its beautiful beaches might be the perfect setting in which to propose to Elizabeth.

Before we could travel to the Bahamas, a medical drama inter-vened. So far as anyone knew, Richard Harris was in good health. He had finished filming the second *Harry Potter* movie and was looking forward to playing Dumbledore in at least two more sequels. Although he had been heard to complain that the part had been tiring, he seemed to be on good form. For a few days in August he devoted considerable energy to preparing his house in the Bahamas for our visit. As a host he took immense trouble to make sure everything was perfect for our arrival, issuing copious instruc-tions to his staff on points of detail.

When Elizabeth telephoned Richard to thank him for these preparations, he did not return her calls for two or three days. Worried by this uncharacteristic non-communication, Elizabeth and her eldest son Damian went over to the Savoy Hotel where Richard was staying. With some difficulty she persuaded a nervous hotel manager to let her into the Harris suite using a pass key. Inside she found Richard spreadeagled on the bed in a dreadful condition, drifting in and out of consciousness and having great difficulty breathing. Doctors were summoned and declared him dangerously ill. An ambulance was called to rush him to the King Edward VII hospital. It was a serious emergency, lightened however by one last-minute touch of humour provided by the patient himself.

When the ambulance men carried Richard out of the hotel, the route of his dramatic exit took his stretcher past the Savoy Grill at precisely 1 p.m., just as a queue of well-heeled luncheon customers were jostling together at the entrance. Until this moment Richard was in an oxygen mask, barely able to breathe or to raise his voice above a whisper. But the actor in him saw an audience. He knew he had a good line to deliver to it, so, pulling himself up on the stretcher, he removed his oxygen mask and gestured to his drips and tubes. Somehow he found the strength to declare *fortissimo* to the Savoy Grill lunch queue, 'It's the food here that's done me in. It's the hotel food!'

This was just about the only moment of laughter that remained in Richard Harris's life. His medical condition was serious and exceedingly complex. Once it could be stabilized he had to go through a plethora of tests, scans, biopsies, lumbar punctures and intrusive investigations some of which involved putting cameras into his body. Several of these procedures required ambulance journeys across London to hospitals which had the required specialist equipment. Everything was hampered by Richard's frail condition, for he was unable to eat any food. Even as he became frailer, he found enough energy to keep arguing with his doctors. At one point he issued all of them with a self-devised questionnaire which was intended to give information to himself about the quality of their medical advice rather than to offer information to them about the causes of his own condition.

Elizabeth was in constant attendance at the hospital during this phase of the crisis. Richard, however, did his best to despatch her to the Bahamas. 'There's going to be no discussion,' he announced. 'You and Jonathan must stick to your holiday plans. I won't have any argument about it.' 'Quite right. There is no argument,' replied Elizabeth. 'We've cancelled our air tickets. There's no way we're going off to the Bahamas leaving you here. Jonathan and I are in complete agreement!' For once in his life Richard Harris did not argue back.

It was right that we did not take that holiday because Elizabeth was constantly needed at Richard's bedside. She was the rock on whom he depended while the doctors carried out more and more diagnostic tests to discover whether his many symptoms meant that he had TB, pneumonia, pleurisy, anaemia, leukaemia or some other form of cancer. As various consultants wrestled to find the right answer, Richard insisted that his illness must be kept secret. He was registered in the hospital under an assumed name, and visitors were initially restricted to his sons, his brothers and Elizabeth. The only non-relatives who saw him at this time were Sean Connery; Peter O'Toole; Dr Terry James, his closest friend; Steve Kennett, his agent; and me.

By the time I visited Richard he had been moved to University College Hospital where the tests finally established that he had Hodgkin's disease, a complicated form of cancer. He was put on a course of chemotherapy whose usual debilitating side effects seemed to have passed him by. That day, he had just finished post-synching (dubbing) several key scenes for the soon to be released *Harry Potter* movie. It had been a mammoth operation to bring Hollywood's finest technicians and state-of-the-art sound technology into the hospital, and Richard should have been exhausted by his day's work, yet he was sitting up in bed laughing, telling stories, and looking forward to future projects with great *joie de vivre*. Apart from a few jokes about handling Elizabeth, the main project on his mind was writing his autobiography. He told me he had enjoyed my book *Pride and Perjury*. 'What I liked most about it was that you made no excuses for your mistakes,' he said. 'I'm going to follow your example.'

Another project we discussed was Christmas. Richard believed he would be out of hospital once the chemotherapy course finished, so he was making lots of seasonal plans for presents, guest lists, number of turkeys and so on. But as he might not be strong enough to travel to the Bahamas, it was agreed that a flat should be rented in London for his Christmas convalescence. Elizabeth quickly found a penthouse suitable for a Hollywood film star in the same Kensington block of flats where she lived. A few days later, she and

I were back at Richard's bedside telling him about the penthouse and the arrangements for moving him in there with nurses when he came out of hospital.

Suddenly Richard lay back weakly on his pillow and said in a low, querulous voice, 'But am I ever going to get out of this hospital?' Although Elizabeth and I responded with words of optimistic encouragement, when we had dinner together afterwards we were in sad agreement that we might have witnessed a defining moment of despair in Richard's battle against cancer.

From then on things got worse. Richard's condition swiftly deteriorated. He was moved to the intensive care unit where he slid into unconsciousness. Eventually he was put on a life support machine. During this period I was outwardly no more than a bystander at this brave man's losing struggle for survival. Inwardly, however, I felt a strange patriarchal pull from him, bringing me closer to membership of his family as his three sons and Elizabeth were keeping their sad vigils at the bedside.

There is an old saying that the sorrows of our lives bind us together far more strongly than the joys. Sharing in Elizabeth's sorrows massively strengthened my feelings of love for her during the ordeal of Richard's last illness. As his teenage bride, the mother of his sons, and in later life his closest friend and confidante, Elizabeth was carrying the heaviest of emotional burdens. At one point she almost cracked under them and had to go into hospital herself with acute stomach pains, but she regained her health and never lost her grace or beauty. I tried to support her in every possible way with a love that seemed to be growing stronger by the day. Although all thoughts of making a marriage proposal to Elizabeth were deferred, nevertheless the fire of our passion was stronger than ever and we both knew it.

On the afternoon of 19 October I went with Elizabeth to the intensive care unit in University College Hospital. Richard was almost unrecognizable, strapped unconscious to a life support machine, to which he was connected by a forest of electronic leads, tubes, drips and other medical equipment. As the machine pumped away to keep him alive, you did not need a doctor to know that Richard was beyond all hope of recovery.

At about six o'clock that evening we started to discuss his last rites. Richard had a strong, if not always obedient, Catholic faith, so his family knew that he would want a priest to give him extreme unction and absolution. The hospital's Catholic chaplain arrived at the bedside. In the presence of Damian, Jared, Jamie, Elizabeth and myself, he carried out his holy office in a ceremony of great beauty and dignity. As Richard's head was anointed with oil in the sign of the cross, his furrowed brow seemed to relax as though he understood that his earthly journey was coming to an end with God's forgiveness and blessing. So with our individual prayers and tears we saw him on his way.

Our departure from the intensive care unit immediately after the last rites coincided with the arrival at the hospital of Master Marlowe Harris, aged five months. This was Richard's grandson, the son of Damian. As soon as I saw the tiny figure of Marlowe in the arms of his mother, the Australian TV star Peta Wilson, I was astonished by the uncanny resemblance of his flowing blond hair and striking features to those of Richard in his cinematic prime. Marlowe's entrance made it feel as though a torch was being passed from one Harris generation to another at a mystical moment of symbolic continuity and renewal.

A few hours later, in accordance with clear medical advice, the decision was taken to switch off the life support machine. In the presence of Elizabeth and their three sons, Richard Harris died at 8 p.m. on Tuesday 20 October 2001.

Enormous new burdens now fell on Elizabeth. Not only was she the focal point of administration for matters such as passing the news to friends across the world, issuing announcements and making the funeral arrangements, she was also the sole trustee and executor of Richard's estate. This appointment, which Richard had asked Elizabeth to accept when making his will several years earlier, could not have been a clearer demonstration of the trust and confidence he had in her.

Supporting Elizabeth through the difficult days leading up to the funeral was another important challenge, for she was emotionally and physically shattered. The speed of Richard's downward spiral had come as an immense shock to her, so I was literally a shoulder to weep on, yet paradoxically Elizabeth's tears for Richard also watered and strengthened the roots of our own deepening relationship.

After Richard's beautiful funeral service in the St Thomas More Church off Chelsea Embankment, life took some time to settle down again. As sole executor, Elizabeth was busy with the administration of the estate. She had to spend a great deal of time on the telephone and visiting agents and lawyers in Nassau, New York, Hollywood and London. I was busy too with authorship, journalism and Christian speaking engagements. But despite these pressures we stayed close. I even took Elizabeth with me on one of the most interesting of my speaking dates which was held in the chapel of HMP Ford.

Thanks to the prison ministry work I had done from Wycliffe and in the USA with Prison Fellowship, giving a talk to an audience of convicts was not an unusual experience for me. For Elizabeth, however, who had never been inside a prison in her life, spending an evening in jail seemed a daunting prospect until she was put at her ease by the socially graceful inmates of Ford.

After we had checked through the security at Ford (extremely light because it is a D-category prison full of ex-accountants and lawyers), we were met by Mick, an inmate bubbling with bonhomie. 'A very good evening to you, Mrs Harris,' he began. 'We have a lot in common because I was a good friend of your late husband Richard. We both grew up in Limerick and I shared many a drink with him.' To make Elizabeth feel even more welcome, Mick added that another prisoner who had known Richard well would be coming to hear my talk in the chapel. He too was looking forward to meeting her. As if to enhance the growing feeling of being at home rather than in jail, when I walked into the chapel I immediately recognized three or four inmates who had been with me in Belmarsh and who were now coming to the end of their sentences in an open prison. These old acquaintances and many other prisoners wanted to shake Elizabeth's hand and talk to her. In the long period of coffee-drinking after my talk, she showed a natural rapport with the inmates she met, listening to their problems with warm and sensitive empathy. As we drove home to London I said to Elizabeth, 'You could be a tremendous help to me in my work in prisons. I think you've got a natural gift for it.' My words have since come true, for Elizabeth has shown her personal and spiritual warmth for prisoners in several jails across the world.

In the 18 months since our reunion at the screening of *Subterrain*, I had seen so many of Elizabeth's gifts, not least the unexpected gift of grace under pressure, that I was more and more certain that I wanted to marry her. So in the last week of November I bought the most elegant sapphire engagement ring I could afford and planned my proposal. The first part of the plan was to take Elizabeth to the theatre, and on to dinner at Annabel's afterwards. There I thought I would pop the question and put the ring on her finger in a quiet alcove off the dance floor, well after midnight when the lights and the music would be low. Annabel's, where I have been a member for 40 years, is one of the most romantic places I know. I particularly like the usually more sedate atmosphere of Saturday evenings, when the club tends to be less crowded and quieter.

On the night of Saturday 1 December, when I arrived with Elizabeth at Annabel's, the atmosphere was not what I was expecting. The place was bursting at the seams with boisterous partygoers who had apparently come from some large office festivity. The only table we could get was close to the dance floor and even closer to the sound amplifiers. Conversation over dinner in these conditions was at first difficult and after a time impossible because of the high-decibel musical selections of the gyrating punters on the dance floor. The secluded alcove I had had in mind for the location of my proposal was heavily occupied by several pairs of heavily writhing bodies. So, abandoning Annabel's far earlier than anticipated, I kept the ring in my pocket until we returned to Elizabeth's flat. There I proposed and was lovingly and immediately accepted as her future husband.

We kept our engagement secret for four more weeks, mainly because we wanted to tell our seven offspring the good news face-to-face. As three of them were living in America, we had to wait until they gathered in London for Christmas. Although we each told our children beforehand, we made the announcement at a joint dinner for both families on Christmas Day. No one seemed surprised and everyone rejoiced, not least my 92-year-old mother whose matchmaking efforts had played a key role in bringing us together. We were on the road to marriage.

1 *Prayers for People under Pressure* (Continuum, 2005).

CHAPTER 15

New Passions on the Road to a New Life

Passion is one of the richest words in our language. Its varied meanings and definitions fill over five columns in the *Oxford English Dictionary*. The first is simply, 'The suffering of pain'. Further down the page the definitions become more complex. They include, 'Any kind of feeling by which the mind is powerfully affected or moved i.e. hope, love, joy, grief ... amorous or sexual affection ... an eager outreaching of the mind towards something ... an aim pursued with zeal ... a word of Christian theology ... a literary composition or speech marked by deep emotion ... a beloved person who is the object of love'.

My Christmas Day engagement to Elizabeth was an act of commitment to the last of these definitions. Exactly six months later on 25 June 2003, Reader, I married her.

Elizabeth and I did not pretend that our journeys to the altar of St Matthew's, Westminster had been free from trials and errors. At the start of the service we sang J.G. Whittier's poignant hymn which opens with the lines,

> *Dear Lord and Father of mankind*
> *Forgive our foolish ways!*

It was a gentle reminder that we both carried a lot of baggage from our colourful pasts. As our vicar and great friend who married us, Father Philip Chester, more tactfully put it in his address, 'This is no fairytale love but a love rooted in the reality of life.'

One of the most joyous realities of our wedding day was the presence of our seven adult children Damian, Jared, Jamie, Alexandra, Victoria, Petrina and William. All of them participated in the service by reading prayers or passages of scripture. The best unscripted moment in the liturgy came when Father Philip asked the question, 'Who gives Elizabeth in marriage to Jonathan?' The three Harris sons stepped forward and shouted in unison, 'We do!' to loud laughter in the church.

We decided to push the boat out and have a big wedding day, so we filled St Matthew's with 200 guests and had another 250 (many of them invited by our children) to our reception at 10 Carlton House Terrace. Its magnificent state rooms and its beautiful roof garden overlooking the Mall were packed with joyful revellers until the small hours.

The friends who came to share in our happiness were drawn from our joint and separate paths in life, particularly from the worlds of politics, journalism and theatre. The famous faces present attracted the attention of the media, notably *Hello!* magazine[1] which featured the wedding on its front cover with 12 inside pages of photographs. Most of our guests were mercifully unknown to the media, including a good sprinkling of old Belmarshians, Standford Hillians and Wycliffeians. By some strange symmetry, identical numbers of ex-Cabinet colleagues and ex-prisoners turned up to the reception. If there had been any more of the latter I would have been extremely worried since the only way they could have managed to be present would have been by escaping!

The size and scope of our guest list said something about the strength of life's friendships and bondings. So did the warmth of the speeches, delivered in turn by Damian, Jared and Jamie Harris, with my son and best man, William Aitken, rounding off the afternoon with something of a tour de force of wedding oratory. Armed with the inside information that Elizabeth and I were spending the first night of our honeymoon at the Ritz Hotel in London, William delivered a line which introduced humour into the historical nightmare of my notorious stay at the Ritz Hotel in Paris eight years earlier. Declared William to the assembled throng, 'I have one word of advice to my father when he carries Elizabeth over the threshold of the honeymoon suite in the Ritz Hotel tonight. It is "tomorrow morning, please make sure you pay your bill!"' He brought the house down.

After dancing the evening away at 10 Carlton House Terrace, enjoying our first night of marriage in the Ritz and meticulously following William's advice the next morning at the cashier's desk, Elizabeth and I set off for the Bahamas. We headed for the beautiful Paradise Island home of Richard Harris which he had first invited us to stay in as a courting couple about a year earlier. We never made that visit because of Richard's terminal illness. Although it was sad that he did not live to see us enjoying his house as a honeymooning couple, we knew that he had given his blessing to our marriage, so we often thought of him during our blissful first weeks as newlyweds, living in luxury and seclusion on his most appropriately named island.

When we unpacked our suitcases after arriving in the Bahamas, I do not think Elizabeth entirely understood why her bridal trousseau had been supplemented by a large number of theological commentaries on the Psalms. They were in our luggage because I had been commissioned to write a new book, *Psalms for People under Pressure*. As I got under way with this project, Elizabeth enjoyed telephoning her girlfriends with the line, 'Guess what Jonathan is doing on our honeymoon? He's writing a book for people under pressure!'

Authorship was opening up a new kind of passion for me. Ever since the publication of my biography of President Nixon in 1993, I had dreamed of enjoying the life of a writer after leaving politics. Although my departure from the political stage had come far sooner and more brutally than expected, the dream lived on. Now it developed a new impetus and a new direction. The impetus came from necessity: writing was my preferred and perhaps only way of earning a living. The direction came from a new urge within me to communicate some of the discoveries I had made about the blessings that can flow from a relationship with God. Whether to attempt such communication through autobiography, historical writing, biography, fiction, non-fiction or books of amateur theology were open questions. All I knew for certain was that I wanted to have a go at some of them. I also knew that certain kinds of critics and cynics would have a field day in ridiculing me if I put so much as a toe into such waters as spiritual writing. Even so I decided to make the attempt.

My first effort as twenty-first-century author was a fragment of autobiography, *Pride and Perjury*. It covered the period between early 1994 and early 1999, starting with my promotion into the Cabinet and ending with my decision to plead guilty to charges of perjury. It was the story of a political, legal and spiritual journey. I hope the first two parts of the story were told with humour and human interest. Perhaps the last part reflected a little too much the zeal of the new convert. This delighted some reviewers and repelled others. One thing I could not complain of was lack of attention. My author's journey took me on the rounds of most of the interesting TV and radio shows, where I was grilled by such luminaries as David Frost, Jeremy Paxman, Kirsty Wark, Tim Sebastian, Jeremy Vine, Michael Buerk and Peter Sissons. The book was serialized in five extracts by the *Sunday Times* which also reviewed it generously, as did many other newspapers and magazines. The most stinking reviews came from two *Guardian* journalists. Under the headline 'NOW THE LIAR IS TRYING TO PROVE HE'S HOLIER THAN THOU', David Pallister described the book as 'yet another elaborate exercise in cunning and cynicism'. This was moderate flak compared to the hellfire poured down on me by Pallister's colleague, David Leigh, who concluded his review in the *Guardian*'s sister paper, the *Observer*, with these words: 'On this evidence it is not God who has taken Aitken over and is speaking through him but the forked tongue of someone else altogether. If his religion is a true one then when that old rogue Aitken snuffs it he could find himself in hotter water and in a hotter place than he had ever imagined.'

It might be deduced from these reviews that the leading lights of the *Guardian* remained in a slightly unforgiving mood towards me. If so, their mindset did not appear to last. What happened next must have caused great wailing and gnashing of teeth to Messrs Leigh and Pallister. Although it would be rash to jump to conclusions about conversion experiences in Farringdon Road, there was clear evidence of a new willingness at the *Guardian* to turn the other cheek. For when I completed the manuscript of my second and quite heavily theological book *Psalms for People under Pressure*, guess who put in a strong £8,000 bid for serialization rights? Well I would never have guessed it, but yes, the *Guardian* did serialize *Psalms for People under Pressure* as a cover story for their G2 section. It was accompanied by a long and friendly profile of me by the paper's top interviewer, Emma Brockes. For good measure the *Observer* came in with a favourable review of *Psalms* by its literary editor. Back in the days of the *Guardian*'s editorial campaign to get me jailed, you would have needed to believe in miracles to prophesy such good coverage.

The good sales of *Pride and Perjury* (over 26,000 so far and still going strong) and of *Psalms for People under Pressure* encouraged my publishers Continuum to sign me up for a four-book contract. The first fruits of this venture have been *Prayers for People under Pressure* (serialized in the *Daily Telegraph*) and this book *Porridge and Passion* whose serialization rights were bought by the *Daily Mail*. So I have been fruitfully busy with my pen.

Meanwhile on the other side of the Atlantic I am slowly becoming recognized as a Christian writer. I do a regular column on spiritual topics for the *American Spectator*. I have recently delivered to my US publishers Doubleday the manuscript of a 300,000-word biography of Charles W. Colson. There are encouraging signs, such as a first print order of 80,000 copies in hardback, that this book *Colson: A Life Redeemed* may do well in both the secular and spiritual bookshops of America.[2] At the time of his imprisonment in 1974 for Watergate-related offences, Colson was the most demonized figure in US politics this side of Richard Nixon. Thirty years later he is the most lionized US religious leader this side of Billy Graham. The story of Colson's journey between these two poles of the spiritual compass is a saga I have loved researching and writing.

Although I am as keen as the next writer to earn a living from my books and articles, I have a sense of motivation for this work which goes deeper than the financial rewards from it. This brings me to another new passion in my life. Evangelism.

In secular circles the word evangelism sounds rather pretentious. Sometimes it has negative associations featuring caricatures like Elmer Gantry, religious snake-oil salesmen, Bible-belt televangelists and the exuberant oversimplifications of happy-clappies. Yet the actual meaning of the term is a simple one derived from the original Greek word for the gospel – *evanggelion*. In the first century this translated as 'good news'. So even in the twenty-first century, evangelism is simply telling the good news or preaching the gospel.

I do not think of myself as a preacher, for I usually give talks not sermons. But through a series of coincidences I seem to have developed into the outreach speaker Wycliffe wanted me to be. There are four main types of audience who invite me to address them. The first are those who come to Alpha course suppers. The second are those at outreach events organized by churches. The third are international audiences. The fourth are prisoners. Between them they keep me busy with well over a hundred speaking engagements each year.

The Alpha course, which started at Holy Trinity, Brompton Church in Knightsbridge, has become a worldwide phenomenon. It is an introductory series of talks on the Christian faith which have now been attended by over 7 million participants across the world, most of whom started the course with little or no knowledge of faith or church. Alpha was a turning point in my own journey [3] back in 1997 and has been a source of much friendship and spiritual growth ever since. These days I teach parts of the course. Often I am the guest speaker at local or regional events promoting it, usually at suppers launching the course which attract audiences in the 150 to 750 range. So at certain times of the year I am extremely busy in the role of an Alpha warm-up man. In the last three years this has taken me to venues as diverse as Manchester United Football Club at Old Trafford; Norwich and Bradford Cathedrals; Sussex Cricket Club; dozens of hotels and restaurants in every part of the UK; many prisons; innumerable churches and church halls of all denominations. Because Alpha requires such close teamwork, the speaker is not all that important but like everyone else in the team he or she needs to do the job well. For reasons known only to God, Alpha has become one of his leading tools in modern evangelism, changing lives and leading tens of thousands of people into a relationship with the Lord each year. I am honoured to be a member of the Alpha team of volunteers.

In addition to Alpha talks of which I do about 20 to 30 a year I also accept a rather larger number of outreach invitations from churches and faith-based organizations. Sometimes I talk on a particular passage of scripture like a parable or a psalm. More often I am asked to give what is called a 'testimony talk', frequently using the personalized title 'From power to prison to peace'. Since I have now given this talk at least a hundred times I should by any rational calculation be bored with it, yet this is far from the case, certainly for me and hopefully for my audiences. This may be partly because the talk is extempore with many variations. But I think it is much more because the Lord, who I am convinced has a sense of humour, so often takes unpromising material from an unworthy speaker and uses it for his own purpose of communicating the good news to individual hearts.

Although I receive more speaking invitations than I can possibly cope with in the UK, I enjoy the dozen or so each year which arrive with the offer of an air ticket and take me to overseas audiences. In the last 12 months I have given talks, or programmes of talks, as far afield as Australia, China, Canada, New Zealand, India, Hong Kong, Belgium, Portugal, Ireland and the United States. My Colson biography and other writings have raised my profile as a speaker in America where I do a fair amount of what evangelicals sometimes call 'down-and-outer ministry' (i.e. in prisons) but rather more of what they call 'up-and-outer ministry'. This latter label applies to audiences of corporate executives, community leaders, media and advertising professionals, medical practitioners, financial services organizations, country club memberships and even the political leaders of Washington, DC. In 2002 I was invited to address the staff of the White House. In President George W. Bush's administration his aides meet once a week in an office on the West Wing to share devotions and to listen to a speaker. I gave them a 20-minute talk on Psalm 130. With the Iraq war looming, some of its verses on patience and other thoughts 'out of the depths' took on a special meaning. At lunch in the White House mess afterwards, the President's staff secretary (the equivalent of the Prime Minister's principal private secretary) told me that my interpretation of the psalm in the context of contemporary political pressures had reached out to many people in the audience and had been 'great evangelism'. Nothing could have pleased me more as an expression of thanks. Yet for all the power and prestige of the White House and other VIP American audiences I am at my happiest when trying to do my amateur evangelism among 'the least of these my brethren' in prison.

Prison ministry is high on my list of passions, partly because it comes low in the priorities of too many churches. I like to work with offenders and ex-offenders, partly because of my own prison experiences, partly because of my friendship with and admiration for Charles Colson, and partly because I feel called to this form of service both practically and spiritually. In practical terms, it covers activities like finding housing and jobs for newly released prisoners (part of my voluntary work for the Caring for Ex-Offenders charity), or sending Christmas presents to some 600,000 children of prisoners with 'Love from Dad' or with 'Love from Mum' under Prison Fellowship's Angel Tree scheme. In spiritual terms, it means working through Prison Alpha and Prison Fellowship to bring prisoners into a relationship with the Lord and so to change the direction of their lives. In this last context, I am fond of a Victorian verse of Christian doggerel which goes:

Some like to live within the sound of church or chapel bell
I want to run a rescue shop within a yard of hell

Because of my enthusiasm for working in such rescue shops, the one kind of invitation I never refuse is one which says 'come and talk to prisoners'. Thanks to my membership of the board of Prison Fellowship International, I now travel all over the world in this service. Strangely I do more of it abroad than at home. This is because several prison governors in the UK have refused to allow me to accept invitations from their chaplaincies. In the early weeks of this year the governors of both Pentonville and Belmarsh prisons in London have banned me from coming to speak to their inmates, yet I can't complain, because in the same period I have been welcomed by the governors of seven other UK jails, so I do not take these rejections personally. They are just more manifestations of the anomalies and illogicalities that are found time and again throughout the uneven landscape of Her Majesty's Prison Service.

Any thoughtful person who has seen as much of Britain's prison system as I have soon turns his or her mind towards the subject of prison reform. This has become another of my new passions. What worries me most is our national complacency about the alarming reoffending statistics. Out of every five prisoners who are released from our prisons, three are reconvicted and back behind bars within two years. Among prisoners in the 18–25 age group, four out of every five released are reconvicted and jailed again within two years. Are there any reforms that could improve this dismal failure rate? I believe that we need to tackle three main practical areas crying out for reform – literacy, work and drugs. All of these subjects are covered in the earlier chapters of this book, but here is a quick summary of an agenda for reform on each of them.

Illiteracy and subliteracy are major ingredients in reoffending. One-third of all Britain's prisoners cannot read or write at all. How can any of them hope to earn an honest living on their release if they cannot even read labels in a warehouse or notices in a factory? The same must be partly true for the next one-third of all prisoners, whose literacy skills are below the level of 11-year-old schoolchildren. What is needed here is a root-and-branch drive to reduce prisoner illiteracy. If resources from public expenditure cannot be made available for this task, then bring in volunteers to give simple lessons in reading and writing to illiterate prisoners. The Prison Service needs to do far more to open its doors to voluntary workers across a whole range of rehabilitative areas. Literacy is one in dire need of attention. As part of the drive to tackle this problem I would like to see far more imaginative use made of remission. At present it comes uniformly and automatically to all inmates who keep out of serious trouble. A scheme by which extra remission could be earned by prisoners who achieve certain educational qualifications including basic literacy and NVQ levels would be well worth introducing into the criminal justice system.

Real work for prisoners is another area of reform that needs attention. The Prison Service fails year after year to meet its promised target of providing four hours a day of 'purposeful activity' for each prisoner. Very little of this so-called purposeful activity is related to genuine work. Only 10 per cent of all prisoners ever get placed in prison workshops, factories or jobs which bear some resemblance to jobs in the outside world. Remedying this failure could have a major impact on the reoffending rate. The Home Office calculates that employment on release from prison reduces the risk of reoffending by between a third and a half.[4] As I saw at first hand, much prison work is a bit of a joke and not much else. Without sweeping reforms in this area, the joke will continue to backfire by increasing the reoffending rate.

The third topic for reform should be tackling drugs in prison. The general view among inmates is that three out of every four prisoners take drugs regularly. This guesstimate may be too low. A recent report by the House of Commons Home Affairs Committee[5] put the serious drug use figure among prisoners at 80 per cent. My observation is that the Prison Service has reconciled itself to losing the battle against prisoner drug abuse. Many governors and rank-and-file prison officers have simply given up trying to stem the tide of drugs entering their jails. Such defeatism will assuredly result in reoffending continuing to rise. Yet a reform agenda of improved security, drug testing and drug treatment could have a huge impact on reoffending in the long term.

One last area of potential reform is Innerchange. This label is well known to American prison specialists because five US states have been pioneering Innerchange prisons since 1997. An independent University of Pennsylvania study shows that over the last eight years prisoners released from the Innerchange Correctional Facility at Sugarland, Texas, have been reoffending at the rate of 8 per cent, whereas the average reoffending rate among all US prisoners is 67 per cent – very similar to the British figure.

Innerchange prisons are a Prison Fellowship initiative which offers the inmates who volunteer for it a concentrated regime of rehabilitation, change, retraining and post-release mentoring. The principles of restorative justice, the practicalities of preparing for a new life of honest work in the community, the teachings of faith-based instructors and the fellowship of outside mentors are all part of the Innerchange programme. The point about it is that it works.

As its founder Charles Colson says, 'You can argue about faith but you can't argue about the consequences of faith. That 8 per cent reoffending rate speaks for itself.'

Faith-based solutions to the problems of prisoner rehabilitation have in the past been regarded with scepticism, if not hostility, by Britain's politically correct prison administrators. But the ground is shifting. The success of Innerchange regimes and faith-based restorative justice courses in jails around the world is changing some attitudes within the UK Prison Service. In early 2005 I attended the opening of Britain's first faith-based Innerchange facility in HMP Dartmoor. It was a day of great rejoicing for those of us associated with Prison Fellowship and Prison Alpha who have been campaigning for this particular experiment to be given a try in a British jail. So watch this Innerchange space at Dartmoor and watch the results of other spiritual initiatives for prison reform, such as the Brixton prison initiative launched by the Catholic bishops in December 2004. It will certainly be one of my passions in the coming years to fight for a reforming agenda in the fields of prison literacy, work, drugs and faith-based rehabilitation programmes.

When I talk to audiences about my ideas on prison reform I am sometimes asked the question 'Are you going back into politics?' Of course I immediately know that my questioner is somewhat politically naïve because there are one or two little obstacles to be overcome before a political career can get started or restarted, such as being approved for candidate selection by a party, selected by a constituency and elected by the voters.

At the time when I came out of prison in January 2000, I had never in my wildest dreams considered the possibility of re-entering the political arena. However, an interesting group of people did give it serious consideration in early 2004. They were my former constituents in the Kent parliamentary district of South Thanet. At the time when the South Thanet Conservative Association was starting the process of selecting a parliamentary candidate, a pro-Aitken faction (which within six weeks proved to be a majority of members of the Association) approached me to ask whether I would be interested in throwing my hat into the ring.

I was hesitant about this idea at first hearing, for I assumed it was an initiative from a small group of old friends of mine endowed with more political nostalgia than realism. However, when I met this group they proved tenacious and energetic in their enthusiasm for an Aitken comeback. When I asked them to produce evidence of what they called 'widespread and cross-party support' for my return they went away first to take soundings and then to organize a petition on my behalf. This petition was headed:

> We the undersigned loyal members and supporters of the South Thanet Conservative Association request that our former Member of Parliament, Jonathan Aitken, should be allowed to enter the selection process for choosing the next Conservative Prospective Parliamentary Candidate for this constituency.

Within a week of this petition being circulated, over 220 Conservative activists had signed it, a remarkable figure considering that the total number of members in the South Thanet Conservative Association was only 335. From that indication and from other favourable signs such as the friendly coverage the petition received in the local press, it was clear that some sort of Aitken bandwagon was rolling in my former constituency.

The local enthusiasm was not matched by similar feelings of goodwill or even neutrality at the national level of the Conservative Party. When the petition was delivered to the Head of the Candidates Department, together with a formal application for my name to be considered in the constituency selection process, it was treated like something the cat had brought in. Conservative Central Office seemed to go into a tailspin of confusion. One party official denied that the petition had been received at all. Another said it had been received but that it had missed the deadline for such applications. A signed and time-dated receipt proved that this was untrue. In some desperation, the same official corrected his version of events to assert that the application had arrived on time but was technically invalid – which was also untrue. By this time the story was making headlines. I wrote an article in the *Spectator* explaining the background to the petition. Most journalists (with the angry exception of Tom Utley in the *Daily Telegraph*) gave the Aitken comeback idea a surprisingly fair wind. In the pages of *The Times*, the *Guardian*, the *Daily Mail* and most of the local and regional press the line seemed to be, 'Why not let the local association and the local voters decide?' This also was the prevailing tone from the numerous TV and phone-in radio programmes on which I appeared during the 48 hours after the petition became public knowledge.

These stirrings of media and popular support for the democratic process to be the judge of my proposed candidature did not find favour with the Conservative leadership. Michael Howard quickly issued a statement saying, 'Jonathan Aitken has many fine qualities but his days as a Member of Parliament are over'. An hour or two later we talked on the telephone. Michael said, 'I am sure you will understand how sad I am at having to do this.' I did understand. The judgemental pressures at the highest levels of the party against permitting any ex-offender to become an approved Conservative candidate were strong and in my case perhaps they were over-whelming. So I issued a statement saying that I accepted Michael Howard's decision with good grace. And that was that, except for a few follow-up pieces in various publications. Of these my favourite was a column by Petronella Wyatt in the *Spectator* who wrote,

> If Mr Howard were genuinely brave he would not have driven Mr Aitken away. But how would it look, senior Tories obviously protested, to accept an ex-jailbird back into the party? I can tell them how it would have looked. It would have looked humane, sensible and, judging by the views of voters I have talked to, would have received the backing of a significant chunk of public opinion.

No doubt there were significant chunks of public opinion on both sides of this argument, so I could not blame Michael Howard for playing it safe. In any case, my feelings of disappointment were fleeting. I was philosophical about being rejected from my old politics because I was getting so much fulfilment from my new passions. Returning to the House of Commons might have been exciting, but then not going back into politics would allow me, as the cliché has it, to spend more time with my family.

For me the old cliché slowly ripened into another new passion. I was painfully aware that family life had not been given its rightful priority during my years of ambitious financial and political careerism. In the aftermath of my fall, I wanted to change that and to give my family their full place at the centre of my heart and being. Marriage to Elizabeth strengthened this determination. Family life was top of her agenda too. So we both wanted to offer a commitment of emotional love and practical support to our entire extended clan. This included not only our seven single children but also two grandchildren, three brothers and sisters, five nephews and nieces, several close cousins, a great-uncle and a grandmother.

The grandmother (my mother – always known as Pempe) was our greatest ally in her enthusiasm for strengthening the bonds of family understanding and unity. Even in her ninety-fifth year she was a busy and hospitable matriarch. Her alliances and intimacies to us touched almost every member of our tribe. A typical Pempe initiative was her encouragement of the romance between Elizabeth's actor son Jared and the actress Emilia Fox. No one was more pleased or less surprised than my mother when Jared and Emilia announced their engagement in the autumn of 2004.

As I have said in earlier chapters of this book, life's sorrows as well as life's joys can strengthen family ties. The Harris–Aitken family found this to be true in painful circumstances when in the winter of 2004–5 we suffered three close bereavements in the space of six weeks. The first was Elizabeth's elder brother Gwilym, Lord Ogmore. He had a check-up for a suspected ulcer at the beginning of December 2004. The tests showed he had cancer. Fifteen days later he was dead. In the week of Gwilym's funeral my uncle, Simon Maffey, broke his hip in a fall. He never recovered from the operation to reset the bones of his fractured femur and died in the intensive care unit of the Middlesex Hospital just before Christmas. The sudden deaths and funerals of these two much-loved family figures took a heavy toll on their respective surviving sisters Elizabeth and Pempe. Yet both rallied in the spirit of 'the show must go on' to perform their customary roles as hostesses for Christmas Eve and Christmas Day family parties. Elizabeth's Christmas night dinner for 20 members of the family in our new matrimonial home was a spectacular production. The stars of it were our youngest and oldest guests. The young male lead was Master Marlowe Harris, aged 2½, who occupied centre stage for most of the evening with proclamations that everyone else's presents should belong to him. Almost a match for Marlowe's *joie de vivre* was 94-year-old Pempe's. After keeping the table in a roar with her stories until well after midnight she departed joyfully, although to me she added the improbable exit line, 'I don't think I'm quite over my winter flu.'

In fact my mother's post-Christmas flu did seem to get worse. She had mysterious pains that led to suspicions that she could be suffering from kidney stone problems, so a scan was ordered for 14 January. At seven o'clock that evening I was in Nottingham, just about to address an Alpha supper of 350 guests, when my mobile phone rang. It was my mother's doctor, Christian Carritt. 'Bad news I am afraid,' she reported. 'Pempe's scan has shown that she has advanced cancer of the pancreas. I think she is unlikely to live for more than another three months.'

My mother faced up to her death with characteristic grace and courage. She refused chemotherapy and other treatments that might have slowed the growth of her tumour. 'I have had a good and long life,' she said with real, not forced, cheerfulness. 'Now I am going to have a good death. But what a nuisance when I have so many things to do.'

What my mother most wanted to do in the closing weeks of her life was to see her old friends, so Maria and I alerted several members of the Pempe fan club to her medical situation. As a result, a stream of visitors poured into my mother's flat. They arrived in such numbers that we had to put a notice on her front door insisting on time limits and a queuing system, so it was champagne and roses all the way. In the last week of Pempe's life the farewell callers included Michael and Sandra Howard; actor Peter Bowles and his wife Sue; the former Editor of *The Times*, Simon Jenkins and his wife Gayle; BT Chairman Christopher Bland and his wife Jennie; Geoffrey and Elspeth Howe; Pam Powell, widow of Enoch Powell; Dame Sue Timson of ITN; Jared Harris and his fiancée Emilia Fox; Damian Harris; two High Court judges; two former inmates of HMP Belmarsh; many regulars from her local pub Chimes where my mother was an institution at her corner table every Saturday; and several stallholders from the Tachbrook Street market near Chimes where she did most of her weekly shopping.

As the end drew near, it was utterly natural for all my mother's immediate family to want to be at her bedside. So her grandchildren Jack, Alexandra, Victoria, Petrina and William dropped everything and came from as far afield as Los Angeles and New York to say their goodbyes. These poignant farewells were a combination of sadness, thanksgiving and joy. The joy came from the knowledge that my mother was leaving behind her a legacy of family life, love and strength.

My mother's final words to me began with the question, through a dreamy haze of morphine, 'Am I just going to slip away like this?' 'Yes, and you are surrounded by love,' I replied, as I held her hand. 'I am very much aware of that,' she said putting an amazing last sparkle into the words 'very much aware'.

She kept that awareness almost to the end. She knew we were all gathered around her in her flat. She understood what we were saying. She felt and reciprocated her family's strong emotions.

After midnight on the day of her death we divided the vigils at her bedside into family watches in pairs. It so happened that her two grandsons, Jack Davenport and William Aitken, were the ones watching over her when she finally slipped away at 4.55 on the morning of 7 February 2005. It was just how my mother would have wanted to go – at home, in physical and emotional touch with the rising generation, carried quietly and painlessly away on a high tide of family love.

A few days later my mother's funeral service took place in St Margaret's Church, Westminster Abbey. It was a moving and magnificent send-off attended by over 400 mourners who transcended all social and generational boundaries. Pempe's close friend and parish priest, Father Philip Chester, who had administered the last rites to her, conducted the service. He delivered a superb homily full of personal, spiritual and humorous insights. Equally superb in its humour, love and understanding of my mother was the address by Sir Christopher Bland. The *Evening Standard* reported its references to past love affairs as 'colourful ... breaking new ground at the normally staid Speaker's Church'. The biggest laugh came from the description of the first kiss my mother was given by my father, then RAF Flight Lieutenant Bill Aitken, in 1938: 'He bet her half a crown he could kiss her without touching her,' said Sir Christopher. 'Then he kissed her passionately, gave her half a crown and said it was well worth it.'

The funeral service was full of family touches, with beautiful readings in strong young voices from three of Pempe's grandchildren, Jack, Victoria and William. My mother would have loved it. Laughter and the love of friends were two key ingredients in her life, and both were in abundance at the reception held after her funeral in the Terrace Room of the House of Commons. But the more I thought about my mother's good life and good death, the more I concluded that her greatest passion was love of family. May the continuation of it be my passion too.

The final new passion of my life is loving God. I know how imperfectly and inadequately I express it and do it. Because I think of myself just as much as a 'failed again' Christian as a 'born again' Christian, I am well aware how much I expose myself to criticism, cynicism or worse when I try to describe what God has done in my life in my talks or writings. Yet that exposure seems a small cost compared to the great gains from being allowed to work in prison ministry, in practical help for ex-offenders, in private prayer groups, and in public areas of Christian service such as lay evangelism.

A few months ago I received a strange sign of encouragement for my evangelistic efforts. The sign came at a large church in Sussex – The Worthing Tabernacle – where an audience of about six hundred people turned out on a cold November evening to listen to my outreach talk. When the time came for the Pastor to thank me at the end of the meeting, he started off at what seemed to be a discordant tangent by talking about the political career of my great-uncle, the first Lord Beaverbrook. The mention of his name startled me for a reason no one could possibly have known about. Earlier in the week my great-uncle Max (Beaverbrook) had appeared in my dreams on two or three successive nights. I had dreamt about him as a newspaper proprietor giving orders to his editors at the *Daily*

Express, Sunday Express and *Evening Standard*. I had dreamt about him as a politician, sitting alongside his great friend Winston Churchill as a fellow member of the War Cabinet in both world wars. I had dreamt of him as a small boy fishing in the lakes and rivers of his native New Brunswick and then running back to the Manse, the home of his father the Reverend William Aitken, whose Bible is one of my favourite family heirlooms.

I can offer no explanation or interpretation of these dreams except to say that in normal daylight hours I quite often think of my 'Uncle Max'. He was a formative influence on me, for I was close to him in the last years of his life when I was an Oxford student, obsessionally interested in politics and journalism. In one of the last letters he wrote to me, dated 1 February 1964, he said, 'Don't be a dull man like your father. Go out and stir up mischief!' Perhaps I may have taken this advice rather too often.

Against the background of such memories, musings and dreams I was extremely surprised to hear Pastor Mark Weeden of the Worthing Tabernacle talking to the audience about my great-uncle. Apparently I was about to be presented with a tapestry featuring some words of wisdom from Lord Beaverbrook which had been specially embroidered for me by a member of the congregation. The words of wisdom went as follows:

> When I was a young man I pitied my father for being a poor man and a preacher of the Word. Now that I am older, I envy him his life and his career. For the evangelist is the man who has the greatest capacity for doing good. If I were in a position to influence the life of a sincere young man today I would say to him: 'Rather choose to be an evangelist than a cabinet minister or millionaire!'

Beaverbrook's words about his father, the Reverend William Aitken, made quite an impact on me, for I have somehow managed to straddle all three of the career choices which my great-grandfather and great-uncle shared between them. I wholeheartedly agree that the work of an evangelistic servant of the Lord is infinitely the most satisfying of these choices. This is because of the deep sense of excitement and fulfilment that comes from being used in the service of God. Despite all my obvious faults and failings, it is my relationship with a loving and forgiving God that has made this possible. This is why the glory of his name and of the transforming power of his love has become the greatest of my new passions.

[1] Among those of interest to the pages of *Hello!* were, from the political world: Michael and Sandra Howard, Norman Lamont, Michael Portillo, Malcolm Rifkind, Norman and Margaret Tebbit, Leon and Diana Brittan, David Davis, Alistair Burt, Greg Knight, Malcolm Pearson, Nicholas Soames, Winston Churchill, John and Louise Patten, Peter and Elaine Rawlinson, John Bercow, Richard Shepherd, and Diane Abbott; from film: Peter Bowles, Frank Langella, Tsai Chin, Victor Spinetti, *Harry Potter* producer David Heyman, Edward Hibbert and, of course, my sister Maria and her son Jack Davenport. Among other guests who attracted the attention of the press were Lady Annabel Goldsmith, BT Chairman Sir Christopher Bland, Sir Anthony and Lady Bamford, Rupert Hambro, Lady Jane Rayne, Prince Khalid bin Abdullah, Bishop Richard Llewellin, Sir Colin McColl, Harold and Lady Antonia Pinter, Wafic and Rosemary Said, former Taoiseach Albert Reynolds, Frank Williams, Petronella Wyatt and my ex-wife Lolicia.

[2] *Colson: A Life Redeemed* will be published in the UK by Continuum in September 2005.

[3] See *Pride and Perjury* (Continuum), pp. 271–4.

[4] Home Office report: *An Evaluation of Prison Work and Training*, 1996.

[5] Report of House of Commons Home Affairs Committee: *The Rehabilitiaton of Prisoners HC 193-1* (2005).

Acknowledgements

I gratefully acknowledge all those whose friendship, assistance and hard work have helped me to write this book.

My prison diary, the main source of the first-hand material used in the first ten chapters, was written every evening during my sentence. My fellow prisoners, most of whose names have been changed to protect their privacy,[1] engaged with me so warmly (occasionally too warmly!) that I would like to thank all of them for their companionship and often friendship, during our shared experiences.

My special thanks to Mickey Aguda, to whom this book is jointly dedicated. I am particularly grateful for his friendship and also for his research in newspaper libraries and elsewhere during the months when I was at work on the prison chapters.

My gratitude also goes to several members of the staff and student body of Wycliffe Hall who in one way and another helped me with the material in the Oxford chapter. I particularly thank the former Principal of Wycliffe Professor the Revd Dr Alister McGrath and Canon Michael Green, my two Oxford tutors, both of whom gave me interviews for this book in early 2005.

The burden of typing and retyping the manuscript was borne with exemplary speed and efficiency by Kate Rainbow. Additional secretarial assistance was given by Helen Kirkpatrick. To both of them, my sincere thanks.

I also thank my publishers at Continuum, particularly Robin Baird-Smith, for all their support, encouragement and even pressure to get the manuscript completed at high speed.

Finally my warmest gratitude goes to my wife Elizabeth who made many excellent suggestions which improved several chapters. For her loving support no praise and thanks can be too high.

Jonathan Aitken
March 2005

[1] The only exceptions are one or two of my fellow prisoners whose names have already been publicly linked to mine and who have no objection to shedding their anonymity.

Source Notes

Chapter 1

Author's prison diaries and private papers   8 June 1999
Letter to Author from Archbishop George Carey   7 June 1999
'Take Lord and Receive' prayer, from *Prayers of Ignatius*
   (Zondervan Press, 1976)
The *Evening Standard*   8 June 1999
BBC *One O'Clock News*   8 June 1999
The *Times*   9 June 1999
The *Daily Telegraph*   9 June 1999
The *Guardian*   9 June 1999
The *Independent*   9 June 1999
The *Daily Mail*   9 June 1999
The *Daily Express*   9 June 1999
The *Mirror*   9 June 1999
Valerie Scott, Letter to Mr Justice Scott Baker   4 June 1999
'Ballad of Sir Andrew Barton' quoted in *Nixon: A Life* by Jonathan
   Aitken (Weidenfeld and Nicolson, 1993) p. 525

Chapter 2

Author's prison diaries and papers   9 June 1999
William Shakespeare *Hamlet* Act 1 Scene 1
Psalm 130, NIV Bible

Chapter 3

Author's prison diaries and papers   9 June 1999
The *Daily Mail*   10 June 1999

The Tablet   11 June 1999
C. S. Lewis, *Mere Christianity* (Macmillan, 1957) Chapter 9

Chapter 4

Author's prison diaries and papers   10 June 1999–21 June 1999
The *Sun*   14 June 1999
The *Mirror*   4 June 1999
Razor Smith: *A Few Kind Words and A Loaded Gun* (Viking, 2004)
   pp. 459–462
Razor Smith *Punch* articles   3 July 1999–17 July 1999
Letter to Author from Robert – aka 'Wolfie'   12 June 2002

Chapter 5

Author's prison diaries and papers   12 June 1999–18 June 1999
The *Daily Mail*   10 June 1999
The *Daily Express*   9 June 1999
Kenneth Rose: *Superior Person: A Portrait of Curzon and his Circle*
   in late Victorian England, (Weidenfeld and Nicolson, 1969)

Chapter 6

Author's prison diaries and papers   14 June 1999–30 June 1999
The *Mirror*   10 June 1999
The *Sun*   12 June 1999
BBC Radio Kent   13 June 1999
The *Spectator* Magazine   26 June 1999
The *Daily Telegraph*   25 June 1999
The *Daily Mail*   25 June 1999
The *Times*   25 June 1999
The *Daily Express*   13 June 1999

Chapter 7

Author's prison diaries and papers	29 June 1999–28 July 1999
Author's letter to Alexandra Aitken	4 July 1999
The *Mirror*	9 July 1999
The *Sunday Mirror*	11 July 1999
The *Sun*	10 July 1999
The *News of the World*	18 July 1999
The *Daily Express*	14 July 1999
The *Times*	26 July 1999
The *Mirror*	22 July 1999
The *Mirror*	1 August 1999
The *News of the World*	25 July 1999
The *Sun*	26 July 1999
The *Mirror*	24 July 1999

Chapter 8

Author's prison diaries and papers	28 July 1999–31 August 1999
The *Sunday Mirror*	25 July 1999
The *Times*	26 July 1999
Wing Cleaners' Manual A Wing Office HMP Standford Hill	
Psalms of David ed. C. H. Spurgeon (Zondervan Press, 1985)	
Psalms for People under Pressure (Continuum, 2004)	
Prayers for People under Pressure (Continuum, 2005)	
The *News of the World*	18 July 1999
The *Mirror*	22 July 1999
The *Mirror*	8 November 1999

Chapter 9

Author's prison diaries and papers	14 July 1999–30 October 1999
The *Times*	16 July 1999
The *Sunday Mirror*	25 July 1999
The *Sunday Mirror*	29 August 1994

HMP Standford Hill *Harvest Festival Notes*	12 September 1999
The *Daily Mail*	11 November 1999

Chapter 10

Author's prison diaries and papers	1 November 1999–
	23 December 1999
James Pringle Letter to author	31 August 1999
The *Times*	27 August 1999
The *Times*	28 August 1999
The *Times*	23 September 1999
The *Sunday Mirror*	15 August 1999

Chapter 11

Author's prison diaries and papers	30 December 1999–
	8 January 2000
The *Sun*	1 January 2000
The *Times*	1 January 2000
The *Daily Telegraph*	1 January 2000
The *Mirror*	1 January 2000

Chapter 12

Author's prison diaries and papers	7 January 2000–31 August 2000
The *Times*	8 January 2000
The *Guardian*	8 January 2000
The *Daily Mail*	8 January 2000
The *Daily Telegraph*	8 January 2000
The *Daily Express*	8 January 2000
The *Sun*	8 January 2000
The *Mirror*	8 January 2000

Dominic Carman: *No Ordinary Man, A Life of George Carman QC* (Hodder and Stoughton, 2002) pp. 225–249

The *Daily Mail*   20 August 1999
The *Guardian*   31 May 2000

Chapter 13

Author's Wycliffe Papers & Correspondence
Alan Clark *Diaries* (Weidenfeld and Nicolson, 1993) p. 314
The *Sunday Times*   1 May 2001
Author's *China Visit Diaries*   1 January 2002–12 January 2002

Chapter 14

The *Daily Mail*   11 July 2002
The *Daily Mail*   19 July 2002
Hello! Magazine   28 January 2003

Chapter 15

Oxford English Dictionary Vol VIII pp. 523–4
J G Whittier 'Dear Lord and Father of Mankind' English Hymnal
    p. 285
Hello! Magazine   8 July 2003
The *Observer*   11 April 2003
The *Evening Standard*   8 April 2000
The *Guardian*   22 January 2004
Home Office Reports and Evaluation of Prison Work and Training
    1996
Report of the House of Commons Home Affairs Committee 2005
The *Spectator* Magazine   10 February 2004

Index

Index